FINANCIAL TIMES
MANAGEMENT

Knowledge   Skills   Understanding

Financial Times Management is a new business created to deliver the knowledge, skills and understanding that will enable students, managers and organisations to achieve their ambitions, whatever their needs, wherever they are.

Financial Times Pitman Publishing, part of Financial Times Management, is the leading publisher of books for practitioners and students in business and finance, bringing cutting-edge thinking and best practice to a global market.

To find out more about Financial Times Management and Financial Times Pitman Publishing, visit our website at:

www.ftmanagement.com

Advanced GNVQ
LIVING AND WORKING IN EUROPE

John Evans-Pritchard

FINANCIAL TIMES
PITMAN PUBLISHING

LONDON • HONG KONG • JOHANNESBURG
MELBOURNE • SINGAPORE • WASHINGTON DC

FINANCIAL TIMES MANAGEMENT
128 Long Acre, London WC2E 9AN
Tel: +44 (0) 171 447 2000
Fax: +44 (0) 171 240 5771
Website: www.ftmanagement.com

A Division of Financial Times Professional Limited

First published in Great Britain in 1997

© Pearson Professional Limited 1997

The right of John Evans-Pritchard to be identified as author
of this work has been asserted by him in accordance
with the Copyright, Designs and Patents Act 1988.

ISBN 0 273 62129 7

British Library Cataloguing in Publication Data
A CIP catalogue record for this book can be obtained from the British Library

10 9 8 7 6 5 4 3 2

Typeset by M Rules
Printed and bound in Great Britain by Clays Ltd, St Ives plc

The Publishers' policy is to use paper manufactured from sustainable forests.

Contents

PART THREE

Element 16.3 Examine customs and cultures in the European Union

PART FOUR

Element 16.4 Investigate different work opportunities among European member states

Preface

Notes for students

This textbook has been written to meet the specific requirements of the BTEC **Living and Working in Europe** option. It covers all of the *performance criteria* and *range* statements. It is laid out so that it broadly follows the four Elements. An assignment is given at the end of each part.

There is some overlap in the range for each element, for example, 'mobility of labour' is in Element 16.1 and 16.3, and 'training' is in Element 16.2 and 16.4. When you use the book for researching data you should read the obvious sections, but also use the index to find other references.

It would be possible to use only this textbook to answer nearly all the tasks set. There are, however, very good reasons why you should use additional materials:

➡ If you wish to achieve a **merit** or **distinction** grade for your work, the marking scheme insists that you use a variety of sources. One textbook is not enough.

➡ All textbooks go out of date because the real world is constantly changing. Your analysis of the EU should be up to date. You should, therefore, be checking the latest data from monthly publications, such as the *Main Economic Indicators* (OECD), and collecting news items and articles from newspapers and magazines.

➡ Whilst this textbook provides considerable data on all of the EU countries, it is simply not long enough to go into great depth. What is being offered is basic data on each part of the range and more detailed examples for particular parts of the range, or for particular countries. For really good work you will need additional details from specialist books, articles, professional bodies, etc., that deal with only one country, or with only one aspect of working conditions such as trade unions.

A lengthy list of resources is given at the end of this textbook. Each assignment also has a list of recommended sources.

Some of the material that you will need will take a long time to collect, either because you will have to find many sources, or because firms and institutions take a long time to reply to your inquiries. You must, therefore, start collecting data early in your course. The final assignment is likely to be the most difficult to find data for. You will need to choose one specific work role, and study its characteristics in four different EU countries. If you do not start this assignment early, you will not have time to collect all the data. You should, therefore:

➡ Check with your teacher/lecturer that this is the right thing to do.

➡ Check what planning you are expected to do.

➡ Read the last part of *Living and Working in Europe*.

➡ Choose the work role and career you wish to study.

➡ Select the countries that you need data for.

➡ Start contacting the appropriate sources.

This textbook also includes many insets from books, newspapers and magazines, as well as Quick Quizzes. All are relevant, and most can be used as part of your assignment work.

France is to move out of step with its continental neighbours by abolishing the difference between winter and summer time. Alain Juppé, the Prime Minister, said the traditional clock change was no longer justified on economic grounds.

Source: The Daily Telegraph (September 1996)

Europe and the EU will continue to be a dominating force in our economic and cultural development and will provide growing opportunities as a job market for you. This course should provide a chance for you to learn and understand how similar and different the EU countries are, and what employment opportunities there are in the EU. Hopefully it will also inspire you to go out and experience the cultures of Europe first hand.

Notes for teachers and lecturers

The major problem that students will have in completing assignments, for any of the Europe units, will be time. Unless the school or college library is very well stocked, some information will be difficult for students to access quickly. The most difficult elements are Elements 16.3 and 16.4.

Element 16.3 requires data taken from all EU countries, and across every part of the *range* and, then, a detailed comparison of customs, cultures and lifestyles in the UK and one other EU country. Element 16.4 requires data, for up to four countries, on what are very specific aspects of working conditions and career progressions. In both cases good data collection, and analysis and synthesis, will only be possible if students are given a sufficiently long time, possibly months, in order to compile what they need. It is strongly recommended that the final assignment (and possibly the assignment for Element 16.3 as well) is given to students very early on in the course, with a relatively generous deadline. Planning will then become an important feature for the students.

Because certain items of the *range* are repeated in different elements, the data for assignments may be found in parts of the book that do not specifically relate to that element. Students should be encouraged to select relevant data from any part of the textbook, and this should then be considered for grading 'variety of sources' and 'synthesis'. On the other hand, for **distinction** work it is expected that students will consult a range of other sources, and this textbook has intentionally given only part of the picture.

The **key skills** for each assignment have been suggested in very general terms. This should allow students to choose which skills they still need to demonstrate and should allow this unit to fit comfortably into the key skills delivery and mapping process.

John Evans-Pritchard
March 1997

Acknowledgements

A great many people have been responsible for the production of this textbook, many of whom are unknown and generally unthanked. Much of the data used in this textbook was recorded by others and put into tables, graphs, articles, books, etc., by people whose names are not recorded. I have given my recognition to the final sources of information below each table, diagram, article, etc., but I would also like to express my thanks to the anonymous people who collected and compiled the information.

I would again like to thank Annette McFadyen and Kara Regan of Financial Times Pitman Publishing for their supportive and efficient work, and I wish Kara well in her new life. I would also like to thank Emmanuel Renauld-Dehlinger and Benoît Imhauser for the forthright details of their own work roles.

Finally, as always, I wish to thank my family for the time, space and support they have given me to write this text. Giles has yet again provided the original inspiration for both the cartoons and the diagrams and Sheila has provided positive support when most needed.

PART ONE

Element 16.1
Investigate infrastructures of European member states

PERFORMANCE CRITERIA

A student must:

1 **compare** the **demographic** profiles of **member states**

2 describe **key economic resources** of **member states**

3 **compare** the **industrial profiles** of **member states**

4 describe, using **illustrations, transport and communications systems** across **member states**

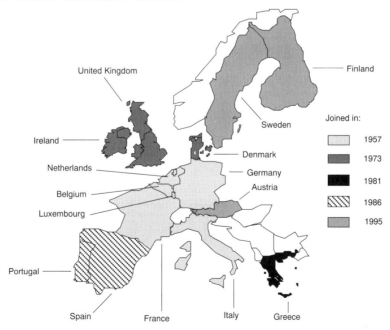

The member states of the European Union (1997)

1 Introduction

The European Union

The Second World War began as a conflict between independent European nations, fighting over fundamental beliefs, both political and economic. On the one hand, there was the desire for power and the belief that armed conflict and conquest could achieve this. The reward would be the power to dictate 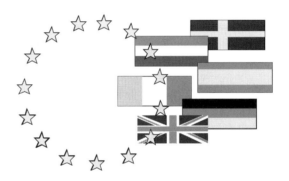 how societies and economies should be run, and who would be allowed to vote, work, own property, make decisions, etc. On the other hand, there was a belief in the freedom of choice, and the principles of the right to free speech, to freedom of movement, to vote, etc. The nations of Europe fought to prove that their own beliefs were right, and, in so doing, they killed over 55 million people and destroyed homes, factories, agricultural land and transport networks. They also introduced the twin horrors of the nuclear bomb and the modern holocaust.

'If Europe is to be saved from infinite misery, and indeed from final doom, there must be an act of faith in the European family. To recreate the European family and provide it with a structure under which it can dwell in peace, safety and freedom, we must build a kind of United States of Europe.'

Winston Churchill, 1946

In the shadow of these atrocities the leaders of the European nations decided that the uniting of Europe through economic and political ties was the surest way of preventing such abominations from ever happening again. This hope was the cornerstone on which the **European Union** was built.

What is now called the **European Union** was set up by the **Treaty of Rome** in 1957. The Union is a group of European countries which has common economic, social and political objectives. The member states have shown their commitment to these common objectives by agreeing to changes which have created new laws and regulations that apply to all the states (*see* Part 2).

The term **European Union** is comparatively new, and has only been used since the Treaty on European Union (Maastricht) in 1992. Before that, the Union has been called the **European Economic Community**, the **Common Market**, and the **European Community**. The number of countries involved has also changed over the years, growing from six major members in 1957 to fifteen major members in 1995. The progression is shown in Figure 1.1 opposite.

Although the name has been changed, the basic objectives of the European Union have remained the same as when it was first established in 1957.

> *Definition*
> A **customs union** is a group of countries that has no barriers to trade with other countries inside the union (except for regulations, such as safety or VAT, that individual countries also impose on themselves). Each member country also charges the same rate of import duty on goods coming into the union from countries outside. For example, a Japanese car coming into France would be charged the same duty if it was imported into the UK or Spain instead.

➡ The creation of a customs union with free trade between member states.

➡ The creation of a common market for factors of production.

➡ The ultimate integration of the separate national economies into a single European economy.

➡ Significant integration of the member states towards political union.

The first definite step on the economic front was in 1945, when Belgium, The Netherlands and Luxembourg established a single **customs union**, generally known as 'Benelux'. This union was designed to reduce trade barriers, such as import tariffs and quotas, between the three countries and thereby encourage trade.

> *Definition*
> A **common market** occurs when a group of nations have removed all their barriers to trade and all the products of the member countries can move freely from one country to another as though they were in the same market place. This means that there must be no barriers to trade and therefore all products and factors, including labour and capital, must be able to move freely. There must also be uniform levels of taxation and eventually a single currency.

When the European Economic Community was created in 1957, it established a customs union for all EEC member states, and every new member state has had to agree to remove all tariff and quota barriers between it and the rest of the community. Currently, Sweden, Austria and Finland are doing this. The long-term objective, however, has always been to create a real **common market**.

In 1996 the European Union was still a long way from achieving this objective, but it had removed many of the barriers, as the examples below demonstrate. It is now possible, in theory, for EU citizens to:

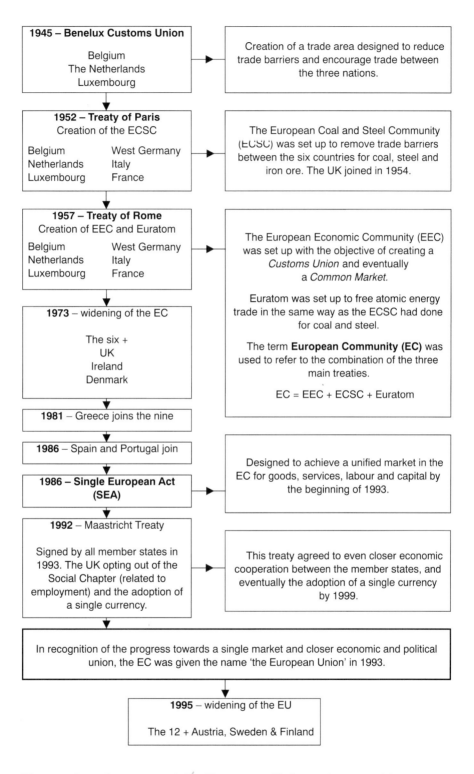

Fig 1.1 Development of the European Union, 1945 to 1995

- work in any EU country that they wish to work in.
- have their professional qualifications recognised in all EU countries.
- invest in firms in any EU country that they wish to.
- sell their products in any EU country on the same basis as national firms sell their products.
- buy goods and services for their own use from any EU country of their choice and only have to pay the taxes charged by that country.
- live in, and own property in, any EU country that they wish.

For full common market status, all the countries would need to treat their citizens and businesses in the same way so that all EU citizens and EU businesses had the same opportunities, rights and responsibilities. That would mean common taxes and benefits, common education and training facilities, common working conditions and even a common form of money. The EU, as yet, does not fully meet any of these conditions, but it is moving towards them.

All of this does make the EU sound like some uniform state where everything is controlled and there is no individuality. This is not true now, and even if we move towards closer political ties, it will not be true in the future. The characteristics of individual countries are significantly different from each other. These differences include language, customs, culture, leisure interests, the role of men and women, the importance of religion and even what people eat and drink. There are also differences in geography, demography, natural resources and the types of industries that individual nations have decided to specialise in.

The importance of the European Union

Figure 1.2 shows the percentage of the world market held by EU countries in selected products and the ranking that this production gives them. It demonstrates that individual EU countries are able to compete successfully with the rest of the world in some areas of production. In terms of total production, however, individual EU countries do not fare so well (*see* Figure 1.3).

Since the Second World War, the USA, Germany and Japan have dominated world production and trade. Individually, these countries have outstripped the rest of the world in terms of economic growth, income, wealth, investment, technological innovation and a host of other indicators that economists put forward as important measures of economic success. Figure 1.3 shows the relative strengths of the different nations in terms of **Gross Domestic Product (GDP)**, the most commonly used international indicator of production and wealth. GDP measures the value of the total production of a country. The national GDP figures have been converted into pounds sterling to make comparison easier.

Definition
Gross Domestic Product (GDP) is the total amount of goods and services produced in a country in a set time period (usually one year).

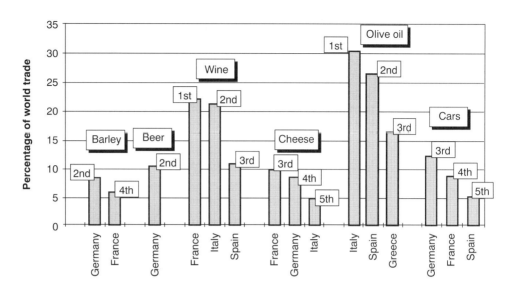

Fig 1.2 Positions in World's Top Ten by production 1994 (selected products)

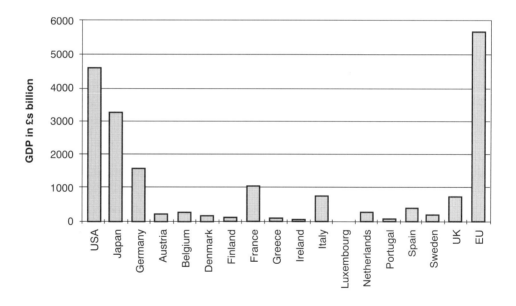

Fig 1.3 GDP for the USA, Japan and EU countries, 1995 (£ billions)
Source: Adapted from Main Economic Indicators (OECD)

It should be clear from this comparison that in terms of total production all EU countries are, individually, relatively small fry compared to the USA. Most EU countries, with the exception of France, Italy and the UK, are also relatively insignificant even when measured against Germany. When combined together, however, the output of the EU places it right back among the world leaders. Figure 1.4 shows that in 1995 the EU became the largest trading block in the world just ahead of the North America Free Trade Association (NAFTA). Indeed, NAFTA was only formed in 1994 by the USA because of fears about the growing strength of the EU. The member nations of NAFTA are the USA, Canada and Mexico. The change in the relative performance of the two trading blocks between 1994 and 1995 is due in large part to the poor growth record of Mexico.

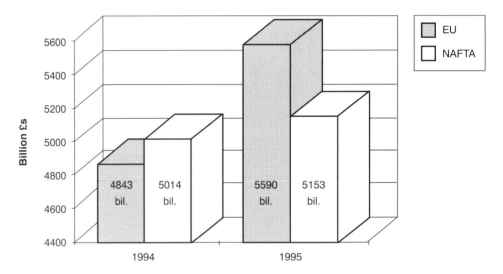

Fig 1.4 Total GDP of EU and NAFTA trading blocks (£ billions)
Source: Main Economic Indicators (OECD)

GDP is a particularly useful measure to take because it shows:

➡ how much is produced in each country and is, therefore, available for providing the inhabitants with their standard of living.

➡ how much income people are receiving and, therefore, how large the potential market is for domestic producers and for importers.

➡ how powerful a country is in terms of being able to control international trade.

Countries with high levels of GDP and large markets have the power to dictate terms to their trading partners, offer incentives to attract foreign investment, gain economies of scale and lower production costs, and invest in research and development in order to find the high-selling products of the future. On their own, the EU nations have found this difficult, but working together, pooling resources and sharing their markets, they have been able to build a union that now has considerable economic strength.

Quick Quiz No. 1

Which EU countries have the following world rankings?

a) Seventh in the production of cucumbers and gherkins.

b) Second in the production of lemons and limes.

c) First in the production of peaches and nectarines.

The answers are given on page 91.

Infrastructure

There is a general rule that applies to the development of all economies:

As an economy becomes more advanced and integrated, it requires more complex systems of trading and greater levels of physical and economic support in order to operate efficiently.

It is these systems and supports that are referred to as the **infrastructure**.

Definition
The **infrastructure** of a country is the underlying network of physical and economic supports that allow production and trade to take place.

The meaning of the term **infrastructure** is potentially very wide and certainly includes all of the items listed in the unit *range*: demography, economic resources, transport and communication systems, etc. **Infra** comes from the Latin meaning 'under' or 'below', and it is used here to indicate all of the elements that are needed to support the structure of a nation's economy.

It is very easy to think of economies as simply two sides of the production cycle, households and firms (as shown in Figure 1.5), with money flowing in one direction and physical production flowing in the other. The real business world is, however, far more complex, and involves training of the workforce, transport of the goods, sources of finance, distribution of goods through wholesalers and retailers, etc.

As economies become larger, they also require greater levels of infrastructure. In the countries of the EU there are hundreds of thousands of producers in the primary and secondary industries and over 3¼ million shops. The EU has a population of over 370 million people, spread across fifteen nations and 3¼ million square kilometres. Over 160 million EU citizens are either in work or looking for work. In order to bring all of these elements of the marketplace together, it is necessary to have a complex infrastructure that will allow producers to get their goods and services to their customers and allow workers, providers of capital, etc., to get to the firms. The term infrastructure will, therefore, include all of the following areas of support:

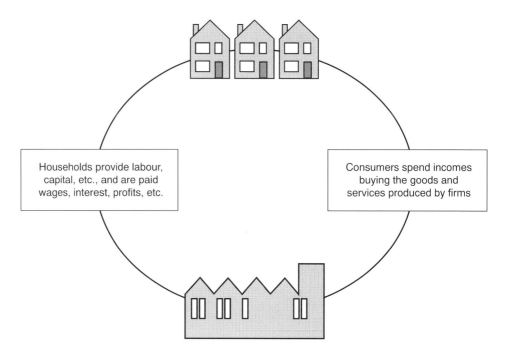

Fig 1.5 Simple production cycle

- Road and rail systems
- Airports and docks

- Advertising channels
- Insurance facilities

- Hospitals and schools
- Water, gas and electricity supplies

- An international postal system

- A system of telecommunications

- A capital market for investment
- A labour market to provide employees
- An educated workforce
- A system of wholesalers and retailers
- A supportive system of taxation
- A system of sound money for exchange
- Law and order to protect against crime
- International agreements to protect trade

In this textbook we will be concentrating on only a few of these areas, and in particular the ones that are specified in the *performance criteria* and the *range*.

In most countries, major parts of the infrastructure are provided by the state, such as education, transport systems and the money supply. This is mainly because individual firms could not afford to pay for them separately. There are some examples of firms providing their own infrastructure, as when whisky firms provide their own water supplies, or a firm producing aluminium builds its own electricity power station, but they are rare. In the EU there is now a growing number of private firms that supply parts of the infrastructure. In the UK, electricity, gas, telephones and now many train services are all run by private sector firms, and many EU countries are following our example of privatisation. Parts of the infrastructure, such as insurance and advertising, have always been mainly provided by the private sector.

2 Demographic features of the EU member states

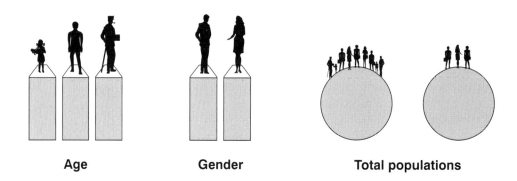

Age **Gender** **Total populations**

The meaning of the term 'demography'

The term **demography** is used to describe the study of population statistics. In the EU there are over 370 million people with a vast range of different characteristics. The basic demographic statistics can, therefore, be divided in many different ways, some of which will be considered in this chapter. Demography includes details about:

➡ The total number of people in countries, where they live, how wealthy they are, etc.

➡ How and why the numbers of people change, through changes in birth rates, death rates and migrations, etc.

➡ How the population is structured in terms of age, gender, location, etc.

➡ How people's way of life, standard of living and cost of living vary from country to country.

➡ Characteristics of the population such as religious belief, customs and cultures (these are dealt with in Part 3).

The **demographic profile** of a country will look at a range of these demographic features. From these it will build up an outline of what the major characteristics of the country's population are – how many people it has, how crowded the country is, what the ratio of men to women is, how incomes are distributed, and so on. This profile will give an overview of the country's population, and will allow comparisons to be made between countries.

Differences in demographic profiles mean that countries will have different economic, social and political characteristics. Each of the measures that are considered below will affect a range of factors inside each country. The ratio of men to women will, for example, affect what clothes are bought, what work is done by each, how old the population is on average (because women tend to live longer), what medical treatment is considered most important (because some illnesses are more common to one sex than to the other), etc. It is important, therefore, to know not only how the demographic profiles differ from one country to another, but what effects these profiles will have on those countries.

Quick Quiz No. 2

1591 people died of rheumatoid arthritis in the UK in 1992. 21 per cent were men and 79 per cent were women. The figures for heart failure and chronic liver disease are given below, but did more men or more women die of each?

	Cause of death	Total deaths	Percentages
a)	Heart failure	5354	68% and 32%
b)	Chronic liver disease	3056	58% and 42%

The answers are given on page 91.

Basic population statistics

All EU countries know the basic facts about their populations because it is the law in each country that births and deaths are registered, and that immigrations and emigrations are recorded. From this data the authorities should be able to calculate how many people there are, their ages, their gender, how long they are likely to live, how many will be available for work, and so on. In addition to this basic record, all EU countries conduct censuses, usually every ten years. These require, by law, that all people are registered, and usually require details about age, sex, where they live, and frequently require details about levels of income, basic household amenities that people have, employment details, etc. These sources provide the data that we will be examining below.

Total population

The fifteen countries of the EU now have a combined population of over 370 million people. Figure 2.1 shows how the people are distributed across the member states. It also shows that the five largest nations, namely Germany, the UK, France, Italy and Spain, have a combined population that forms almost 80 per cent of the total EU population.

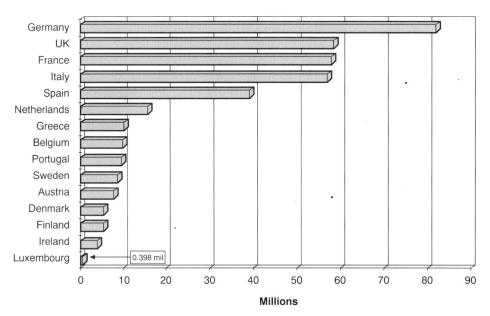

Fig 2.1 Population of the EU member states, 1994
Source: Adapted from Main Economic Indicators OECD

Size is very important when it comes to population because people are the raw material of economies. Total population affects the economy of a country in two major ways:

➡ It is the population that provides the labour needed to produce a country's goods and services. The labour force is a vital part of the natural infrastructure of the economy (*see* Chapter 3). The more people there are of working age, the more there is that can be produced. Labour makes the products and is, consequently, a major part of the **supply** side of an economy.

➡ It is the population, with its income, that buys the goods and services that are produced and hence provides the market for the producers. Population has the income and is, therefore, a major part of the **demand** side of the economy.

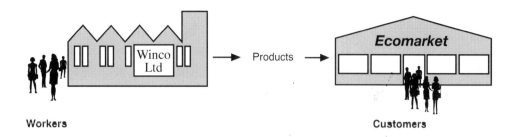

Workers   Products   Customers

In terms of the total number of people, the EU (371 mil.) is currently the fourth largest market in the world, behind China (1,166 mil.), India (883 mil.) and the North American Free Trade Area (NAFTA) (378 mil.). In terms of spending power (as indicated by total GDP), the EU is the largest marketplace in the world (*see* Figure 1.4). This gives the EU considerable economic power and benefits:

➡ High levels of population provide a workforce with a wide range of skills.

➡ Division of labour is possible and this helps to increase the levels of productivity and of total production.

➡ High levels of population provide large markets for producers.

➡ With large markets firms can mass produce and gain economies of scale.

➡ When there are many income earners and consumers this allows governments to raise adequate taxes to pay for a good welfare system and for infrastructure projects to improve the economy.

Large populations are not, however, purely beneficial. There are also potential problems:

➡ When the economy is performing badly, there will be high levels of unemployment and the need to pay unemployment benefits through additional taxes or by borrowing money.

➡ If there is limited land, high levels of population will lead to overcrowding, congestion and pollution.

➡ People have different customs, cultures and beliefs, and with more people there will be more differences. These can lead to conflicts, as with racial, religious and political discrimination, riots and even wars.

➡ More specialisation means that more people are needed to help provide finance, transport, wholesaling and retailing, etc., and it might be argued that these people would be better employed actually producing new products.

Countries can have either too many people or too few people and both of these situations can cause problems.

Over-population occurs when there are too many people in a country, causing a strain on the national resources. It will be characterised by high unemployment, falling standards of living, congestion, pollution, etc.

Under-population means that there are too few people in the country, leading to a lack of manpower and a lack of production. Again the standard of living will fall and will be accompanied by inflation, difficulty in competing internationally, too many imports, etc.

When the UK joined the EU in 1973, the major argument given in support of our joining was that it would increase the size of our market from about 55 million to what was then 250 million. Since 1973 the EU population has continued to grow and six other countries have joined. With the Single European Act and the removal of most trade barriers by 1993, the EU has become a very valuable marketplace for the UK. But it is not a completely uniform marketplace. Nearly all the EU nations have their own distinct language, which means that producers trying to sell their products in EU markets have to advertise, write instructions, contents, guarantees, etc., in up to thirteen other languages. Because the EU is not yet a real common market, international traders are still faced with fifteen different currencies and fifteen different sets of indirect taxation on VAT, alcohol, petrol and tobacco.

When these differences are considered, the size of each country's population becomes important to firms choosing their markets. If a UK firm decided to sell to a foreign market of 80 million people, it could sell in Austria, Belgium, Denmark, Finland, Greece, The Netherlands, Portugal and Sweden, with all the different currencies, taxes, laws on marketing and languages, and still not find 80 million people. Alternatively, it could sell in just one country, Germany, and find a population of over 80 million people, with one official language, one currency, uniform marketing laws and standardised taxes.

Quick Quiz No. 3

English is the most widely understood language in the EU, with 83 per cent of secondary school children studying it as a foreign language. Which EU countries have the highest percentage of secondary school children studying each of the following languages as a foreign language?

a) English (96%)   **b)** French (69%)   **c)** German (58%)

The answers are given on page 91.

■ Changes in total population

In 1990 the population of West Germany increased by about 17 million people as East and West Germany were unified. Normally, however, a country's population will only increase when the number of people born is greater than the number of people dying (i.e. the birth rate is above the death rate), or when the number of people coming to live in the country is greater than the number of people leaving to live elsewhere (i.e. there is net immigration into the country). These factors are explained in the next section.

Table 2.1 Percentage growth in population (1977–1993)

	%		%
Germany *	33.2	Spain	4.9
Greece	11.3	Portugal	4.8
Netherlands	10.4	Austria	3.0
France	8.5	UK	2.6
Luxembourg	8.3	Belgium	2.4
Ireland	7.1	Denmark	2.0
Finland	6.7	Italy	2.0
Sweden	5.7		

* NB This figure is so high because of the reunification of West and East Germany in 1990
Source: Adapted from Euromonitor

Table 2.1 shows that over long periods of time, all nations' populations tend to grow. This will have important effects on the economy and way of life, such as:

➡ the size of the market

➡ the size of the labour force

➡ the number of people per square kilometre (population density)

➡ the demands being made on scarce resources

➡ the ability to introduce specialisation, economies of scale, etc.

Over shorter periods of time, countries do experience falls in their total populations, as shown for Portugal in Figure 2.2. The population of Portugal fell, on average, by 0.1 per cent for each year between 1984 and 1994. While that might not seem to be a very big fall, it does add up to over 1 per cent of the total population over ten years, or about 100,000 people. Generally this occurs because less people are being born, and that affects many industries that cater for babies' and children's needs, such as baby clothes, toys, or nursery education.

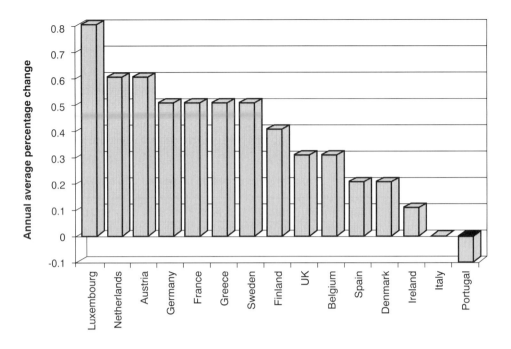

Fig 2.2 Annual average population change, 1984 to 1994
Source: Adapted from Main Economic Indicators OECD

When individual years are considered, falls in population are more common, but still relatively unusual. In the UK the total population has fallen only once in the last 250 years, and that was in 1975/76. In other EU countries falls in population occur more frequently. In both Germany and France at the moment there is negative population growth. Italy also has a falling total population, with one of the lowest birth rates in the world.

This up-and-down pattern of the population can make it very difficult for producers trying to expand their markets because they can never be totally certain how many people there are going to be to sell their products to.

■ Birth rate and death rate

> **Definition**
> **Birth rate** measures the number of children born per 1000 of the population in one year.
> **Death rate** measures the number of people who die per 1000 of the population in one year.

If we are to understand what will happen to the size of a country's population in the future, and hence the size of its potential markets, it is important to know how the birth rates, death rates and migration numbers are likely to change.

Figure 2.3 shows that for all EU countries, except one, the birth rate was above the death rate in 1992. In other words, in all of these countries the total population rose in that year. The exception was Germany, where the birth rate was

10.0 per 1000 of the population and the death rate was 11.0 per 1000, so more people were dying than were being born. As Germany had a population of just over 81 million people in 1992, that meant a fall in total population of about 81,000.

In January 1996, the *World Programme* of the BBC reported that what was former East Germany now had the lowest birth rate in the world. The low birth rate was caused by worries about the economy and whether or not couples could afford to have children. To encourage couples to have more children the government offered prospective parents a one-off payment of 1000 DM for each child born. The initiative was not a success. Potential parents felt that the high rates of unemployment and low incomes were still too much of a risk. Funds for paying this birth bribe have now run out.

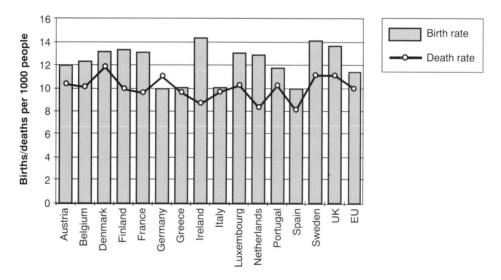

Fig 2.3 Birth and death rates in EU countries
Source: Adapted from the Demographic Year Book

Changing birth rates and death rates will have major effects on the country concerned. Less people being born will mean:

➡ falling demand for maternity products, baby products and, as the years pass, a range of toys and educational products.

➡ less expenditure for governments on maternity hospitals, maternity leave and education.

- more tax for governments as women continue at work.
- more incomes left to buy non-baby items and hence an increase in demand for these products.
- in about sixteen years' time there will be less school leavers and less people available for the workforce. If there is unemployment that will be a good thing, but if there is a shortage of labour, production will be affected and the standard of living will fall.

In countries where the number of people born is rising, the effects will be reversed.

At the other end of the age scale, the death rate usually changes because of the number of old people dying. In EU countries people are living longer and longer so the death rate tends to fall. As the number of old people rises, this causes:

- increased expenditure for governments on pensions and medical care.
- reduced government incomes as people stop working.
- less people in the workforce as people retire.
- a change in demand patterns with older people tending to prefer more conservative products, such as gardening items.
- a change in where people live, as retired people often move south and towards the coast (*see* page 23).

■ Infant mortality

Definition
Infant mortality occurs when a child dies within one year of its birth.

One particular death rate is considered to be an especially valid measure of the standard of living in a country. **Infant mortality** measures the number of babies that die before they are one year old. This is normally measured per 1000 births. It is used as a valid measure of the standard of living because it reflects important elements of a country's environment, such as the level of health care, the diet of mother and child, the levels of disease, war and famine in a country, etc.

Figure 2.4 shows the differences in infant mortality for the EU. Portugal has the worst figures but this is still relatively good in world terms, ranking only 26th down a list of 140 countries.

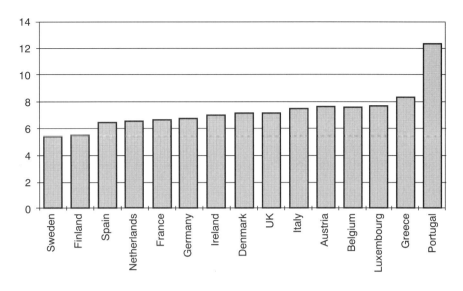

Fig 2.4 Infant mortality in the EU (deaths/1,000 births), 1993
Source: Adapted from the World Health Statistics Annual (WHO)

■ Migration

Definitions
Immigration occurs when foreigners move into a country and become residents there.
Emigration occurs when people who are resident in a country leave and become residents in another country.

The size of a country's population can also change because of the movement of people into the country (**immigration**) and out of the country (**emigration**). International migrations occur when people take up long-term residence in a new country. Other forms of migration take place when residents move from one part of the country to another. Tourism is not counted as migration because it is only temporary.

Between 1986 and 1992, more than 200,000 EU citizens migrated to the UK to live, and almost 150,000 UK citizens migrated to other EU countries. Although this sounds a lot, the net flows in each year were relatively small (*see* Figure 2.5).

For the EU as a whole, the relatively high standard of living has meant that it is an attractive place to live and work, or to seek political asylum. Figure 2.6 shows the numbers coming into ten EU countries in recent years, mostly from the former Soviet block (3 mil.), the former Yugoslavia (2½ mil.), Turkey (3 mil.) and North Africa (2 mil.).

Figure 2.6 shows that Germany has received the most immigrants but it also shows that Belgium and Austria have received very high numbers of immigrants considering the relatively small sizes of their own populations.

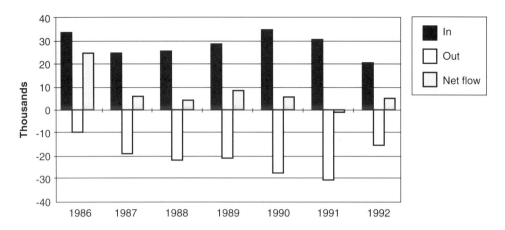

Fig 2.5 Flows of migrants into and out of the UK, 1986 to 1992

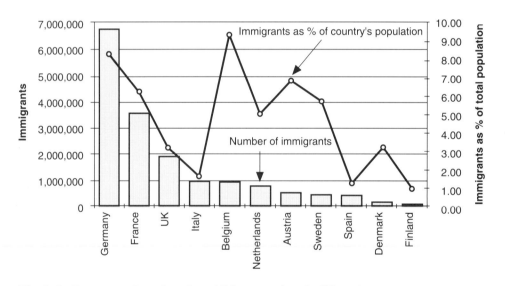

Fig 2.6 Recent migration into EU countries (millions)

The level and nature of migration can have profound effects on an economy:

➡ When there is net emigration it is generally the young, and usually young males, who leave the country. This can drain away the new generation of workers and leave the country short of skilled, young, adaptable labour.

➡ Frequently immigrants come from different ethnic backgrounds and may demand different goods and services. Unfortunately this also, sometimes, leads to discrimination and even racism.

➡ Where a country is over-populated, net immigration is likely to make the problem worse, causing unemployment, dependency ratios to rise, etc. Where there is under-population, net emigration will again make the problem worse.

➡ As people move from one country to another they will frequently require new training in language, different local skills, etc. They must also understand the new culture, laws and customs. This will create demand for the trainers, but a cost for the individuals, or for the state if the training is provided by the public sector.

The importance of identifying regional changes

Using average figures for the whole of a country can give a very distorted picture of what is actually happening within different parts of the country. In the UK we have, in the past, had considerable movements of people from the north to the south, and from the country to the towns and cities. In more recent years people have tended to move out of the city centres into the suburbs, or even further, and commute to work. There has also been a significant movement of retired people towards the south. If the country as a whole is taken, these shifts in population from one region or area to another will not be registered.

Europe gears up for the Florida effect

Following the introduction of a single currency there could be a significant migration of people from northern to southern Europe, similar to the influx of people into Florida. The barriers are currently lack of understanding of:

1. how houses are priced
2. how one buys houses in different countries
3. how much it costs to own and run a house abroad

But these restrictions are crumbling as understanding grows. For workers, those who will find it easiest to move will be home workers such as artists and IT specialists.

Source: The European (August 1994)

To see more thoroughly what is going on inside a country it is necessary to examine the regional and local changes in that country. This has been done for Portugal below.

In the years from 1981 to 1991, the total population of Portugal grew from 9.82 million to 9.86 million. The underlying causes of this change are shown in Figure 2.8. The rise in population through births and deaths was then significantly reduced by net emigration. But this only tells part of the story. If individual regions are examined the underlying changes and causes vary considerably.

Fig 2.7 The regions of Portugal

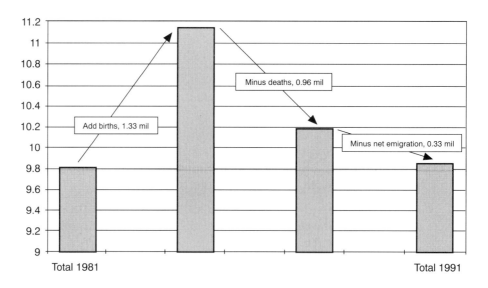

Fig 2.8 Causes of change in Portugal's population, 1981 to 1991

Table 2.2 shows how the total population for Portugal has changed (per annum) for every 1000 people in the country over the same time period. It also shows how the figures have changed for each region of Portugal.

Table 2.2 Regional annual changes in Portugal's population (1981 to 1991) per 1000 of the population

	Births/1000	Deaths/1000	Net migration/1000
Portugal	**13.5**	**9.8**	**–3.3**
Norte	15.5	8.8	–5.2
Centro	12.6	11.2	–3.6
Lisboa	11.9	9.4	–1.0
Alentejo	10.9	12.2	–4.9
Algarve	12.6	12.3	+4.7
Açores	18.7	11.3	–9.9
Madeira	16.1	9.9	–5.6

Source: Adapted from Eurostat

When the individual regions are considered, they reveal some dramatic differences in the rates of change. The birth rate runs from a low in Alentejo (10.9 births/1000) to nearly double this (18.7 births/1000) in the islands of the Acores (Azores). Death rates are lowest in Norte and highest in Alentejo and Algarve. The highest natural rate of growth is in Acores, where 7.4 more people are born per thousand than die per thousand, but there is then a net emigration of 9.9 people per thousand. In Alentejo the natural growth rate is actually negative, with more people dying than are being born. In the Algarve there is net immigration, probably through the increased number of people retiring there. The highest net emigrations are in Acores and Madeira, which reflects the limited availability of jobs and the need to move to the mainland to find work.

To form an accurate picture of what is happening inside Portugal, it is clear that a breakdown of the changes in the regions is also needed. Figure 2.9 shows the overall effects of the changes in Table 2.2 for each of the regions over the ten-year period from 1981 to 1991. The growth rates varied from − 6.1 per cent (Alentejo) to + 5.1 per cent (Algarve). If smaller areas had been taken they would reveal even more diverse figures. Pinhal Interior Sul had a fall of 15.7 per cent in its population over the same period.

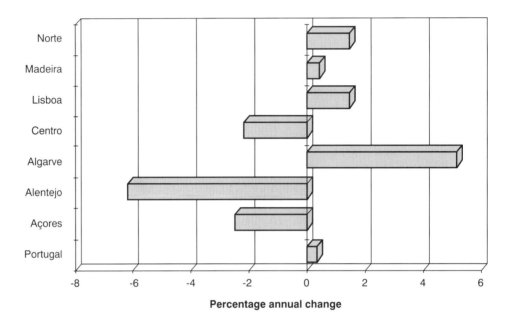

Fig 2.9 Population growth rate for Portugal by regions, 1981 to 1991

The structure of the population

The structure of the population shows how the total population is divided into certain categories, such as male/female, different age bands, the type of work they do, and where they live. The occupational structure will be covered in Chapter 4.

■ Age structure

The age structure of a country is frequently shown in the form of an age pyramid, as in Figures 2.10 (a) and (b), which also distinguishes between the number of men and women in each age band. Figures 2.10 (a) and (b) show the number of people in year groups from one year old to 99 years old, taken from the latest full census for the UK and Finland, respectively.

The population structure is typical of most developed countries in recent years, and applies to nearly all of the EU countries. One might expect that with higher and higher ages there would be progressively less people in each year group, but this is not the case any more. The wavy borders, from year to year, indicate variations in the birth rate. At point (b) on the graph for the UK there is a very high number of 43 and 44 year olds, which shows that there were an unusually large number of births in 1947 and 1948, immediately after the Second World War. This is the group that has been nicknamed the 'baby boomers'.

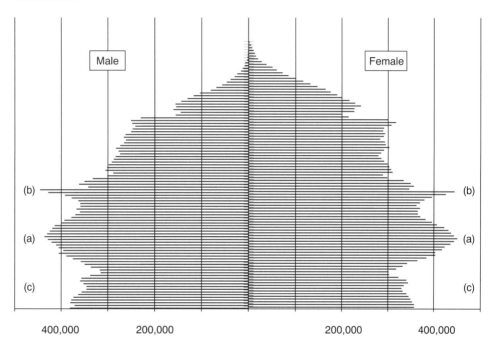

Fig 2.10(a) UK, distribution of population by age and gender, 1991
Source: Adapted from the Demographic Year Book (UN)

> *Definition*
> An **ageing population** is one where the average age of the population is rising.

The general pattern is that there are now less people in each age group at the bottom of the structure, at point (c), than there are in the older year groups, at point (a). This means that there are not enough babies being born to replace their parents' generation. Normally this would cause the total population to fall, but people are living longer. One dramatic effect of this is that the population is, on average, gradually growing older. The UK, and most EU countries, have an **ageing population**.

The age structure of a country, and particularly how many people there are in each of the age groupings, will influence many parts of the economy:

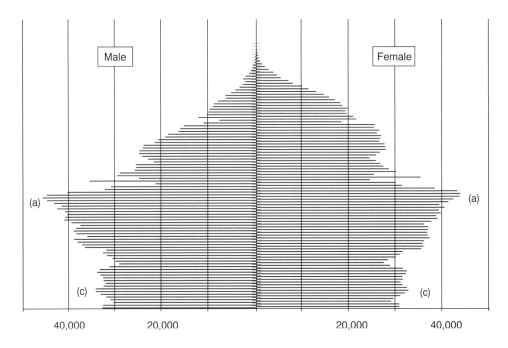

Fig 2.10(b) Finland, distribution of population by age and gender, 1991
Source: Adapted from the Demographic Year Book (UN)

➡ People of different ages like to buy different goods and services.

➡ Often age dictates what people are allowed to buy, as with drinking alcohol, driving vehicles on public roads, watching certain films, etc.

➡ The working population is mainly limited by the age at which the government permits children to leave school, and by the age at which they insist that people retire.

Quick Quiz No. 4

What is the standard retirement age for men and women in the UK?

The answers are given on page 91.

➡ Age also affects the ability of people to work, particularly in physical jobs.

Definition
The **dependency ratio** indicates how many people, on average, are supported by the income of each person who is working.

➡ The two extremes of age – school age and retirement age – are the times when the government pays out most money to support people, or to pay for services such as education and medical care.

➡ The age structure also indicates what the **dependency ratio** is likely to be, as this is calculated, in part, on the basis of how many children and OAPs have to be supported.

→ The level of people's incomes tends to change with age, with the highest incomes being earned by people between the age of 45 and retirement.

Figure 2.11 shows that the basic breakdown of the age structure in all of the EU member states is very similar. In each case there is a relatively small group of people below the age of sixteen, and a growing number of people above the age of 65. Sweden, with 17.4 per cent of its population above the age of 65, has the highest percentage figure in the world for people in this age bracket. Ireland, with only 11.6 per cent, still has the 29th highest percentage of any country in the world. This is typical of developed countries. Developing countries have populations that are skewed the other way. This is shown, for comparison, by Zaire.

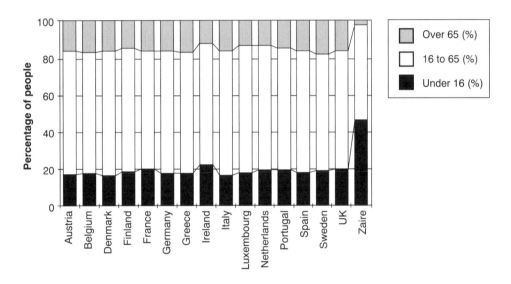

Fig 2.11 Age structure of EU countries by three main age groups, 1995
Source: Adapted from OECD

■ Life expectancy

Age structure is also related to how long people may be expected to live, or to what is called their **life expectancy**. This is another measure of the standard of living within a country, because as medical care, diet, housing, welfare support, etc., improve, people are likely to live longer.

Life expectancy for all EU citizens, both male and female, is in excess of 70 years. Figure 2.12 shows that women in all EU countries fare better than men. It also shows how the countries differ.

Quick Quiz No. 5

How many people are there in the UK over the age of 100 years?

(1) 700   (2) 7000   (3) 70,000

The answer is given on page 91.

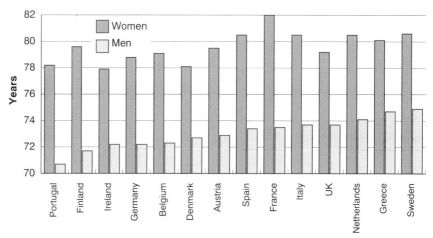

Fig 2.12 Comparative life expectancy in the EU
Source: Adapted from the World Health Statistics Annual (WHO)

Figure 2.12 shows that Portugal has the lowest life expectancy for men at 70.7 years, but this still puts Portugal into only 33rd place in the world league table out of 140 countries. The lowest figure for women is in Ireland, at 77.9 years, and that puts Ireland into only 23rd place in the world league table.

When the life expectancy figures change, this will have significant effects on economies. On average, people in the EU live ten to fifteen years beyond the normal age of retirement. Living longer is likely to have all of the following effects:

➡ There will be a growing number of older people who need support and care.

➡ As governments find it more and more difficult to pay for the increased pensions, they will insist that people provide for their own old age through private pensions.

➡ Populations will become more conservative, both in their voting habits and in terms of what they wish to buy.

→ Markets that cater for the needs and wants of the elderly will grow. The *grey market* is perhaps the fastest-growing market in the EU because many older people have built up considerable pension funds and basic wealth.

→ Eventually EU governments will wake up and realise that it is both necessary, and sound economics, to encourage people to work beyond the current retirement ages. The age of retirement will, therefore, be raised.

■ Gender structure

Both in the UK, and in the EU, legislation has been passed that makes discrimination on the basis of a person's sex illegal. This should mean that men and women have equal opportunities in the workplace, and are able to earn comparable levels of income. In reality, however, this is still very far from being the case in the EU. Various examples of the continued discrimination against women are cited in this textbook. Some discrimination, however, is made with the full consent of the two sexes, and gender remains an important distinction for many parts of economic life:

→ Many products are still distinguished on the basis of gender, such as clothes, magazines, drinks, sports and leisure activities.

→ Despite the so-called modern man and modern woman, most of the household tasks of cooking, washing and shopping, etc., are still done by the woman, and most of the DIY and car maintenance tasks are done by the man (*see* Figure 10.5). This fact will affect how goods and services are packaged and promoted and who is targeted.

→ Despite the Equal Opportunities Acts, it is still mainly women who do keyboarding and clerical work in offices, teach in primary schools, and are nurses, and it is still mainly men who work on building sites and are engineers and politicians (*see* Figures 2.13 (a) and (b)).

→ Motherhood, and some strong European traditions, mean that men still significantly out-number women in the workforce.

→ Although the Equal Pay Act is supposed to ensure that men and women are paid equally for similar types of work, women generally have much lower incomes than men. This is compounded by the fact that many women do not work, or only work part-time.

Because gender does make a difference in the workplace and in markets, it is useful to know how many men and women there are, what ages they are, what incomes they have access to, etc. Some of these points are considered in Chapter 10. Table 2.3 shows how the relative numbers of women to men change as the population gets older. This is given for the UK (1991) and Finland (1990). It also shows that generally more boys are born than girls. This is nature's way of compensating for the fact that women tend to live longer than men.

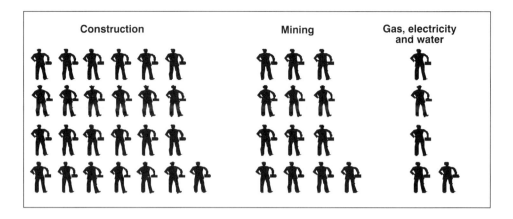

Fig 2.13 (a) Number of men for each woman in different EU industries
Source: Adapted from *Statistic Yearbook*, 1995 (UN)

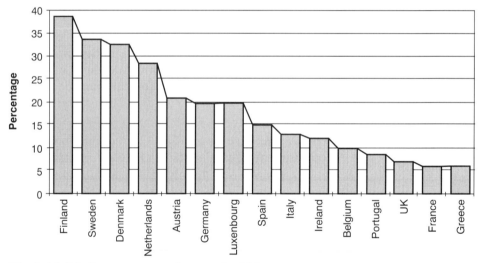

Fig 2.13 (b) Percentage of seats held by women in national parliaments, 1994
Source: Adapted from the Human Development Report (UN)

Traditionally it has been the man who has been the 'bread-winner', but in the last 20 or 30 years this has changed dramatically. It is now the norm for women to have jobs outside the home, and in an increasing number of cases women earn more than their male partners. Gender is, nevertheless, still a major discriminatory factor in the workforce. Further details are given in Chapter 3.

Table 2.3 Number of women for every 100 men in different age groups

Age range	UK	Finland
0 to 20 years	96	96
21 to 40 years	101	96
41 to 60 years	101	100
61 to 80 years	127	152
81 to 100 years	245	274
Over 100 years	579	481
Total population	107	106

Source: Adapted from *The Demographic Year Book* (UN)

■ Location of the population

Figure 2.1, on page 14, showed how the population was distributed, in total terms, across EU countries. It did not, however, indicate how the population was distributed within countries. The location of the population is important because it will affect all of the following:

➡ The need for housing, shops, schools, etc.

➡ The need for transport and communications systems to link major centres of population.

➡ Where the major markets for goods and services will be.

➡ Where the major sources of labour will be found.

➡ How crowded an area will be and hence the effects on congestion, pollution, etc.

➡ The need to provide people with jobs, welfare and security.

Definition
Population density measures the average number of people who live on a set area of land, usually one square kilometre. It is calculated by dividing the total population by the total area of land.

Table 2.4 shows how many people are located in each EU country in relation to its area and hence how crowded each country is. This is referred to as **population density**. Countries like Sweden and Finland have very large land masses but relatively few inhabitants. This gives them very low population densities. In contrast, Belgium and The Netherlands have relatively small areas of land even though their populations are not very large. This results in high population densities.

Table 2.4 Relative population densities in EU countries, 1993

	Pop./mil.	Area/sq. km.	Density/ sq. km.
For EU total	368.7	3,238,350	114
Finland	5.1	337,030	15
Sweden	8.7	449,964	19
Ireland	3.6	70,283	51
Spain	39.1	504,782	77
Greece	10.4	131,944	79
Austria	8.0	83,849	95
France	57.7	552,000	105
Portugal	9.9	92,082	107
Denmark	5.2	43,069	120
Luxembourg	0.4	2,586	146
Italy	56.1	301,225	186
Germany	81.2	357,039	227
UK	58.2	244,046	238
Belgium	10.0	30,513	328
Netherlands	15.3	37,938	403

Source: Adapted from Main Economic Indicators (OECD)

Table 2.4 gives an average population density for the whole of each country. Most people live in towns and cities. This means that urban areas will have population densities that are well above the national average, and rural areas will have population densities that are well below the national average. The proportion of people living in urban areas affects their individual population density. Figure 2.14 shows the proportion of people in each country who live in urban areas.

Quick Quiz No. 6

One traditional English nursery rhyme is about domestic overcrowding and high population density. Which one is it?

The answer is given on page 91.

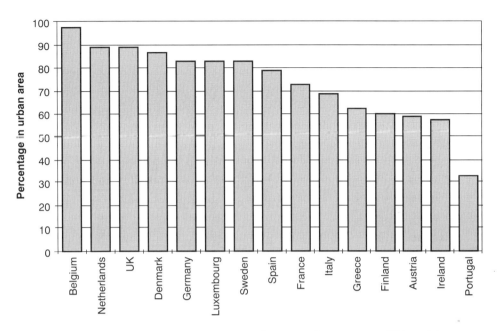

Fig 2.14 Percentage of population living in urban areas, EU 1993
Source: Adapted from Main Economic Indicators (OECD)

The effect of this crowding into urban areas means that rural and urban population densities are widely different. In Germany, for example, where the national population density was 227 people/sq. km. in 1993, West Berlin had a population density of almost 4,400 people/sq. km., but in the whole region of Niedersachsen it was only 150 people/sq. km. For the regions of Portugal, the population density varies from 317 people/sq. km. in the 800 sq. km. islands of Madeira, to only 20 people/sq. km. for the whole 27,000 sq. km. of rural Alentejo. The 12,000 sq. km. of Lisbon is the industrial and commercial centre of Portugal, and has 276 people/sq. km.

The largest city in every EU country is its capital city. Figure 2.15 shows the percentage of each country's population that lives within the capital city. During the working day the populations of most of these cities are dramatically swollen by the influx of commuters from dormitory towns and villages.

Figure 2.15 shows that the percentage of the population living in the capital city is lowest in Berlin and highest in Athens. The two sets of figures show that, generally, it is the countries with the smallest total populations that have the highest percentage of their populations in the capital cities. This is mainly due to the fact that large countries tend to have more than one major city. Only the UK, France, Germany and Italy have three or more cities with populations of over one million people (*see* Table 2.5).

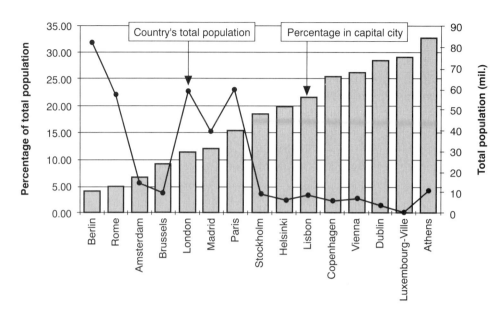

Fig 2.15 Total population of EU countries (mil.) and population of capital cities as a percentage of total population
Source: Adapted from EUROSTAT and OECD

Table 2.5 Cities of over 1 million residents, selected countries

UK		France		Germany		Italy	
London	6.4 mil.	Paris	9.3 mil.	Berlin	3.4 mil.	Rome	2.8 mil.
Manchester	1.7 mil.	Lyon	1.3 mil.	Hamburg	1.7 mil.	Milan	1.4 mil.
Birmingham	1.4 mil.	Marseilles	1.1 mil.	Munich	1.2 mil.	Naples	1.2 mil.
Liverpool	1.1 mil.						

When population density is taken down to the level of the family, what may be most important is how many people are living in one household. Figure 2.16 shows the average number of people per household for EU countries in 1992. This will determine how crowded their living accommodation is. It must of course be remembered that some people have small houses and some people live in mansions or castles, and as the population gets older, there are more likely to be retired people living in one- or two-bedroom flats or bungalows.

 The largest residential property in the EU, other than palaces, is St Emmeram Castle in Regensberg, Germany. In total, it has 517 rooms.

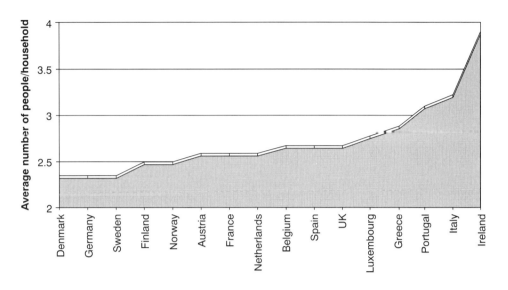

Fig 2.16 Average number of people/household in EU countries, 1992
Source: Adapted from Eurostat

Population density provides important data in both economic and social terms:

➡ For businesses it provides details of where the highest concentrations of people are to be found, and therefore where the best markets are likely to be. Household size will also indicate where advertising and promotion are likely to reach the most people.

➡ The highest areas of population will also indicate where the greatest labour supply is likely to be found.

➡ Population density is likely to be a major indicator of where over-population and under-population will be found.

➡ Population needs to be supported with infrastructure, so population density will indicate where the highest areas of expenditure are likely to be.

The way of life and cost of living in different EU countries

An important part of any demographic profile must be the conditions in which the people live – how wealthy they are, what values they consider important, what standards and costs of living they have, etc. Some points, on infant mortality and life expectancy, etc., have been covered above, but the wider issues of the way of life and the costs and standards of living are considered in Chapter 12.

3 Key economic resources of EU member states

Introduction

In an economy, all products are produced from four basic factors of production: **land**, **labour**, **capital** and **enterprise**. The definitions of these terms are very wide, and together they cover **everything** that is used in the production process. Figure 3.1 shows how these factors might be combined to produce a bar of chocolate. Only four examples of each factor of production have been given. There are in fact a great many more elements involved in this kind of production.

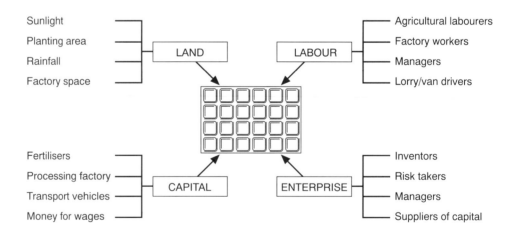

Fig 3.1 Factors of production for a bar of chocolate

Land is anything that is provided as the *free gift of nature*. This does not just apply to the land itself, but includes water, air, sunlight, rainfall, wild animals and the minerals of the earth. Each of these is vital to some kind of economic production:

➡ It is the purity of the water in the Scottish Highlands that makes Scotch whisky world famous.

➡ It is the reliability of the sunshine in Spain and Greece that attracts so many tourists to these countries.

➡ It is the natural deposits of uranium in Germany and France that allow them to produce 8 per cent and 7.5 per cent respectively of the world's total production of uranium.

➡ It is the temperature and precipitation in the Alps that make Austria, France and Italy such popular skiing resorts.

➡ It is the climate of Italy and France that makes them the world's greatest producers of wine.

Land is provided by nature and the amount of land is therefore fixed. All mankind can do is to change how much of it is available for use in the production process. Increasing the availability of land is what happens when farmers build greenhouses to use the warmth of the sunlight for longer periods during the winter, or when a country like The Netherlands reclaims land from the sea and turns it into productive farmland.

Labour is that part of the production that is carried out by people. It includes both their physical and mental efforts. Countries that have large numbers of well-educated people of working age who are highly motivated to work, will gain a significant advantage over small countries where the

work ethic is considered of little importance. The total quantity of labour that is available in a country will depend on a variety of factors:

➡ How many people there are in the population.

➡ How many people are available for work. This will depend on school-leaving age, retirement age, family commitments, etc.

➡ How many hours they are prepared to work.

➡ What skills they have gained through education and training.

➡ What physical skills they have, which will be affected by diet, exercise, living conditions, etc.

➡ What incentives people are given in the form of incomes, perks, etc.

➡ What disincentives people are given in the form of taxation of their income, state benefits for not working, how hard or boring the work is, etc.

> **Definition**
> **Capital** is anything, other than land, labour or enterprise, that aids future production.

Capital has a very wide meaning, and basically includes everything that has not been provided by the other three factors. Capital's special characteristic is that it is something that helps future production, rather than simply satisfying current consumer demand. A guitar used by a commercial band will create music that can be sold in the entertainment industry, so it is described as a *capital good*. A guitar bought for someone to

play at home for his or her own pleasure does not produce anything that can be sold commercially and is, therefore, described as a *consumer good*.

Capital will include all of the following inputs into the production process:

- Money
- Raw materials
- Plant
- Equipment
- The power source
- Maintenance contracts
- Infrastructure
- Goodwill

Enterprise or 'entrepreneurship' is really a specialised form of labour, but it does have major characteristics that separate it from other types of labour:

- The entrepreneur is the person who **takes the risk** in the production process, and the person who will lose money if the firm goes bankrupt.
- The entrepreneur is usually the person who **comes up with the original idea**, as Richard Branson did for Virgin, and Anita Roddick did for the Body Shop.
- Ultimately the entrepreneur is **responsible for the running of the business** and is therefore likely to have a major managerial role in the firm.
- Normally the entrepreneur will also **put in the original capital**, and it is that which is, initially, at risk.

With a small business, such as a sole trader, the entrepreneur is likely to carry out all of these functions, but with a large business there is generally specialisation. Expert managers will be employed. Risk will be partially taken by insurance firms. Capital will be lent by banks. New ideas will come from the research and development departments.

Differences in natural resources across the EU

The basic natural resource of a country is its area. Figure 3.2 shows how the 3,238,350 square kilometres of land in the EU are divided between the member states. It also shows just how large France, Spain and Sweden are. These three countries occupy 46.5 per cent of the total EU land mass. It must, however, be remembered that the area of sea around a country is often as important as the land mass. The UK has gained considerable wealth from the sea, both in terms of fishing and resources such as North Sea oil, and Greece has developed merchant shipping fleets, off-shore oil fields and valuable tourism because of its sea borders.

It is not just the size but also the nature of the land that determines how valuable it is. It is the purity of the water in Scotland that allows the whisky

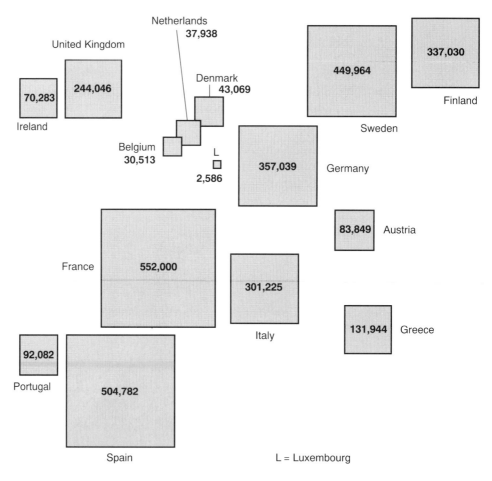

Fig 3.2 Relative land area of EU member states (sq. kms)
Source: Adapted from Main Economic Indicators OECD

and salmon industries to flourish. It is the reliability of the sunshine in the Mediterranean countries that attracts the huge number of tourists each year. It is the height of the Austrian Alps that provides ski slopes throughout the winter months.

Some EU countries are richer than others simply because they are lucky enough to have valuable natural resources. These resources allow the nations to develop productive, income-generating industries that raise the standard of living. Products may be produced for the home market, directly providing a standard of living, or they may be produced for export, generating income that can be used to buy imports which will also provide a standard of living. Figure 3.3 shows countries that have significant natural resources in certain raw material deposits.

	Oil	Iron Ore	Coal	Zinc	Lead	Gas	Marble	Gold	Copper	Silver
Austria		✓	✓	✓	✓					
Belgium			✓			✓	✓			
Denmark	✓					✓				
Finland		✓		✓	✓			✓		✓
France		✓	✓		✓	✓			✓	
Germany			✓			✓			✓	
Greece	✓	✓	✓			✓	✓			✓
Ireland			✓	✓	✓	✓				
Italy			✓	✓	✓					
Netherlands	✓					✓				
Luxembourg		✓								
Portugal							✓		✓	
Spain	✓	✓	✓							
Sweden		✓		✓	✓				✓	✓
UK	✓		✓			✓				

Fig 3.3 EU countries with natural resources (selected raw materials)

Table 3.1 shows the major productions of coal, petroleum and natural gas in the European Union. These basic products form the raw materials for all of the following industries:

➡ Electricity generation
➡ Domestic heating
➡ Chemicals
➡ Transportation
➡ Steel

**Table 3.1 Production of coal, oil and natural gas
(mil. tonnes of oil equivalents), 1990**

	Coal		Oil		Natural gas
Germany	121.4	UK	91.6	Netherlands	54.5
UK	55.9	Denmark	5.9	UK	40.9
Spain	17.9	Italy	4.6	Italy	15.6
France	7.6	Germany	3.9	Germany	13.4
Greece	6.4	France	3.4	France	2.5
Bel/Lux	1.7	Austria	1.2		
Austria	0.8				
Italy	0.2				

Source: Adapted from BP

The contrast in natural resources is most clearly shown when the production of something such as hydro-electric power is considered. The raw materials listed in Table 3.1 can be imported, but hydro-electric power comes from the natural domestic resources of water and relief. Table 3.2 shows the total production of hydro-electric power in each country, and the percentage that this forms of the country's total energy consumption.

Countries also develop their own bases of natural resources by adapting the land. All of the following are examples of where land has been adapted to provide productive resources:

➡ The Dutch and British have reclaimed land from the sea to create the polders of north Holland and the Fens.

➡ The British breed pheasants, partridges and grouse for the UK gamebird industry.

➡ The Austrians, Italians and French cut down forests and landscape their mountains in order to produce ski runs.

➡ The French dam their estuaries in order to tap the tidal energy and create electricity.

Quick Quiz No. 7

a) Which two EU countries have most horses?

b) Which two EU countries have most asses?

The answers are given on page 91.

Table 3.2 Production of hydro-electric power (billion kilowatts and percentage of domestic energy production)

	Production bil. kW	Percentage of domestic energy
Sweden	73.1	50
France	57.4	14
Italy	35.1	16
Austria	34.5	64
Spain	26.2	17
Germany	19.5	3
Finland	10.9	20
Portugal	9.3	33
UK	7.1	2
Greece	2.0	6
Ireland	0.4	1
Belgium	0.3	0.2
Luxembourg	0.1	0.9
Netherlands	0.1	0.2
Denmark	0	0

Source: Adapted from *The Nations of the World*

➡ The Finns and Swedes cut and replant their forests, ensuring renewable sources of timber.

➡ The Greeks, Italians, French and Spanish have cultivated the natural trees of the Mediterranean to produce olives and citrus fruits.

An example of the adaptation of natural resources is shown by the levels of livestock that each EU country has developed. Figure 3.4 shows the three main forms of livestock in each country. To allow easy comparison this is shown in terms of how many pigs, sheep, cattle or chickens there are for each member of the population.

All countries have some natural physical resources. Many of these have more than one use and therefore allow the country to develop a range of industries. Figures 3.5 (a) and (b) show some of the potential uses for water and sunlight. A similar pattern of resource use could be drawn for forests and timber, coal, oil, limestone, wind, land itself, and so on.

To understand how natural resources might be of value to a country, it is useful to relate the natural resources that exist in each country to the industry

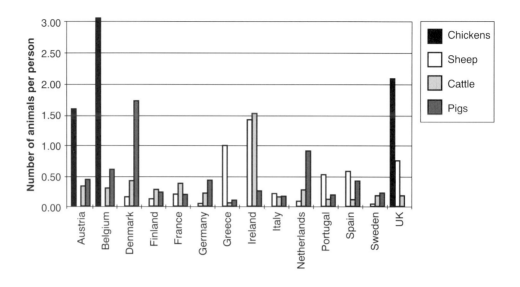

Fig 3.4 Number of units of livestock for each person in the country
Source: Adapted from *Eurostat*

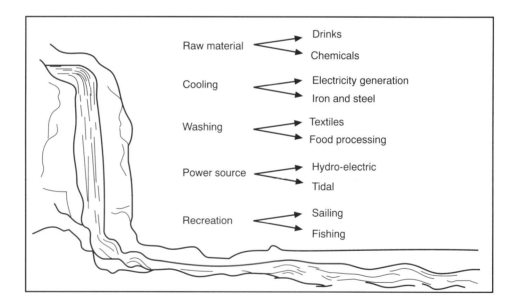

Fig 3.5(a) The use of water for industry

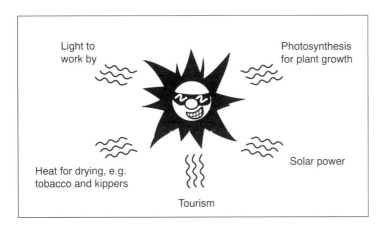

Fig 3.5(b) The use of sunlight for industry

that is found there. The UK has major resources of coal. This provides the raw materials for electricity generation, and through that the power source for producing products that use high levels of electricity, such as aluminium. Finland has a large resource of timber from which newspapers and furniture are made, both of which form a large part of Finnish exports.

Table 3.3 shows the major industries for all the EU countries. Readers should attempt to work out what natural resources are needed to produce these products, and whether the country has its own supply of these resources or whether it will need to import them.

Natural resources are vital to countries because they form the basis on which countries create their own wealth. They do this in the following ways:

➡ They form the raw materials and power sources of domestic industries (e.g. coal and iron ore for the iron and steel industry of the Ruhr in Germany, forests and timber for the Swedish furniture industry, water for the hydro-electric power plant at Dinorwick in Wales).

➡ They can be sold as exports which fund the purchase of imports that the country needs or wants (e.g. exports of oil from the UK or iron ore from Sweden).

➡ They directly increase the standard of living of the country by providing products that the country wants (e.g. water for Scotch whisky drinkers, snow for French skiers in Val d'Isère, olive oil for Italian and Spanish cooks).

➡ They encourage foreign firms to set up in the country by providing an attractive environment, or the resources the foreign firms need (e.g. Shell and Burmah drilling for oil in the North Sea).

Table 3.3 Major industrial production in EU countries

	Au	Bel	D	Fin	Fr	Ger	Gr	Ire	It	L	N	P	Sp	Sw	UK
Electronics	●	●	●	●	●	●	●	●	●		●			●	●
Pharmaceutical	●	●							●		●				
Engineering	●	●	●	●	●	●	●		●		●	●	●	●	●
Aerospace		●			●				●		●				●
Gas refining			●								●				●
Oil refining			●								●				●
Chemicals	●		●	●	●	●	●		●		●	●	●	●	●
Textiles	●	●	●	●	●		●		●		●	●	●		●
Automobiles		●			●	●			●		●	●	●		●
Telecommunication		●									●		●		
Wine production					●		●				●	●			
Iron & steel	●						●								●
Banking & finance										●					●
Computers					●	●			●						●
Pulp & paper			●				●							●	
Ship building				●	●		●	●			●	●			●
Fish processing			●								●	●			

Differences in human resources across the EU

The total population for each EU country will show how big the labour force is likely to be, but this is only part of the picture. Many people in the population are either unable to work (because they are too old, too young, disabled, in prison, etc.) or unwilling to work (because they are raising a family, continuing their education, living off past earnings, etc.). In terms of the key economic resources, the number of people in the **workforce** is more important than the total number in the population.

Figure 3.6 shows the participation rates for men and women in the EU countries. Participation rates indicate the number of people of working age who are in the workforce, either working or registered as looking for work. The data clearly confirms that more men than women work, but it also shows that rates, particularly for women, vary considerably from country to country.

Chapter 2 showed that there is still a fairly traditional split in terms of men and women working in specific jobs. This is also true for the major sectors of industry – primary, secondary and tertiary. Table 3.4 shows how many men there are in each sector for each woman who is working. Remember when interpreting the data that there are more men working in total.

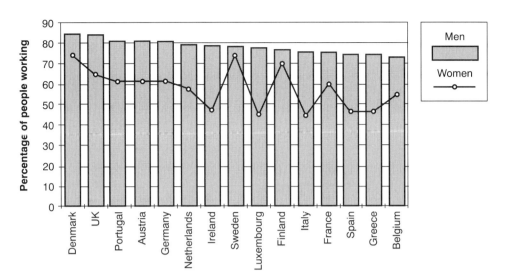

Fig 3.6 Participation rates for men and women in the EU, 1994
Source: Adapted from Main Economic Indicators (OECD)

Table 3.4 Number of men working for each one woman working in EU industry (1992)

	Total		Primary		Secondary		Tertiary
Greece	2.0	Ireland	11.1	Lux'bourg	9.6	Greece	1.7
Ireland	2.0	UK	3.7	Spain	5.0	Spain	1.3
Italy	2.0	Austria	3.2	Netherl'ds	5.0	Ireland	1.2
Lux'bourg	2.0	Denmark	3.0	Italy	4.4	Italy	1.2
Spain	2.0	Belgium	2.9	Belgium	4.2	Lux'bourg	1.2
Netherl'ds	1.6	Spain	2.8	Greece	3.6	Netherl'ds	1.1
Belgium	1.5	Sweden	2.8	Ireland	3.6	Belgium	1.0
Austria	1.4	Netherl'ds	2.7	Sweden	3.5	Austria	1.0
Germany	1.4	Italy	2.7	France	3.1	Portugal	1.0
France	1.3	Lux'bourg	2.4	UK	3.1	Germany	0.9
Portugal	1.3	France	2.0	Austria	3.0	France	0.9
Denmark	1.2	Finland	1.9	Finland	2.7	Denmark	0.8
UK	1.2	Germany	1.7	Denmark	2.6	UK	0.8
Finland	1.1	Greece	1.5	Germany	2.5	Finland	0.7
Sweden	1.1	Portugal	1.1	Portugal	2.0	Sweden	0.7

Source: Adapted from *The UN Statistics Yearbook* (1995)

Figure 3.7 shows that there is also still a wide variation in how people earn their livings, with up to 25 per cent earning their living from agriculture in Greece and as little as 2 per cent earning their living from agriculture in the UK.

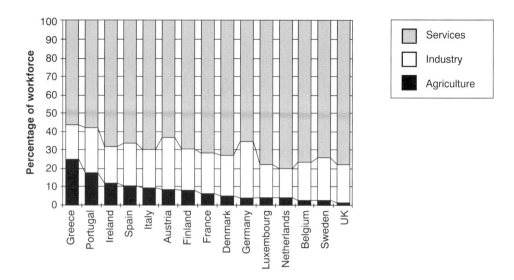

Fig 3.7 Breakdown of workforce into main sectors of industry, 1994
Source: Adapted from OECD

These average national figures do give a rather distorted picture of what actually happens in individual regions, or sub-regions, inside a country. Figure 3.8 shows how different specific areas of Italy are. The average employment figures for Italy as a whole have been given and then the two areas with, respectively, the highest figures for agriculture, industry and services. The differences are very dramatic, and show how misleading national averages can be.

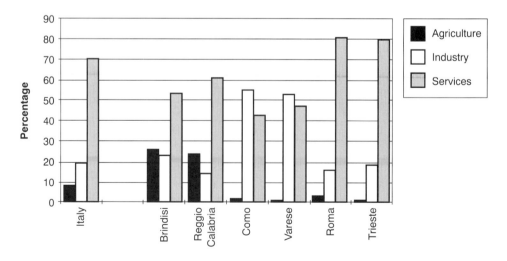

Fig 3.8 Variations in employment in selected areas of Italy, 1994
Source: Portrait of the Regions (EUROSTAT)

■ Mobility of labour

For some people the potential job market has become pan-European, and they see jobs in other countries as being as good, if not better, than ones in their own country. There are also a growing number of firms that actively seek employees from other countries.

Worker mobility

It has always been a basic principle of the Community that an EC citizen should be free to choose where to live and work. This freedom is now a reality. It is, however, unlikely to lead to a large movement of people from one member state to another. When restrictions on working in other countries have been removed in the past, few workers have been stimulated to seek jobs in other EU countries.

Source: The Single Market (Office for Official Publications of the European Communities)

This is not a new phenomenon. Spanish agricultural workers traditionally used to pick grapes, starting in Spain, working northward through France and finishing three months later in Germany. Workers from Ireland built many of the roads in the UK.

Linguists Required

A successful translating/interpreting business is expanding its freelance translators database. Professional native-speaking linguists required.

Today Germany has a large group of Turkish workers, and France has a large group of Algerian workers. Where translation and interpreting work is required firms often prefer to employ foreign native speakers.

Most worker mobility, however, takes place within countries. All regions, in all EU countries, show movements of workers in and out of the region, but generally internal mobility is highest in the UK. In Germany and France the major patterns of movement have been from north to south. In Spain, Madrid is the main focus of migration, and in Italy workers are moving away from the southern regions.

Worker mobility can be found in all of the following situations:

➡ Workers moving from one country to another.

➡ Workers moving from one part of their own country to another part.

➡ Workers living in one place and travelling to work in another, i.e. commuting.

➡ Workers moving from one kind of work to another.

➡ Workers moving from office and factory work to working from home.

European Union law (*see* Part 2) gives all workers in the EU the right to work in any member country that they wish to. This should, in theory, encourage workers to seek work in other countries and increase the level of worker mobility. In reality there is relatively little movement between countries, due mainly to the fact that most workers do not want to work abroad, and that those who do often find real barriers (e.g. language) and artificial barriers (e.g. qualifications) erected against them.

 More than 11,000 people succeeded in having their higher education qualifications recognised in another EU country between 1991 and 1994. Of these, nearly 6000 successfully applied to work in the UK. 3800 of these were teachers, encouraged to come to the UK by the high demand here for teachers.

Entry into France has been more difficult as there has been discriminatinon against foreigners and the French have been breaking EU regulations by insisting that teachers go on a French training course. Germany has also refused to recognise teaching qualifications from non-university colleges. Each *Land (plural: Länder)* in Germany decides its own teacher recruitment policy and after more than five years six *Länder* still have not passed the laws required by the EU. Greece now recognises qualifications for some health and legal professions, but not for teachers.

The main reasons for the movement of labour from one area to another, or from one country to another, are:

➡ The opportunities of earning higher wages.

➡ Persecution in, or dissatisfaction with, the country that one is currently living in.

➡ The wish for better working or living conditions.

➡ The simple desire to live and work in another country.

➡ Economic pressures caused by high levels of unemployment.

➡ The desire to gain wider experience and build up a valuable curriculum vitae.

4 Industrial profiles of EU member states

There is often considerable confusion about what the word **industry** means in the context of business. The problem is caused by those who classify industry as only the *manufacturing* of products, as in the production of iron and steel or the making of textiles and clothes. In the study of business, industry correctly refers to all parts of the production process. For example, in the production of chocolate bars all of the following branches of industry will be included:

➡ The *cocoa industry* producing the raw materials for the chocolate flavouring.

➡ The *sugar beet* or *sugar cane* industry providing the expected sweetness of chocolate bars.

➡ The *transport industry* transporting the raw materials and the finished products.

➡ The *confectionery industry* actually producing the range of chocolate products.

➡ The *advertising industry* providing the promotion for the product.

➡ The *finance* or *banking industry* providing finance, sources of capital and investment opportunities.

➡ The *insurance industry* covering the risks of theft, public liability, fire, accidents, etc.

➡ The *wholesale* and *retail industries* providing the channels of distribution needed to get the product from the producers to the consumers.

➡ *Government* providing legislation that will protect consumers from ingredients that would harm them, raising taxes on the sale of chocolate products and funding firms that are willing to locate in depressed regions of the country.

Because every part of production is included in the term 'industry', it is necessary to sub-divide the different parts of a country's industrial production in order to build up a distinct industrial profile of that country. This division can be done in a number of ways but the basic division is into **primary**, **secondary** and **tertiary** industry and, in some classification systems, **quarternary**. The basic meanings of these different categories of industry are given below:

➡ **Primary industry** involves the **extraction** of basic natural resources through four main areas of production:

- agriculture
- fishing
- forestry
- mining

These industries may create products that consumers want directly, as when people buy mackerel from Cornish fishermen in Penzance or Mevagissey, or they may create the raw materials that will be processed into other products, as when chemical firms use fish bones to produce bone-meal fertiliser.

➡ **Secondary industry** involves the **processing** of the raw materials provided by primary industry into new products. Findus takes breadcrumbs, originally produced from grain, and slices of cod, and processes them into partially cooked cod fishfingers.

➡ **Tertiary industry** involves either the **support** industries that ensure that primary and secondary products reach the consumers (industries such as transport, wholesaling, retailing, advertising, banking, etc.), or industries that offer a **service** direct to the consumer (such as private banking, travel agents, hairdressing, entertainment, etc.).

➡ **Quarternary industry**, where the term is used, refers to service industries that are not directly related to the production of consumer products, but are necessary to allow the smooth functioning of trade. Such functions would include government, taxation, the provision of law and order, basic education, and so on. (NB This term was invented by an economist and will not be found in a dictionary.)

Figure 4.1 shows the division of production for each EU country in terms of agriculture, industry and services. This is very similar to primary, secondary and tertiary, except that mining is included as part of secondary rather than as part of primary. This has to be done because that is how some EU countries make the classification for their own statistics.

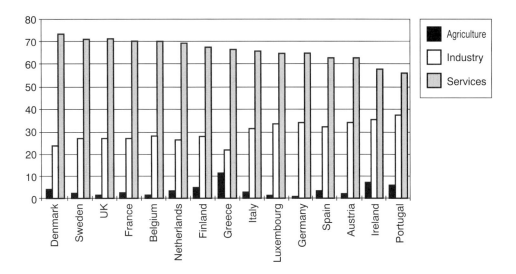

Fig 4.1 Division of EU countries' production, 1993
Source: Adapted from Main Economics Indicators (OECD)

The graph has been ranked in terms of the service industries, showing Denmark with the highest percentage. All EU countries have a high percentage of tertiary industry, even Portugal where the service industries comprise 56.4 per cent of its GDP. Greece, with 11.8 per cent of its GDP from agriculture, has the largest percentage gained from agriculture, and also the lowest from secondary industry at only 22.2 per cent. The country with the highest percentage of GDP created in secondary industry is Portugal, with 37.8 per cent.

The division of production into primary, secondary and tertiary is a very broad division. Most countries break down the classification of their own industries into far more detailed sections. They will, for example, distinguish between pig breeders and cattle breeders, or between retailers of electrical equipment and retailers of newspapers.

The EU has now accepted a standard classification, called the *Nomenclature générale des activités économiques dans les Communautés Européennes* or **NACE**. Our own classification, the Standard Industrial Classification (SIC), was changed in 1992 to follow the NACE classification. This is shown in Table 4.1 below. Both NACE and SIC closely follow the United Nations international classification standard (ISIC). The minor differences occur because the UN classification has to apply to all activities in all nations across the world.

Table 4.2 shows how the GDPs of Austria, France and Greece are divided by this wider category, although even here some categories are combined.

Table 4.1 The new Standard Industrial Classification of activities (SIC)

	Type of industry involved
A	Agriculture, hunting and forestry
B	Fishing
C	Mining and quarrying
D	Manufacturing
E	Electricity, gas and water supply
F	Construction
G	Wholesale and retail trade; repair of motor vehicles, motorcycles and personal and household goods
H	Hotels and restaurants
I	Transport, storage and communication
J	Financial intermediation
K	Real estate, renting and business activities
L	Public administration and defence; compulsory social security
M	Education
N	Health and social work
O	Other community, social and personal service activities
P	Private households with employed persons
Q	Extra-territorial organisations and bodies

Table 4.2 Percentage division of GDP by NACE categories (1994)

Category	Austria	France	Greece
A & B	2.3	2.9	13.7
C	0.2	0.5	1.2
D	24.5	21.3	15.4
E	2.9	2.4	2.6
F	8.2	5.5	6.6
G & H	16.5	15.6	13.7
I	6.6	6.2	7.0
J & K	19.8	22.4	11.3
L	14.2	16.9	10.9
M to Q	4.7	6.3	17.6

The importance of individual industries and firms in the EU

It is also important to know what power certain firms and industries have, both within the country and within the EU. Some firms are so powerful that they can control markets in terms of price, quality, the range of goods on offer, what pay rate workers will receive, etc. They may even be able to make governments offer them preferential tax rates, or grants and subsidies to set up in certain parts of the country. Generally, the firms that have this power control the major part of the market. In terms of *size*, they are market leaders. Having the largest 'size' in the market usually suggests the highest percentage of sales. Size can be measured by any of the following criteria:

➡ Monopoly power
➡ Market share
➡ Sales revenue
➡ Capital value of the firm
➡ Number of employees
➡ The physical area covered by the factory

Definition
The theoretical definition of a **monopoly** is that there is only **one** firm in the industry. The UK government defines monopoly as any firm that has **25 per cent or more** of the sales of the industry. Economists define monopoly as any firm that has the **ability to dictate market conditions**, especially the price that goods will be sold at.

Definitions
A **price taker** is a firm that must accept and follow the price that exists in the general market for its product.
A **price maker** is a firm that chooses the price for the market, and other firms have to follow suit.

Size in industry is about market power. While Ford, Rover, Vauxhall, Peugeot-Talbot, Nissan and Toyota might dominate the volume car production of the UK, it is still Rolls-Royce that dominates the luxury car market in the UK. The firms that dominate markets are the ones that have monopoly power.

For most EU firms and industries, the markets in which they operate are highly competitive. Prices are dictated by the market, and the individual firms are **price takers**. These prices affect what levels of pay employers can afford to offer their workers, the quality of the products they can afford to make, how far they can risk expanding their sales area, etc. Competitive markets will tend to have a large number of small producers. This is the norm, across the whole of the EU, for agricultural production, and for direct services such as hairdressing, plumbing, local shops, etc.

By contrast, Table 4.3 shows the relative sizes of the single largest firms in each of the EU countries. Size is being measured here by the sales revenue. The rank shows how big the firms are (in sales terms) compared to all EU firms. It is to be expected that the largest firms will be found in the largest countries. This explains the low ranking for Denmark and Ireland. There is, however, an important social dimension here as well. Traditionally Denmark, Ireland and Portugal have had small local firms. Often they have been family firms, as in agriculture. In Germany, France and the UK similar firms exist, but the economy as a whole is dominated by the large firms, producing the highest proportion of the GDP.

Table 4.3 Largest firm (by sales turnover) in each EU country (1995)

Rank	Country	Name of firm	Sales turnover (£ billion)	Type of industry *
1	Germany	Daimler Benz	43.3	Motor vehicles
3	UK	British Petroleum	33.4	Oil and gas
5	Netherlands	Royal Dutch/Shell **	31.3	Oil and gas
10	France	Elf Aquitaine	25.1	Oil and gas
15	Italy	Fiat	21.7	Motor vehicles
49	Sweden	Volvokoncernen	9.6	Motor vehicles
70	Belgium	Delhaize	7.9	Retailing food/drink
126	Austria	OEMV	5.0	Oil and Gas
130	Finland	Neste	4.8	Oil refining
184	Spain	Iberdrola	3.7	Electricity/power
244	Portugal	Petrogal-Petroleos De Portugal	2.8	Aircraft
349	Ireland	CRH	1.9	Wholesaling textiles
439	Denmark	FLS Industries Aktieselskab	1.5	Engineering services

* NB Most of these firms produce a variety of products. This list gives the main activity.
** Royal Dutch/Shell is jointly owned by The Netherlands and the UK.

Most of the largest firms are involved in petroleum and gas production or the manufacture of motor vehicles. These are large-scale operations requiring high capital investment and mass production. Countries like Denmark have little involvement in these kind of industries and so their firms tend to be small. This point is made even clearer when total sales revenue of the **ten largest firms** in each country is compared in Figure 4.2.

The size of firms is clearly influenced by the size of the populations of the countries, although The Netherlands and Sweden both have unusually large firms. This is to be expected because the larger the population of the country the greater is the immediate market. It must of course be remembered that all of these large firms also sell outside their own country.

Tables 4.4 (a), (b) and (c) (*see* page 60) consider the size of firms in specific sections of industry: food retailing, telecommunication services and banking. For the retailing of food and drink it is clear that countries such as France and the UK have moved over to the supermarket (and hypermarket) as the main method of selling to consumers. The German firms tend to be department stores rather than supermarkets. Countries like Spain and Greece still sell food and drink mainly through smaller shops. France still retains specialist *boulangeries* and *pâtisseries*.

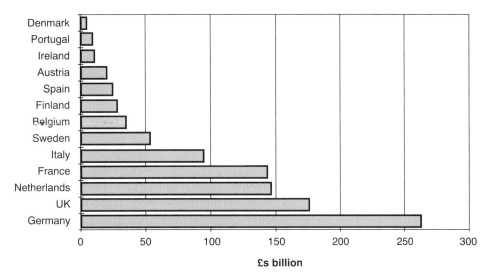

Fig 4.2 Sales revenue (£ billions) of the ten largest companies in EU countries, 1995

Quick Quiz No. 8

In 1995 three EU beer companies were in the top ten producers in the world. What was the name of

a) the Dutch company, ranked second?

b) the Belgian company, ranked sixth?

c) the Danish company, ranked eighth?

The answers are given on page 92.

With telecommunication there has, until recently, been little competition, and firms have tended to be state-owned monopolies. This explains why the largest firms are found in the largest countries. Again Sweden is an exception, but this reflects the fact that Sweden is the third largest country, by area, in the EU and therefore needs a wide telecommunication system. With the banks many countries actually have a large number of small banks competing with each other. France and the UK are dominated by a few very large banks. Generally banks tend to be fairly capital intensive and the sales per employee are therefore fairly high.

Table 4.4(a) Major firms in food and drink retailing in EU countries

Firm	Country	Sales (£ bil.)	Employees	Sales (£000s)/ employee
Carrefour	France	14.9	76,100	196
Sainsbury	UK	11.5	131,300	87
Koninklijke Ahold	Netherlands	10.8	79,900	135
Tesco	UK	10.2	108,100	94
Karstadt	Germany	10.1	108,300	93
Kaufhof	Germany	8.0	61,900	129
Delhaize	Belgium	7.9	12,400	639
Casino	France	7.6	45,100	168

Table 4.4(b) Major firms in telecommunication services in EU countries

Firm	Country	Sales (£ bil.)	Employees (1000s)	Sales (£000s)/ employee
Deutsche Telekom	Germany	25.5	225,400	112
France Telecom	France	15.4	154,500	99
British Telecom	UK	14.0	148,900	145
Cable & Wireless	UK	5.2	41,100	126
Telia	Sweden	3.3	1,156	2848
Posten	Sweden	1.9	52,251	36

Table 4.4(c) Major firms in banking services in EU countries

Firm	Country	Sales (£ bil.)	Employees (1000s)	Sales (£000s)/ employee
Crédit Lyonnais	France	22.4	71,400	313
Crédit Agricol	France	19.6	72,600	271
Deutsche Bank	Germany	18.6	65,100	286
Banque National de Paris	France	17.9	57,100	313
HSBC Holdings	UK	14.0	106,900	130
National Westminster	UK	13.3	97,000	138
Rabobank Nede	Netherlands	7.1	38,100	185
Abbey National	UK	5.6	16,700	337

The tables also show the number of employees in each firm. The sales/employee show how labour intensive the firms are. The Swedish firm, Posten, shows that postal services, which require many postmen and postwomen to collect, sort and deliver mail, is very labour intensive. Telia shows how automated the telephone system is in Sweden.

All of the industries mentioned above are large-scale industries. Many types of production tend to be small scale, such as agricultural production where most agricultural products are produced by small firms, and often by one farm owner (as in Austria). In Denmark, Portugal and Greece, agriculture still forms a high percentage of total production and these countries tend to have many small production units. In the UK, however, agricultural production is becoming more and more concentrated into larger units. Table 4.5 shows the largest companies in farming in the EU. Of the top 30, all but three are in the UK.

Table 4.5 Large-scale agricultural producers in the European Union

Rank	Firm	Sales (£ mil.)	Employees	Sale (£000s)/ employee	Headquarters
1	Buxted Chickens	63	738	85	Suffolk
2	Moorlands Foods	58	927	63	Yorkshire
3	Dean Farms	57	758	76	Yorkshire
4	Nickerson Group Rothwell	55	1,069	52	Lincolnshire
5	Van Hegningen Bros	45	698	64	Sussex
6	Cherry Valley Farms	37	863	43	Lincolnshire
7	Doubs Bétail Et Viande (Fr)	34	46	729	Franche-Comté
8	A.E. Button & Sons	32	391	81	Norfolk
9	Middlebrook Mushrooms	23	1,042	22	Leicestershire
10	Albert Hall (Farms)	21	23	897	Yorkshire
19	Centre Sud Elevage (Fr)	17	4	4354	Midi-Pyrénées
30	Avicola De Galicia (Spain)	14	165	82	Galicia

Total sales are very small compared to the manufacture of vehicles or supermarket sales. The sales per employee also tend to be low, showing a labour-intensive industry. The two French firms and Albert Hall (Farms) mainly manage other farms and there are, in fact, many other workers employed, but not directly by these firms. Large farm units are, however, rare in the EU and most agricultural production units remain very small, generally with less than ten employees and sales of less than £1 million.

The location of EU industry

The location of industry within a country reflects a wide range of factors. At its most basic, industry can only locate where it is economical to do so. In Finland and Sweden there are huge areas of land where there are no industries and no people. In Austria there are mountains so steep and high that even skiing is not possible. On an economic basis, what really matters is 'Will production be profitable?' – and that depends on the raw materials available, the supply of labour, capital and enterprise and whether there is a market to sell to. Because these factors vary considerably from one EU country to another, so does the type of industry to be found there. And, because location factors vary considerably within countries, different industries will be found in different regions and areas (*see* Figure 3.8).

Primary industry is located where the natural resources are found:

➡ Coal is mined in the Ruhr and Lippe in Germany, but the greatest reserves in the EU are found in the UK (e.g. Yorkshire and Nottinghamshire). Belgium produces coal in Kempenland; France in the Nord-Pas-de-Calais between Béthune and Valenciennes; and Spain in the north-west in Leon-Oviedo.

➡ Sweden is the major producer of iron ore in the EU, mined in the north at Kiruna and Gällivare. France, Spain and Austria also mine iron ore.

➡ Oil and gas is found in the North Sea and is extracted by the UK, Denmark and The Netherlands, as well as Norway. There is also some oil extracted off the coast of Thàsos in Greece, in Weser-Ems in Germany and Aquitaine in France.

➡ Almost 75 per cent of Finland's land area is covered with forest, as is 75 per cent of central Sweden. All EU countries have some area of commercially grown forest and produce timber (*see* Figure 4.3).

➡ Fishing is mainly carried out in the sea, although inland fish farming is becoming more common. The major fishing nations (*see* Figure 4.4) are, therefore, those with large sea borders, and the fishing industries tend to be located in the major fishing ports (*see* Table 4.6).

Heavy secondary industries, which produce on a large scale and rely on specific raw materials and power sources, will locate where those raw materials and power sources are to be found, or close to where the materials can be imported. Examples of such industries are the iron and steel industry, the aluminium industry and oil refining. Today many of the original sources of iron ore, coal, etc., have disappeared, and the heavy industries only remain in the same place because it would be too expensive to move them. Often the power source has changed from coal to electricity, which is available through the national grids. Table 4.7 shows major centres for the production of iron and steel across the EU.

Table 4.6 Major fishing ports in some EU countries

	Major ports
Belgium	Ostende
Denmark	Esbjerg, Hantsholm, Hirtshals, Thyboron, Skagen
France	Boulogne, Concarneau, Guilvinec, La Rochelle, Lorient
Germany	Bremerhaven, Cuxhaven, Emden, Rostock
Italy	Barletta, Chioggia, Pescara
Netherlands	Ijmuiden, Scheveningen, Vlissingen
Portugal	Matosinhos, Portimão, Setúbal
Spain	El Ferrol, Gijon, La Coruna, Santander, Vigo
United Kingdom	Aberdeen, Grimsby, Hull, Lowestoft, Peterhead, Plymouth

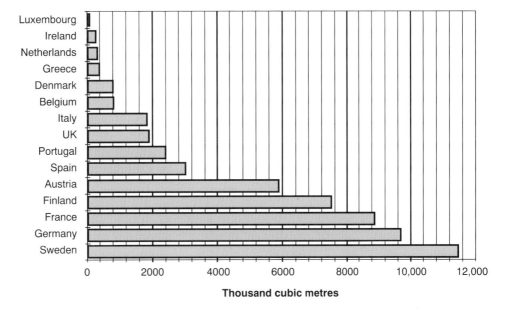

Fig 4.3 Timber production in EU countries, 1993
Source: Adapted from the *Guinness European Data Book*

Quick Quiz No. 9

What is the basic raw material of aluminium called and which is the only EU country that has sizeable reserves of the raw material?

The answers are given on page 92.

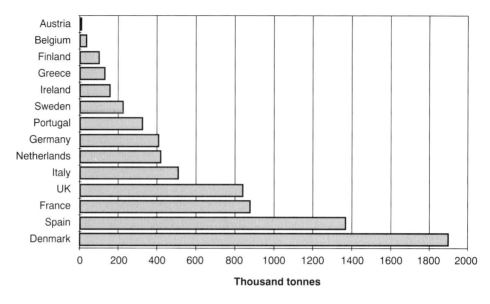

Fig 4.4 Fish catches in EU countries, 1995
Source: Adapted from the *Guinness European Data Book*

Large-scale secondary industries that process or assemble raw materials and components made in other industries will tend to locate where there is a high level of skilled, cheap labour available and where markets are relatively close. The car industry, for example, has traditionally been located where there were engineering skills, but today the new Japanese car firms are primarily attracted by where they will receive the best government grants, tax incentives, and subsidies. Most EU countries have major car production units, as shown in Table 4.8.

Table 4.7 Location of some major iron and steel plants in the European Union

Country	Location
Austria	Linz, Graz
Greece	Thessaloniki
Portugal	Porto, Lisbon
United Kingdom	Middlesborough, Sheffield
France	Marseilles
Italy	Taranto
Luxembourg	Luxembourg
Germany	Ruhr
Denmark	Frederiksvaerk

Denmark has only one steel producer, Dansteel, which is located at Frederiksvaerk, north-west of Copenhagen. Seventy per cent of production is exported mainly to Germany, Norway, Sweden and the UK.

Table 4.8 Location of major vehicle assembly plants in the European Union

Country	Location
Belgium	Antwerp, Brussels, Charleroi
Spain	Barcelona, Madrid, Valencia, Vigo, Zaragoza
Portugal	Porto, Lisbon, Setubal
United Kingdom	London, Birmingham, Coventry, Oxford, Sunderland
France	Paris, Lille, Lyons, Strasbourg
Italy	Milan, Turin, Naples
Germany	Ruhr, Berlin, Frankfurt am Main, Stuttgart, Munich
Sweden	Gothenburg, Stockholm

Definition
A **footloose industry** is one where the location factors do not dictate where firms will locate. They can locate where they want to.

Other secondary industry is far more 'footloose', such as light engineering or computer hardware and software production. These industries tend to be spread widely around countries, attracted by such factors as low rates and rents, a skilled workforce, and access to good communication systems. In the UK the computer industry is to be found in towns like Newbury and Swindon on either side of the M4 corridor, but also in Glasgow, Edinburgh, Cambridge, Oxford, Bristol, Cardiff and London. Electronics firms will be found in most large towns and cities across the EU. In Italy plants can be found in Turin, Milan, Genoa, Venice, Firenze, Rome, Naples and Palermo, to name just a few.

The presence of industry tends to attract both workers and other firms to the area. Over time major centres of industry develop in certain sections of countries. The main concentrations of secondary industry in the EU are shown in Figure 4.5.

Tertiary industries either serve primary and secondary industry, or provide direct services to consumers. They therefore tend to locate where the other industries are located, or where the consumers are living, or where they buy their goods and services. Tertiary industry will, therefore, be found in most parts of all EU countries.

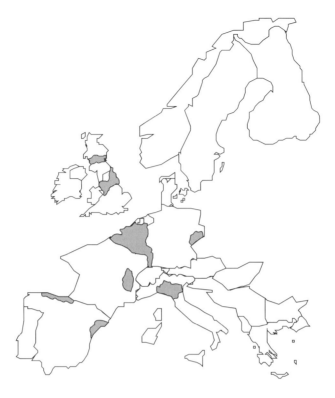

Fig 4.5 Major areas of secondary industry in the European Union

The growth of telecommunications, and particularly the use of modems, now allows some service firms to locate anywhere in the EU, as long as they have telephone connections with their customers. These are the ultimately 'footloose' firms. There are, however, many other small enterprises that are footloose because they need few raw materials and these are widely available. Their potential customers are also spread widely across the country. Examples would include the small craft firms, such as potters, glassblowers, woodworkers, artists, etc., producing for the tourist market and often choosing to locate primarily on the basis of where is a nice place to live.

In the past there were very clear divisions between countries and regions in terms of what was being produced. In some areas these divisions still exist, especially with heavy industries, but in many cases the divisions have completely disappeared as firms have become first international and then multinational. Where there is tertiary production most firms are now footloose. To understand exactly where, how and why firms are located at their particular locations in the EU, it is necessary to make a careful study of the individual firms and the individual areas. In the town of Whitchurch in Hampshire (4000 inhabitants), for example, the following secondary firms are to be found:

- Woolding Vineyard – one of the growing number of wine producers in the UK
- Testbourne Joinery & Kitchens Ltd – making specialist furniture
- The Whitchurch Silk Mill – producing silk cloth and silk garments
- Malcolm Lambden Engineering – producing farm and garden machinery
- R. J. Wiltshire – clock maker
- G. J. Smith Bros – builder

A similar study could be carried out for any foreign town or city to find out exactly what types of industry were located there.

There is, however, a danger that simply taking the name of a firm and the general range of products that it is known for will lead to inaccurate data. It is important to check or validate the data that one is collecting.

One major reason for this is that many firms are now multinationals and have production units in a number of countries. It is also difficult to work out exactly how much of any one product comes from any one country. This point is illustrated, in Table 4.9, by looking at where the ten firms that sold the most cars in the UK in 1995 actually got their cars from.

Table 4.9 Origin of main cars sold in the UK (1995)

Name of company	Country of parent company	Countries from which cars, or major components of cars, are being supplied
Citröen	France	France – Spain
Fiat[1]	Italy	Japan – UK – USA – Italy
Ford	United States	Belgium – Germany – Spain – UK – USA
Nissan	Japan	Japan – Spain – UK
Peugeot-Talbot	France	France – Spain – UK
Renault[1]	France	France
Rover[2]	Germany	UK
Toyota	Japan	Japan – UK – USA
Vauxhall[3]	United States	Belgium – Finland – Germany – Spain – UK – USA
Volkswagen	Germany	Germany – Spain

[1] Fiat is in discussions with Renault about merging their firms and manufacturing centres.
[2] Rover Group is now owned by BMW and is essentially a German company, even though it does not actually manufacture in Germany.
[3] Vauxhall is the UK subsidiary of the US giant General Motors.

5 Transport and communication systems in the EU

Transport and communication systems provide the principal physical infrastructure of economies. Without them all production would be local and small scale, and international trade would cease to exist. Transport systems such as road, rail, air and water networks provide the channels of physical distribution for both people and goods, and through these they allow economies to prosper and grow. Communication systems, such as post, telephone and now the Internet, provide the channels for exchanging information, and in today's sophisticated economies are as important as the transport systems.

Quick Quiz No. 10

Which ports, in which EU countries, do ferries go to from the following UK ports? Some may go to more than one country.

a) Folkestone

b) Harwich

c) Plymouth

d) Swansea

The answers are given on page 92.

■ Trans-European Networks (TENs)

The Treaty of Rome stressed the importance of having well-integrated transport and communication systems. The importance was emphasised again by member countries in the Maastricht Treaty, where the concept of Trans-European Networks (TENs) in transport, communication and energy supplies was established. Financial support is now provided to help the creation of these systems with the aim of stimulating growth, competitiveness and employment.

Transport

Priority has been given in transport projects to the development of:

➡ A high-speed rail network linking the major centres of commerce across the EU.

➡ The combining of different types of transport, such as road and rail, by ensuring that where one system stops the next begins.

➡ Road-building programmes that ensure that all the major cities of the EU are linked.

➡ The development of waterway systems that allow users to operate their craft in different countries.

Communications

The main objectives here have been to support projects that help to break down some of the current barriers to communication between member states:

➡ To promote the high-speed transmission of information on the *high-speed super-highways*.

➡ To ensure that all national systems are compatible and will allow the transmission of information in all forms, e.g. text, data, film, voice and image.

Energy distribution

The principal objective here is to ensure that energy systems are interconnected, and through this achieve:

➡ Better use of existing capacity.

➡ Security of supplies by creating a wider grid system.

➡ The reduction of the need to import energy supplies from non-EU countries.

➡ Better control of pollution.

A network for citizens

In another consultative document, the Commission opens discussion on how best to encourage inter-linking public transport services across the EU that are reliable, flexible and accessible. According to Neil Kinnock (EU commissioner with responsibility for transport), over the last 20 years car ownership in the 15 EU countries increased from 232 to 435 for every 1,000 people. He said it was imperative to increase the quality and management of public passenger transport to levels which encouraged those now dependent on cars to use these alternatives.

The provision of public transport is the responsibility of national, regional and local authorities, but the Commission believes that it has a role to play in four areas: the promotion of information sharing and best practice; research and development; funding mechanisms where links which interconnect with local systems and which promote public transport could be given priority; and legislation.

Source: *European Focus* (March 1996), KPMG

Transport systems in the EU

Good transport systems are vital for the physical movement of people and goods. They are also a major factor in the economic prosperity of a country. Transport systems allow:

➡ regions that produce surplus products to sell them in other markets

➡ firms that need raw materials, labour, etc., to obtain them from other areas

➡ individuals who want to work in other areas a way of travelling there

➡ consumers to take holidays away from home

➡ shops and other retailers to sell a variety of goods from a wide range of sources

➡ consumers the opportunity of buying a variety of products from different areas, regions and countries

It is tempting to think of transport systems as simply lines drawn on maps, creating links between geographical locations. In the real world it is generally the quality of the transport link that the users feel is most important. Users will be interested in all of the following factors:

➡ How much does it cost, and is it the cheapest method of acceptable travel?

➡ Does it provide the quality that is needed in terms of comfort, reliability, etc?

➡ Is it the fastest method of transport, and is that what is wanted?

➡ How convenient is it to use? Does it start and end where it is needed?

➡ How does it link with other transport systems?

➡ What is its safety record?

➡ What alternative transport facilities are available?

The usual way of comparing transport systems in different countries is to list the total length of the systems (the total kilometres of roads or railways, etc.), or to list the usage of the systems (the number of passengers using the trains or the number of arrivals at airports, etc.). These basic figures will be given below, but it must also be remembered that countries have different total areas (in sq. km.) and have different total populations. Transport systems could be compared using any, or all, of the following measures:

➡ Overall length (now generally measured in km.).

➡ Kilometres of system per sq. km. of land area. (This will indicate how well, on average, the country is covered by each system.)

➡ Kilometres of system per head of the population. (This will indicate how much of each system is, on average, available to each citizen.)

➡ The number of people using each kilometre of system. (This will indicate how much each system is used, and would also include tourist use.)

- The amount of road system, rail track, etc., available for each car, train, etc. (This will indicate how crowded the systems are likely to be.)
- The number of cars, trains, etc., that are using each kilometre of system. (This will indicate how crowded the actual systems are, or how efficiently systems are used.)
- The average speed for a journey of a set distance. (This allows time comparison between different systems.)
- The area of the country covered by the system, and how much of the country is within, say, five kilometres of the system. (This indicates convenience for the users.)

■ Road systems

Over 85 per cent of all EU goods and passengers are transported using roads. For most short journeys individuals and firms will use roads because transport is *quick*, it goes from *door to door*, it is relatively *cheap* and roads offer *good access* because there are far more roads than any other form of transport. With the reduction of custom controls between EU states, the building of high-quality motorways and the linking of national road networks, many people now consider that roads provide a system of transport that is as fast and convenient as rail or air. For long distances, however, rail or air travel is still very much faster.

Figure 5.1, shows the quantity of road system, by length, in each EU country. Figure 5.2 shows the length of road per 1000 people in each country. As can be seen by comparing the two graphs, the amount of total road system is fairly meaningless unless one also considers how many people may be using it. The numbers in Figure 5.2 indicate the rank that each country had in Figure 5.1. Four of the original top five countries – Germany, the UK, Italy and Spain – are now in the bottom six countries.

It must also be remembered that the quality of the roads is important. Generally in the UK we are well served by both our motorways and our 'A' roads, and frequently by our 'B' roads. The main problem is congestion, as will be confirmed by anyone who has driven around the M25 during the 'rush hour'. In France the motorways are probably better than those in the UK, but the non-motorway traffic is frequently directed through endless small towns with single carriageways, traffic lights, and poor road surfaces. In Germany, travel on the *Autobahn* is usually fast, generally with no upper speed limit, but the secondary roads are congested and have mainly single carriageways.

Table 5.1 shows the total length of motorway in each country, the amount of motorway for every 1000 people, and the amount of motorway for each square kilometre of land. It therefore shows how well the people are served by motorways and relatively how much of the country is covered.

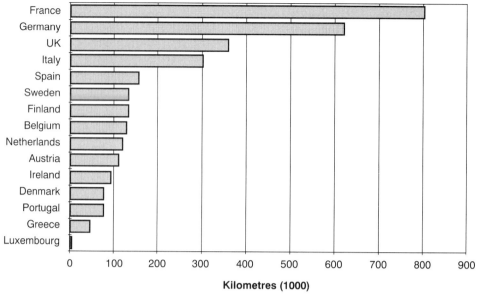

Fig 5.1 Kilometres of roads in EU member states
Source. Adapted from The Nations of the World

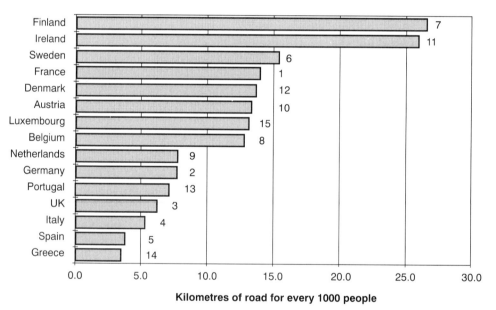

Fig 5.2 Amount of road for every 1000 people

➡ For the number of people in Finland the motorway system is reasonable but it does not cover much land area because so much is uninhabited.

➡ In Greece there are many islands where it is not economical to build motorways.

➡ In Ireland there is relatively little heavy industry so motorways are not as economically important as elsewhere.

Table 5.1 Quantity of motorways (in km.) for EU countries (1990s)

	Kilometres of motorway (1000s)	Kilometres of motorway/1000 people	Kilometres of motorway for each sq. km. of land
Austria	1449	181	17.3
Belgium	1649	165	54.0
Denmark	653	126	15.2
Finland	249	49	0.7
France	7080	123	12.8
Germany	10,955	135	30.1
Greece	91	9	0.7
Ireland	32	9	0.5
Italy	6214	111	20.6
Luxembourg	84	221	32.5
Netherlands	2092	137	55.1
Portugal	454	46	4.9
Spain	2558	65	5.1
Sweden	936	107	2.1
United Kingdom	3181	55	13.0

Source: Adapted from Eurostat (OECD)

The heaviest traffic use on roads is in excess of 50,000 vehicles per day and includes the following major routes:

Manchester ← → Birmingham ← → London

Cardiff ← → London

Leeds ← → London

Calais ← → Paris ← → Lyon ← → Marseilles

Öostende ← → Brussels ← → Cologne

Rotterdam ← → Amsterdam (and both to) ← → Cologne

Hamburg ← → Cologne

Hamburg ← → Frankfurt ← → Basle ← → Geneva

Cologne ← → Frankfurt ← → Nürnberg ← → Munich

Milan ← → Genoa

Milan ← → Bologna ← → Florence ← → Rome ← → Naples

Source: Economic Commission for Europe

All capital cities have traffic flows that are described as 'heavy' and generally have routes to other cities and towns with flows of over 25,000 vehicles per day. Around the capital cities themselves, as with the M25 around London and the Périphérique around Paris, daily traffic flows are huge, with hundreds of thousands of users.

With the completion of the Channel Tunnel, the London to Folkestone M20 has become the favourite route to both the Channel Tunnel terminus and the ports of Folkestone and Dover. The Channel Tunnel itself is a rail system and has therefore removed some traffic as people use the passenger connections from London. The

> ### Europe to Africa by tunnel
>
> Spain and Morocco have agreed to dig a $4 billion rail tunnel under the Mediterranean to provide the first direct land link between Europe and Africa. Work on the 38 km. tunnel, crossing under the Strait of Gibraltar, will start next year and should be completed by the year 2010.

Source: The European (February 1996)

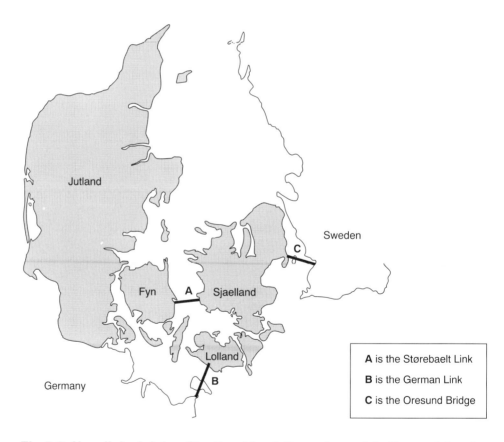

A is the Størebaelt Link
B is the German Link
C is the Oresund Bridge

Fig 5.3 New links joining Sjaelland (and Copenhagen) to the mainland

Channel Tunnel has made the first land link between mainland Britain and most of the rest of the EU. There is also a plan to link the island of Sjaelland, where Copenhagen is situated, to Sweden. Sjaelland would also be linked to the mainland region of Denmark at Fyn and possibly directly to Germany (*see* Figure 5.3). This would give Sweden a direct link to the rest of the EU.

■ Rail systems

Generally the rail systems of the EU are still state owned or heavily subsidised (but *see* cutting) and this has helped to increase investment in the rail systems and keep prices down. The policy of the EU is to establish a high-speed rail network linking all Europe's major cities by the year 2015, with over 15,000 kms of track. France already has the TGV (*Train à Grande Vitesse*) high-speed system running from Paris to Lyon, Tours, Calais and Brussels. Belgium, Germany, Italy and Spain also have high-speed train systems and even the UK has plans to develop systems.

> **Railway liberalisation**
>
> The European Commission has proposed that railway freight should be liberalised throughout the EU. Operators would be free to offer internal services within another member state as well as between countries.
>
> International passenger services would also be opened up to competition, but domestic passenger trains would not be affected. The Commission hopes that introduction of more competition will help to reverse the decline in railways, which have seen a steady fall in passenger and freight traffic over the last 25 years.

Source: European Focus, (September 1995), KPMG

Many of the EU rail systems now operate at speeds of up to 200 km./hr and the TGV up to 300 km./hr. These speeds, and the lower prices, have begun to encourage both motorists and users of air travel to consider trains as an attractive alternative. For the transport of *bulk* goods *over long distances,* rail travel is still economical for firms. The main disadvantages of rail travel, however, remain that:

➡ trains only cover part of each country, so road transport is usually also needed

➡ trains have to run to schedules and are therefore not always available when people want them

Quick Quiz No. 11

Many of the major EU cities now have *metro* systems. In the UK we have metro systems in London, Glasgow and Liverpool. Which are the only two EU countries that do not have metro systems in their capital cities?

The answers are given on page 92.

- luggage is difficult to carry and store on trains
- train systems are very capital intensive and, unless they are subsidised by the state, are likely to be costly to run and expensive for the users

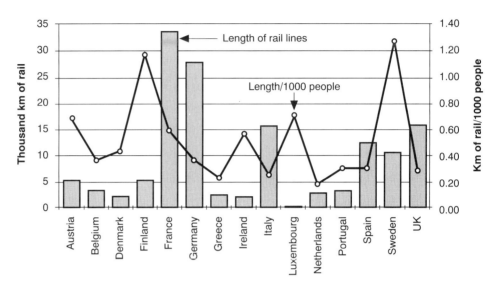

Fig 5.4 Length of rail track in EU countries, 1991
Source: Eurostat

■ Rail systems in each EU country

- **Austria** has a fast and efficient system with most lines electrified. It benefits from being in a central location in Europe with links to Paris, Amsterdam, Munich and Milan. From Salzburg trains leave hourly to Munich and express services run to Italy via Innsbruck or Villach.

- **Belgium** has fast and usually hourly trains connecting all main towns and cities. International lines cross Belgium between France and The Netherlands, and between the United Kingdom and Germany.

- The **Danish State Railways (DSB)** is supplemented by a few private companies and together they create a dense network of train services. In remote areas rail transport is closely integrated with bus networks.

- **Finland**'s extensive rail system reaches all main centres of the country and offers high standards of comfort and cleanliness.

- In France the state-owned **Société National des Chemins de Fer Français (SNCF)** national railroad, is generally recognised as Europe's best national train service, with the **TGV** being fast, punctual and widely spread. The TGV now runs from Paris to Lyon (The Sud Est), to Brittany (The Atlantique) and Lille, Calais and the Channel Tunnel (The TGV Nord). Intercity express trains are not as frequent and local trains are often considerably slower.

- In **western Germany** all major cities are linked by fast intercity services and some by the new **Intercity Express (ICE)** train service. In **eastern Germany** the railway system is still being updated.

- In **Greece** trains are slow and railway networks are limited. The main line runs north from Athens to former Yugoslavia. It divides into three at Thessaloniki. The main line continues on to former Yugoslavia, a second line goes east to the Turkish border and Istanbul, and a third line heads north-east to Bulgaria.

- In **The Netherlands** fast, frequent and comfortable trains operate throughout the country. Intercity trains run every 30 minutes and regular trains run to the smaller towns at least once an hour.

- In **Luxembourg** the size of the country means that rail services are very limited, but there are good international connections to Paris, and to Brussels and then to Amsterdam. The connection to Koblenz opens routes to most German cities.

- In **Ireland** much of the rail system has been cut back in recent years, but it still provides a good coverage. Main routes radiate from Dublin, going to Cork, Galway, Limerick, Tralee, Killarney, Westport and Sligo, and across the border to Belfast.

- In **Italy** the fastest service on the **FS (Ferrovie Italiane dello Stato)**, the state-owned railroad, is the Intercity. The major domestic network runs down the north and the south coast. **Espresso** trains usually make more stops and are a little slower. **Interregionale** and **Regionale** are slowest of all. International links run from Milan to all the neighbouring countries, and from Genoa to Marseilles and from Bologna north through Austria.

- The **Portuguese** railway system is surprisingly extensive for such a small country. Trains are clean and leave on time, but there are few express runs except between Lisbon and Oporto. The major international route passes through Spain and north to Bordeaux and Paris.

- The **Spanish** railroad system, **RENFE**, is now far more efficient. The **talgos** are by far the quickest, most comfortable and the most expensive trains, and operate internationally between Barcelona and Paris, and Madrid and Paris. The **expresos** and **rápidos** are internal and are slower but cheaper.

- **Sweden**'s rail network, mostly electrified, is highly efficient with trains operating frequently, particularly on the main routes linking Stockholm with Gothenburg and Malmö.

- In the **United Kingdom** the **Intercity** service is now one of the fastest in Europe. Other services are somewhat slower. Links with the rest of the EU are now through the Channel Tunnel. The main parts of the service are now in private ownership, under a franchising system.

■ Air transport

Over long distances air travel is still the quickest means of travel. Over short distances the advantage of speed is lost because it takes so long to get to and from the airport. For a typical journey this is between two and a half and three hours. Figure 5.5 shows the busiest air routes in the EU, with much of the air traffic based in London, Paris and Frankfurt. London (with nearly 70 million passengers per year) and Paris (with over 45 million passengers per year) have by far the largest passenger numbers. Frankfurt (with over one million tonnes of freight per year) has the largest freight figure in the EU.

Quick Quiz No. 12

What are the names of the two airports in

a) Paris?

b) Milan?

The answers are given on page 92.

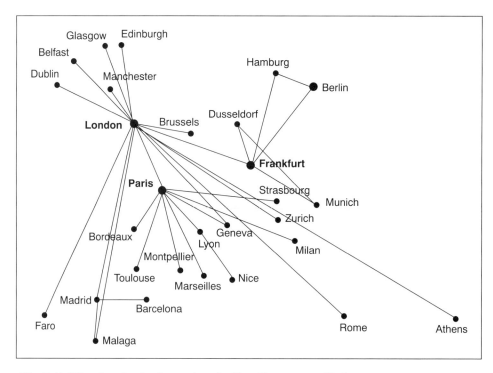

Fig 5.5 The busiest air routes in the European Union
Source: Commission of the EU

Table 5.2 shows the number of passengers using the major airport in each country. It must be remembered that many minor airports also have very large numbers of passengers, such as over ten million in Manchester and Munich, and these are not listed.

Table 5.2 Airport passenger numbers in each EU country's major airport

	Passengers (mil.)		Passengers (mil.)
London (Heathrow)	42.6	Copenhagen (Kastrup)	9.3
Frankfurt (Main)	28.7	Brussels (Zaventem)	6.9
Paris (Charles de Gaulle)	22.5	Athens (Athinai)	6.3
Madrid (Barajas)	15.9	Helsinki (Vantaa)	5.5
Rome (Fiumicino)	15.6	Vienna (Wein-Schwechat)	5.5
Amsterdam (Schipol)	14.9	Lisbon (Portela de Sacav em)	5.0
Stockholm (Arlanda)	14.9	Luxembourg (Findel)	0.9

Source: Commission of the EU

■ Sea and inland waterways

For some countries, and for most of the islands that form parts of countries, sea transport is vital. Ireland and large parts of Greece have no land connections with the rest of Europe. Major areas of some countries also have no land links, such as:

➡ Sjaelland (pop. 2.2 mil.) in Denmark

➡ The Balearic Islands (pop. 0.7 mil.) in Spain

➡ Sardinia (pop. 1.7 mil.) and Sicily (pop. 5.0 mil.) in Italy

➡ Corsica (pop. 0.25 mil.) in France

The UK, although now linked through the Channel Tunnel, still transports most of its goods by sea, even from the EU. Most of the Swedish population lives in the south of Sweden and the easiest routes to the rest of the EU are by sea. Figure 5.6 shows the major sea and inland waterway routes for western Europe. Table 5.3 provides details of how many kilometres of inland waterway are still used in the EU.

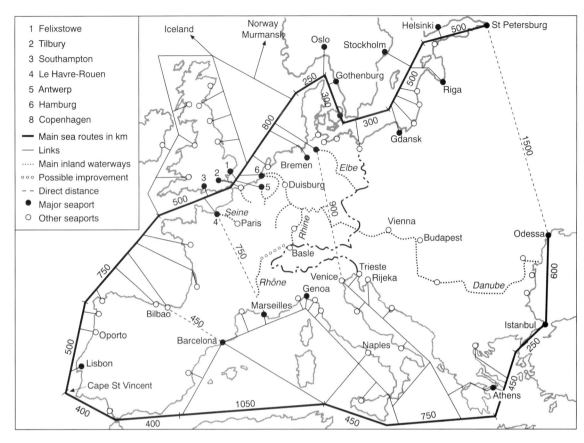

Fig 5.6 Sea and inland waterway routes
Source: Cole

Table 5.3 Length of inland waterways (km.) in EU countries

	Length (km.)		Length (km.)
France	8500	Belgium	1949
Germany	6700	Spain	1045
Finland	6237	Portugal	820
Netherlands	5046	Austria	446
United Kingdom	3200	Ireland	429
Italy	2400	Denmark	417
Sweden	2052	Luxembourg	37

Source: Adapted from Eurostat

Source: European Focus (September 1995), KPMG

Water transport tends to be very slow compared with other methods of transport, but it does allow for the relatively cheap transport of bulky goods. In the EU there are generally faster and cheaper alternatives so use of water transport is limited. For trade between the EU and non-EU countries sea transport is a major element.

For most countries, however, road and rail transport remain the methods preferred by passengers. The breakdown in terms of how many miles are travelled, on average, by each person is shown in Figure 5.7. These include travelling to and from work. For travel to countries outside the EU (not shown here), the main method of transport is by air.

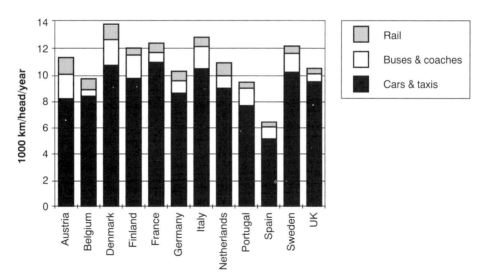

Fig 5.7 Passenger miles travelled by road and rail in EU countries, 1993
Source: Department of Transport

Communication systems in the EU

The major forms of **communication**, both inside countries
and between countries, have historically been the postal
system and the telephone system. These have developed
over time to include telegrams, faxes, and now modems and
the Internet, and, through a separate development, satellite
communications. The term 'communication' is, however, much wider than
just postal and telecommunication systems, and a full study of the EU
communication systems must include other methods of providing and
exchanging information. In medieval England it was the town crier who gave
people information; today it is done through newspapers, magazines, books,
radio, television, window displays, posters, leaflets, etc.

■ The EU postal system

All EU countries have well-developed postal systems although the speed
with which post will be transmitted does vary considerably. Each national
system is now fully integrated with all other EU postal systems so that the
same basic process is involved in sending a letter or parcel from Cardiff to
London, or to Lyon or Lisbon. Differences are relatively minor, but still
important. They will include all of the following:

➡ The time it takes for mail to arrive.

➡ The price charged in different countries.

➡ The way the address should be written.

➡ The times and frequencies of delivery.

➡ The services offered in different countries, e.g. there is no second-class
post in Ireland.

➡ Different countries will have different regulations about their mail, e.g. it
is still necessary to fill in a customs declaration for all items containing
goods that are sent to Andorra and Gibraltar although they are both
technically now part of the EU.

➡ The level of competition available in the postal services. In the UK post
with a price of less than £1 can only be delivered, legally, by the state-
owned Post Office.

The Spanish (*correo*) delivery service has a reputation of being one of
the slowest and most unreliable in Europe, with deliveries taking
anything from a few days to a few weeks or months (or mail
disappearing altogether).

Source: Living and Working in Spain by David Hampshire

Quick Quiz No. 13

In 1995 the latest posting dates given by the Royal Mail for posting Christmas airmail to EU countries was 14 December for nine of the countries. Which **five** EU countries were given the earlier deadline of 11 December?

The answers are given on page 92.

The kind of differences that exist are shown by the following example. Where mail is **registered** it is covered against loss or damage as it is transported and delivered by the postal services. It is, however, only covered up to a certain monetary limit and that limit is determined by the country in which it will be delivered. Some countries have much lower upper limits than the average, as can be seen in Table 5.4.

Table 5.4 Upper limits for registered post in EU countries (1996)

	Limit (£)		Limit (£)
Austria	2200	United Kingdom	2200
Denmark	2200	Italy	1500
France	2200	Ireland	1100
Germany	2200	Finland	800
Greece	2200	Luxembourg	800
Netherlands	2200	Spain	500
Portugal	2200	Belgium	450
Sweden	2200		

Source: Royal Mail

The costs of postal services in different countries change fairly frequently. The UK raised its postal charges again in July 1996 to 20p for second-class post and postcards and 26p for first-class post and airmail letters to the EU (weight not over 20g.). The differences in basic postal costs across the EU, however, remain fairly consistent. The UK has the lowest postal charges. Figure 5.8 shows how much more expensive (in UK pence) it is to send post in the other EU countries. Spain has similar costs to the UK, but Sweden's charges are about double this. Luxembourg, Sweden and Spain charge the same price for postcards as they do for letters.

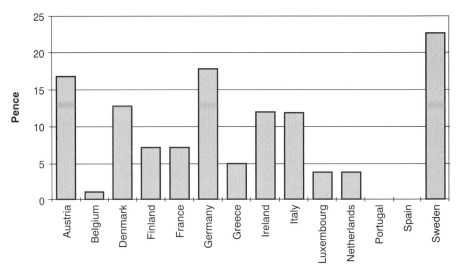

Fig 5.8 The relative costs of sending first-class post (up to 20g.) in the EU
Source: Adapted from *Fodor's Europe*

The European Commission has now set conditions for all EU postal systems. These include the following targets:

➡ 80 per cent of domestic mail should be delivered within one working day
➡ 90 per cent of mail delivered between EU states should be delivered within three working days

The Commission also stresses that competition remains the long-term objective, but agrees that state postal systems will continue to have monopoly rights (if they wish to) when it comes to:

➡ items that weigh up to 350 grams and have a price of not more than five times the basic rate
➡ domestic delivery of mail received from other member states
➡ direct mail items

■ The EU telecommunication systems

Definition
Telecommunication is communication over a long distance by cable, telegraph, telephone or radio waves (including satellite transmissions).

The word **tele** comes from the Greek, meaning far off or from a distance. Today it is used to describe communications using electronic transmission (as with the lines of a telephone system) or radio transmission (as with television or satellite transmission). In all parts of the EU there are sophisticated **telecommunication** systems, and all parts are interconnected with the systems in other countries. As with the postal systems there are minor differences:

- The times of day when reduced rates apply.
- The price charged for phoning to different countries.
- The meaning of the tones for ringing, engaged, etc.
- The services offered in different countries, e.g. you cannot make collect calls from public telephones in Austria.
- The level of competition available in the telecommunication services.

As with the postal service, the European Commission wishes to increase the level of competition in the EU telecommunications industry. On 1 January 1998 the £100 billion a year EU telecommunications industry must be fully opened to competition. Spain, Portugal and Greece, having the least developed systems, are allowed additional years before they have to comply. This liberalisation will signal the end of state control over telecommunications, as private and multinational companies are allowed to compete for a slice of this potentially highly lucrative market. A directive has been given to member states insisting that providers of telecommunication services must be given total access to existing national networks. Belgium, Ireland and Luxembourg voted against the proposal but, under majority voting rules, will still have to apply it.

 Spain has one of the lowest number of telephones per head of population (around 400 telephones per 1000 people) in Western Europe, with a total of 15 million lines in service, although the number of calls per person is high. The Spanish aren't habitual telephone users (it's too expensive) and don't usually spend hours on the telephone. Many businessmen prefer to meet in person or exchange letters, rather than conduct business over the phone.

Source: Living and Working in Spain by David Hampshire

In 1996, Singapore Telecom, TeleDanmark and Ameritech had already taken a joint 49.9 per cent stake in Belgacom. In November 1996 Deutsche Telekom were forced to sell £6.5 billion worth of shares to eager international speculators. In the UK more than 150 different firms already operate in the UK telecommunication industry, although British Telecom and AT&T still dominate the market. As the EU gears up to sell off the state-owned systems, or open them up to competition, banks, cable television networks, gas and electricity firms, railway companies, computer firms, etc., will all manoeuvre to be ready to pounce and profit. Other forms of telecommunication, such as data transmission and satellite communication, are already fully liberalised.

The number of televisions owned per person in EU countries is given on page 206, but the use of television as a means of communication is perhaps best shown by how important advertising firms think it is. Figure 5.9 shows advertising expenditure on the main types of media. The data shows that different countries have different levels of communication available. Greece has only eleven major newspapers, and the population is widely spread, so television is the major media. Denmark is well served with television facilities but advertisers know that customers pay more attention to adverts in newspapers, even though there are only seven major newspapers. 'Other' includes cinema advertising but only Portugal (with 11.8 per cent) uses this as a major form of advertising. All other EU countries spend less than 1 per cent on cinema advertising.The data here should be considered together with the data on pages 206 and 211.

 Although the Italian postal service is known for being particularly slow, Italy's other forms of communication, at least in the cities, are more efficient. Fax machines, courier services and telephones are the most popular means of communication.

Source: Italy, Eyewitness Travel Guides

 The **Hermes** joint venture will create a broadband telecommunication network along the side of the rail networks of ten European countries. This will create direct competition with the existing post and telecommunication systems in these countries.

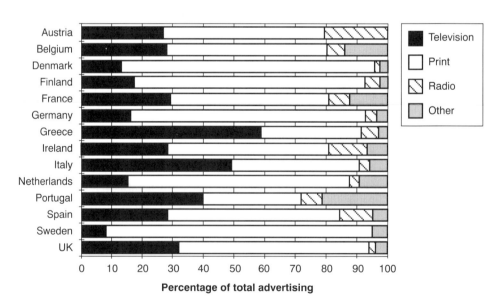

Fig 5.9 Percentage of advertising expenditure by media, 1992
Source: Adapted from European Marketing Data, 1995

Data transmission and information services

The greatest development in communication in the 1990s has been the linking of data sources through modems and the Internet. Many businesses and private people still do not fully appreciate the magnitude of this form of communication, but finally the European Commission has.

Trans-European Telecommunication Networks

The implementation of trans-European telecommunication networks is an essential condition for the operation of the single market, the strengthening of the Union's economic and social cohesion, and the establishment of the information society. The convergence of information and telecommunication technologies and industries, together with the liberalisation of the telecommunication sector, also creates enormous opportunities for the development of new networks, applications and services.

Source: The Information Society Project Office
http://www.ispo.cec.be/ispo/ispois.html

E-mail and the Internet have become the true 'information super-highways' of modern communications, matched only by the new developments in satellite and cable multi-media communications. All of the main figures quoted in this textbook are available, somewhere, on the Internet. All that is required is connection to the existing telecommunication networks via a modem, a good PC and an Internet provider. Currently the Internet and e-mail have the following advantages over other forms of communication:

➡ They provide access to vast quantities of data.

➡ They are very much faster than post.

➡ They usually operate 24 hours a day.

➡ If the right provider is used they are relatively cheap.

➡ It is possible to send animated pictures, video, etc.

Quick Quiz No. 14

What is the meaning of the following computer technology terms?

a) modem

b) e-mail

c) www

The answers are given on page 92.

There are, however, significant disadvantages as well:

➡ Many people and firms are not yet connected.

➡ Locating information can be very time consuming, and hence expensive.

➡ Basic hardware costs are fairly high if one is starting from scratch.

➡ Security can be compromised as communications are intercepted and hacked into.

➡ It does cut out much of the human contact element.

➡ Viruses can wipe valuable software and even damage hardware.

> A total of 8000 homes in Britain are getting wired to the Internet every week, according to new research published this week. But the total number of net-equipped homes is still less than 10 per cent of the homes that possess a home computer.

Source: The Times (August 1996)

Details of software and Internet sites that may be useful sources of information for data on the European Union are given in the resources section at the end of this book.

ASSIGNMENT 1
Investigate infrastructures of European member states

Your study for this assignment will compare the United Kingdom and one other EU member state. You must make your comparison by presenting details of the two countries and assessing their similarities and differences. Each task must form part of a presentation which can be oral (but supported with suitable illustrations) or written. You can work in pairs, or in groups, but where this is done each person must study a different EU country.

TASK 1

➡ Present demographic profiles of each of the countries.

➡ Compare the demographic profiles.

TASK 2

➡ Research and present details of the key economic resources of the chosen countries.

TASK 3

➡ Present industrial profiles of each of the countries.

➡ Compare the industrial profiles.

TASK 4

➡ Present details of how the transport and communication systems of the chosen countries are linked with the other EU member states.

➡ Ensure that your presentation for this task is supported with illustrations.

➡ Record points of interest in relation to how these systems link together, e.g. travel times, number of passengers, charges, private and commercial use, and so on.

Sources of information

This textbook, atlases and road maps, travel guides, country guides, Eurostat publications, national statistics published by the OECD, UN, etc., demographic publications, geography textbooks, personal experience from holidays, newspaper and magazine articles.

Key skills available for testing

- **Application of Number:** Statistical data will be collected and used for comparisons. You should be able to show numeracy skills for all three elements.

- **Communication:** Where you are working in pairs or groups Element 3.1 can be covered. Written presentations will allow you to show skills for Element 3.2 and 3.4. The use of images is particularly important here and you should cover many of the listed images.

- **Information Technology:** Information technology can be used to support all of the tasks in the assignment, and will cover Elements 3.1, 3.2 and 3.3. The presentation of your research should use graphs, tables, etc., where appropriate.

Answers to Quick Quizzes

No. 1

a) The Netherlands produced 500,000 tonnes of cucumbers and gherkins in 1993.

b) Italy produced 710,000 tonnes of lemons and limes in 1993. Spain was ranked sixth with 597,000 tonnes.

c) Italy produced 1.6 million tonnes of peaches and nectarines in 1993 to be the world leader. Greece was ranked third with 1.1 million tonnes.

No. 2

a) Heart failure: men 32%   women 68%

b) Chronic liver disease: men 58%   women 42%

No. 3

a) Both The Netherlands and Austria have 96 per cent studying English.

b) Ireland has 69 per cent studying French. 98 per cent of Flemish (Belgian) students study French but it is an official language in their country.

c) Denmark has 58 per cent of its secondary students studying German.

No. 4

The normal age of retirement for men is 65 and for women it is 60. The European Court has, however, insisted that women who wish may continue to work until they are 65. Many people also take early retirement, and some people continue to work beyond the retirement age.

No. 5

In the 1991 census of the UK, there were 7,159 people aged 100 or more. 1,055 were men and 6,104 were women.

No. 6

There was an old woman who lived in a shoe
She had so many children she didn't know what to do
She gave them some broth without any bread
She whipped them all soundly and put them to bed

No. 7

a) Germany has 477,000 horses and Italy has 250,000 horses.

b) France has 269,000 asses and Portugal has 170,000 asses.

No. 8

	Company	World ranking	Million hectolitres
a)	Heineken	2nd	64.3
b)	Interbrew*	6th	35.1
c)	Carlsberg	8th	31.6

* Interbrew is best known for its production of Stella Artois

No. 9

Aluminium is made from bauxite. The only substantial quantities found in the EU are in Greece, which has about 3 per cent of the total world reserves of bauxite.

No. 10

a) Folkestone ferries go to Boulogne (France).
b) Harwich ferries go to Zeebrugge (Belgium), Esbjerg (Denmark), Hoek van Holland (The Netherlands), Hamburg (Germany) and Göteborg (Sweden).
c) Plymouth ferries go to Santander (Spain) and Roscoff (France).
d) Swansea ferries go, in the summer, to Cork (Ireland).

No. 11

In Ireland, Dublin has no metro system, but it does have a rapid rail transit system.
In Luxembourg, Luxembourg city has no separate rail system.

No. 12

a) Paris's two airports are Orly and Charles de Gaulle.
b) Milan's two airports are Linate and Malpensa.

No. 13

The five EU countries that needed three additional days for their Christmas post to be safely delivered were Finland, Germany, Greece, Italy and Spain.

No. 14

a) modem stands for '**modulator/demodulator**' and is a device to allow the conversion of *digital signals* into *audio tones*, i.e. in this case, computer output to telephone input, and vice versa.
b) e-mail stands for **electronic mail**, and is the use of computer links to allow people to send messages to one another.
c) www. stands for **world wide web**, and is the major Internet connection to and from computer data sites all over the world.

PART TWO

Element 16.2
Investigate the impact of European legislation on employment practices

PERFORMANCE CRITERIA

A student must:

1 **compare education and training practices** and **employment practices** within member states

2 describe the **effects of European legislation** on **mobility of people and goods** between member states

3 **evaluate** the **effects of key European legislation** on **employment practices**

4 explain the **effects of social and legal policy** within a chosen occupational area

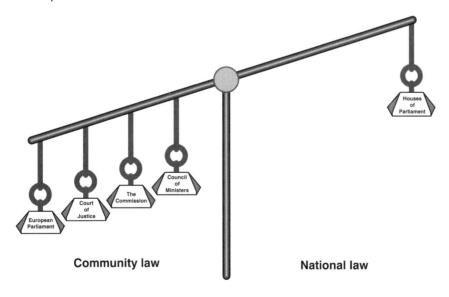

Community law   National law

6 Introduction

European Union legislation

Definition
Laws, in this context, are rules laid down by governments and custom, that must be obeyed, otherwise individuals may be fined, imprisoned or made to obey them.

All EU countries are subject to a variety of **laws** which dictate our rights and responsibilities, and also the way that we are expected to behave. There are also many different types of law affecting employment conditions, the buying and selling of products, the taxes we pay, what we are or are not allowed to do and say, etc.

The basic laws that apply to individuals, firms and governments of the EU are:

➡ **Community laws.** These are laws created by joint agreement between all EU countries. Most of these laws apply to all EU countries but there are examples where some laws are modified by individual nations, or not yet fully adopted.

➡ **National laws.** These are laws created by the individual countries, and apply specifically to those countries, but also to anyone who is resident or travelling in the country.

➡ **By(e)-laws or local laws.** These are laws created by local or regional authorities and apply to all local residents and people living or travelling in the area.

➡ **Customs and culture.** Many of society's rules are not laws in the sense that they must be obeyed, nor that one can be prosecuted in court for ignoring them, but they do dictate how most of us live. These are the customs and culture we were brought up with (*see* Part 3).

There are now a growing number of laws which are made by the European Community as a whole and which apply to the whole of the EU. Most of these laws relate to aspects of the economy, such as freedom of trade and working conditions. This is because the European Community was originally set up as an economic union rather than a political or social one. The importance of these new laws is considerable because there is a general rule that *where Community law and national law (or local laws or customs) conflict, it will be the Community law that must be obeyed.*

Community and national laws

From 1 January 1996 coaches have to obey a 60 mph maximum speed limit on UK motorways. At the same time they were banned from using the fast lane on three-lane motorways.

The maximum speed limit was set by **Community law** and applies to coaches using any EU motorway. The limit was set after a series of coach crashes which showed that coaches were unstable at high speeds.

The banning of coaches from the fast lane of three-lane motorways was made by the UK government and is a **national law**, applying only to UK motorways. The reasoning behind this ban was that, if coaches can only travel at 60 mph and are allowed in the fast lane, other traffic travelling at 70 mph will pile up behind and this will cause congestion and might lead to accidents.

The only legal exception to this general rule is where nations have opted out of specific EU legislation, as the UK has done with the Social Charter (*see* below). The UK has come in for considerable criticism from other EU nations for not accepting these parts of Community law, but UK government officials point out that where we are obliged to implement the law we have a better record than most of the countries who are our leading critics. Figure 6.1 suggests that there is some truth in what the UK officials say. The low figures for Austria and Finland are because they have only just joined the Union and it takes time to bring in all the new rules and regulations.

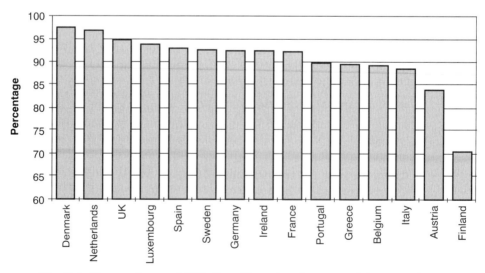

Fig 6.1 Percentage of EU directives implemented by member states
Source: From the Annual Report (1996) of the European Commission

■ The different sources of Community law

Community laws are created in the main institutions of the EU, the Commission, the Council of Ministers, the European Parliament and, through judicial decisions, in the European Court of Justice. In some cases laws automatically become the laws of the member nations. In other cases it has been necessary for each national government to approve the law within their own parliament first.

Quick Quiz No. 1

In the UK our main law-making body is called 'Parliament'. In which EU country is it called the

a) Cortes?

b) Eduskunta?

The answers are given on page 153.

The legislative process involves all four of the major institutions of the EU, but the Council of Ministers, representing the individual nations, is the body that has the greatest power.

■ The Council of Ministers

The Council of Ministers is made up of ministers from each member state. Which government minister attends the meetings will depend on what is being discussed. If, for example, the discussion related to monetary union or budgets, it would probably be the finance ministers who attended. The Council of Ministers is the main legislative body and **decides on all major matters** and on matters that are of particular interest to one country.

> EU Social Affairs Ministers have reached political agreement on the text drawn up by the European social partners (UNICE – employers; ETUC – trade unions; and CEEP – public enterprises) on **parental leave**. This will entitle both men and women to take unpaid parental leave for up to three months and to a given age, which could be as high as eight years (to be defined by the Member States and/or the social partners).

Source: European Focus (May 1996), KPMG

Most proposals have to be agreed unanimously before they can be passed, but decisions of less importance can be passed by a simple majority vote, and sometimes by a qualified majority vote (one that is weighted in terms of the size of the member countries). Under the creation of the Luxembourg Accords in 1965, it is possible for any member nation to insist that proposed measures include matters of particular interest to them. This will then require unanimous voting, and the measure can be rejected if any member nation votes against it.

Sources of Community law

Community law is created in four ways:

1 When the member nations create new laws by **signing major treaties** and **conventions**, e.g. The European Convention for the Protection of Human Rights (1950), The Treaty of Rome (1957), The Single European Act (1986), The Treaty on European Union (Maastricht), 1992.

2 Through **regulations** passed by the Council of Ministers and/or the Commission. These regulations automatically become Community law and all member nations must obey them, e.g. regulations that give powers to the Commission to control and prevent mergers of large firms (1992).

3 Through **directives** issued by the Council of Ministers or the Commission. These directives are binding on member states, but the exact details are left up to the governments of each country, who make them into national laws, e.g. the European Directive on Product Liability has been made part of UK law in our Consumer Protection Act 1987.

4 Through **decisions** issued by the Council of Ministers or the Commission. These decisions are made about specific matters and relate to specific people, companies, etc. They are binding on those people.

THE COMMISSION
MAKES PROPOSALS

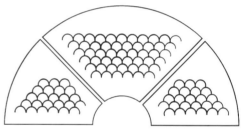

THE EUROPEAN PARLIAMENT
GIVES OPINIONS AND PROPOSES
AMENDMENTS

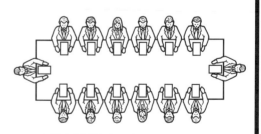

THE COUNCIL OF MINISTERS
DECIDES

Source: DTI The Single Market – 'Brussels can you hear me?'. Crown Copyright

■ The Commission

This body has the express purpose of pursuing the interests of the Community as a whole. It is made up of commissioners – two from each major EU country and one from the rest. In 1996 the two UK commissioners were Leon Brittan and Neil Kinnock. Generally, the legislative function of the Commission is to **propose or start new measures**, but there are some areas of legislation where the EU treaties have given them greater power. The main areas of additional power come through the wishes of the Union to harmonise standards and trade practices across the EU, and this role has been given primarily to the Commission. The Commission is also given legislative powers when the Council of Ministers creates a framework of legislation and then leave the details to the Commission.

The European Commission has agreed on a list of 318 agricultural and food products that will now be protected from imitations. Where these names are approved, only registered producers in the designated geographical area will be allowed to call the products by their specific name. Examples include 'tonne de Savoie' (Savoie tuna) and 'prosciutto di Parma' (Parma ham).

■ The European Parliament

Since 1979, members of the Parliament have been elected every five years on a national party political basis. The number of Euro MPs representing each country is determined by its size. Initially the Parliament's function was to **review proposed legislation and make recommendations**, and this remains a major function. Its legislative power now takes one of three forms:

➡ The right to be consulted. Where this applies laws can only be passed after the Parliament has been allowed to **discuss them first**.

➡ The right to co-operate with the Council of Ministers. Where this applies the Parliament can **reject proposed legislation**. This legislation can then only be passed if the council agrees unanimously.

➡ The right to co-decisions (granted under the Treaty of European Union). Where this applies the Parliament has the power to **stop certain laws from being passed if it rejects them**.

As a result of concerned individuals putting pen to paper and petitioning the European Parliament, France was forced to recognise physiotherapy qualifications obtained in other member states, Greece was forced to allow Union citizens equal rights on entry to museums, and Belgium was forced to amend its VAT laws.

Source: Foreign & Commonwealth Office

■ The Court of Justice of the European Community

The European Court of Justice generally consists of one judge from each member state, plus one extra. Its main role is to judge on Community law. When it does this it will interpret the law in certain ways and, once it has done this, that interpretation will become the law for all other similar situations. The European Court of Justice thereby creates law through what is called **precedence** or **case law**.

Quick Quiz No. 2

Where is the European Court of Justice located?

The answer is given on page 153.

 In 1991 the European Court of Justice first ruled an EU member state could be forced to pay compensation to individuals if they suffered losses because the state itself failed to implement EU laws correctly. This has been confirmed by a further ruling from the court in 1996, which extended the right to companies as well. As a result, the UK government will now have to pay compensation to Spanish fishermen for illegally banning them from British waters in 1989, and the German government will have to compensate the French brewery, *Brasserie du Pêcheur*, for illegally preventing it from exporting beer to Germany.

■ Inter-Governmental Conferences (IGCs)

The leaders of the European Union meet regularly in conferences to decide what direction the EU should be taking, and to discuss any urgent matters that have arisen since the previous meeting. In the summer meeting of 1996, international terrorism was discussed following the blowing-up of the TWA Boeing 747 off the coast of New York. Forty-three French citizens lost their lives.

In addition to these regular meetings, the leaders of the EU have also set up Inter-Governmental Conferences designed to make decisions and proposals on specific matters. The first IGC was set up to pursue and speed up the process of economic and monetary union. The second, agreed in 1991, was set up to recommend changes that would lead to greater political union. These IGCs are on-going and produce a series of suggestions on how EU law and agreements should be changed.

 In March 1996 the Inter-Governmental Conference to review the Maastricht Treaty was launched in Turin in Italy. This discussed the citizen and the Union, majority voting and the role of the European parliament, and foreign and security policy.

7   Key EU legislation

The impact of European Union legislation on individuals, firms and governments is huge, and affects most aspects of our lives in one way or another. In the month of July 1996, as well as the general discussions about movements towards a single currency, closer political union, the ban on the export of British beef, increased controls to protect the environment, and the maximum number of hours people should be made to work, the following specific matters were also being discussed:

➡ A **white paper** making the EU railway industry more competitive.

➡ New regulations on exhaust emission from vehicles.

➡ Better protection for workers in the chemical industry.

➡ The extension, by five years, of property rights on pesticides.

➡ A **green paper** on regulations in the food industry.

➡ More unified pension provisions across the EU.

➡ Specifications for the manufacture, composition and re-use of packaging materials.

➡ Labelling of food to give detailed information about any sweeteners being used.

➡ Management of the fish stocks in the Mediterranean Sea.

These are only a minute sample of the measures that are in operation and being brought into operation. Many of them will have either direct or indirect effects on the workplace and how job functions are actually carried out, how well workers are protected, the benefits that they are entitled to, etc. It is impossible in a book of this length to do more than scratch the surface of European Union legislation. Below, the major pieces of legislation are considered, as well as some examples of legislation that deals directly with employment practices. After each area of legislation a summary is given which explains how employment practices are likely to be affected.

The three major EU Treaties

Three major agreements have set up the bulk of the legislation that we are now bound by under Community law. These three agreements have laid down the basic objectives for the European Union:

The Treaty of Rome (1957)

The Treaty of Rome created the basic philosophy of the European Union – the belief that nations working together can achieve more than nations working separately and against each other. This treaty gives:

- the Community the right to make laws that apply to all the member nations
- the individual the right to take any other individual, firm or government to court if they break Community law

The Treaty of Rome established the European Economic Community, and the European Atomic Energy Community, both of which were essentially economic agreements. It also created the four institutions that run the Union. Article 2 of the treaty set the target of a 'common market' for the member states, and Article 3 set out specific objectives designed to help achieve common market status. These included:

- The elimination of customs duties and quotas on trade between the member nations.
- The fixing of common external tariffs for goods imported into any part of the Union.
- The removal of barriers to the free movement of people, services and capital from one member nation to another.
- The creation of a common policy for agriculture and for transport.
- The monitoring and control of competition to make it fairer.
- The creation of a European Social Fund to improve employment opportunities and raise workers' standards of living.
- The creation of a European Investment Bank to support new developments in the Union.

 The UK did not agree to join the EEC in 1957 because it still had very close links with its Commonwealth partners. By the early 1960s it had realised its mistake, but then the EEC (especially France) did not want the UK. It took until 1973 before the UK could join, by which time, most of the laws, aims and institutions had already been set in stone.

Many of these objectives were achieved very rapidly, as with the removal of tariffs and quotas, the scrapping of work permits for EU citizens working in other EU countries, and the creation of the Common Agricultural Policy (CAP). Other objectives have taken a great deal longer to achieve, and have needed additional legislation and treaties (see below) to give them renewed importance. Some objectives are still to be achieved – it is still necessary to carry a passport or identity card when abroad, resident permits are needed when living abroad for long periods, and certain jobs are still only available to nationals.

The Single European Act (1986)

This act restated the objective of progressing towards a free single market across the EU, where trading in other member states would have **no artificial barriers**. In doing this, it laid down specific rights and benefits for individuals and firms, and set a date for these to come into effect – 1 January 1993. The specific rights and benefits included:

➡ The right to free movement of goods and services, which means that EU citizens can buy goods and services abroad and import them into their own country without having to pay taxes on them (if they are for their own use).

➡ The right to work in any other EU country with the same rights as nationals.

➡ Increased consumer protection.

➡ Improved health and safety controls in the workplace.

➡ The right to set up business in any EU country that one wishes to.

➡ The removal of barriers to trade across national boundaries, allowing firms to transport goods on a Single Administrative Document (SAD). Also see the Schengen Agreement on page 106.

➡ The movement towards European standards for products in terms of quality, labelling, safety, etc., and adoption of a Community trademark system.

➡ Allowing firms from other member countries to compete for government contracts (normally called 'public procurement').

➡ Closer levels of VAT and excise duties (e.g. on alcohol, tobacco and petrol) across the EU.

All of these objectives have now been met, with the exception of the last one, where indirect taxes are still widely different. This explains why so many UK citizens go to France to buy their wine and beer.

> ## Standardisation
>
> Following the standardisation of the document for transporting goods (SAD), and the move towards a standardised identity card and driving licence for all EU citizens, the Commission has now (June 1996) proposed a standardised form for the medical services that are available to citizens travelling in other EU countries. Soon the E111 will be a form of the past.

The Treaty on European Union (1992) – Maastricht

Definition
Subsidiarity is the principle that decisions should be made by those (usually national governments) who are closest to the people who will be affected. Only laws that affect everyone in basically the same way should be made at a Community level.

This treaty gave the Community new powers and introduced the concept of Union citizenship. It also changed the name of the Union from the European Community to the European Union, emphasising the importance of united policies and closer economic and political ties. At the same time it attempted to protect the right of individual nations to decide on matters that did not need a centralised Community decision. This concept is called **subsidiarity**, and explains why many laws which the traveller, worker, resident or business will be bound by when in another EU country are decided by the national or even local government and not by Community law.

> ### Quick Quiz No. 3
>
> The Treaty on European Union is frequently called the Maastricht Treaty because that is where the leaders of the EU met to agree to the proposals.
>
> Whereabouts in the EU is Maastricht?
>
> *The answer is given on page 153.*

The main objectives of the treaty are still in the process of being implemented. They include:

➡ The creation of Union citizenship, and the rights that go with this.

➡ Additional powers in areas such as the Trans-European Networks (*see* page 68), education and vocational training, consumer protection and health.

➡ The commitment to an economic and monetary union, with the planned creation of a single European currency (now to be called the Euro) by 1 January 1999.

➡ The development of common foreign and defence policies.

➡ Closer co-operation on legal matters, immigration policy and police matters.

➡ The agreement to speed up the movement towards the conditions laid down in the social charter (agreed in 1989) to protect employees' working conditions (*see* page 115).

The European Union citizen

The term **European Union citizen** was created by the Treaty on European Union (Maastricht) in 1992. This treaty made every person who was a citizen of an EU member state also a citizen of the European Union as a whole.

EU citizens are defined by the rights that EU citizenship gives to them. These rights include:

➡ The **right to freedom of movement** throughout the EU.
➡ The **right to reside** in the EU country of one's choice.
➡ The **right to work** in the EU country of one's choice.
➡ The **right to vote and stand as a candidate** in municipal and European Union elections.

These rights are given in addition to the national rights that citizens have because they are citizens of particular countries.

These three treaties have been brought into effect by a seemingly endless stream of regulations, directives and other supporting treaties, most of which have in some way affected the conditions in which firms practise and in which people work. The details given below outline the main areas that have been affected.

The right to freedom of movement of people, goods, services and capital

■ The free movement of people

All Community citizens now have a basic **right to free movement** into and out of any member country. This means that citizens from one EU country cannot be prevented from entering another EU country. There are inevitably some exceptions to this general rule, such as:

- citizens who are thought to be a security risk
- citizens travelling without a valid passport
- citizens travelling without sufficient funds to support themselves
- citizens with certain notifiable diseases

Quick Quiz No. 4

The right to free movement of goods, services, capital and persons has been extended to all members of the European Free Trade Area (EFTA) except Switzerland. Which are the other three EFTA countries?

The answer is given on page 153.

Generally, however, the European Union has become a much more open area and EU citizens travelling within the EU will now find that the following changes have been made:

- When travelling abroad they can change as much of their own currency into any other EU currency as they wish.
- National driving licences are now valid in all EU countries and there are plans to introduce a standard European licence.
- EU citizens need only carry a passport or national identity card in order to travel in the EU – no visas are required. When crossing national borders, citizens of countries who have signed the **Schengen Agreement** merely display a green sticker and they may then pass through without the need to show any other identity. By 1996, eight of the fifteen EU nations had signed the agreement; the UK, fairly typically, had not. Austria signed in 1995.

> **Schengen Agreement – border controls abolished**
>
> Since March 1995, citizens can move freely between the seven [now eight] member states who have signed the Schengen Agreement. The checks at the internal borders of the Schengen area have been abolished for all citizens. Identity checks, however, play a role in the European governments' efforts to prevent international crime. Tough negotiations remain before the other member nations will be ready to end their internal border checks. As things stand the situation can hardly be said to be satisfactory since the objective of "free movement" is not applied throughout the EU. The real single market has still to be achieved.

Source: EUR-OP News (1995)

- Customs controls have all but disappeared and this means that:
  - i) Luggage is no longer inspected.
  - ii) All goods purchased in the EU can be transported without having to be declared.

iii) There is no tax on goods imported from other EU countries as long as they are for the purchaser's own consumption.

iv) The only indirect taxes (such as VAT or alcohol duty) that have to be paid are those in operation in the country where the products are purchased.

➡ Credit cards can be used extensively across EU countries and in Automatic Telling Machines (cash points).

➡ Travellers carrying the E111 form will be entitled to medical care in the event of illness or accident while travelling in the EU.

Schengen Agreement – border dispute

Threats from President Chirac of France that he might keep French border controls in place after the end of 1995 have angered his neighbours. Any action of this kind would indefinitely suspend the Schengen Treaty.

Source: The Times (September 1995)

Banning of alien bees stings Danes into action

Ditler Bluhme, a Danish schoolteacher and bee owner, has claimed that EU legislation allows bees to fly freely through any of the twelve EU member states, and that the Danish Ministry of Agriculture has no right to ban his bees from the Island of Lasø. The Danish Ministry claims that his bees are threatening the survival of the larger, native, Danish brown bee. The European Commission has now been asked to decide if bees have free-flying rights in the EU.

Source: The European (September 1994)

The right to freedom of movement is also extended to the movement of labour and money. All EU citizens now have the **right to work** in any EU country of their choice (see below). They also have the right to move their savings, investments or capital to any EU country that they wish. This has meant that the factors of production used in industry are now far more mobile than they were.

Table 7.1 shows, for the UK, just how many trips are now taken abroad to EU countries – a total of over 26 million in 1993. It also shows that most of these were for holidays, but a substantial number were for business. The high number of visits to friends and relations in Ireland is because there are a great many Irish people working in the UK. The very high comparative figure for 'other' trips to France is primarily for the purpose of purchasing cheap alcohol and other goods from French supermarkets and stores. In the same period the UK received about 11.5 million visits from residents of other EU countries, mainly from France (2.5 mil.), Germany (2.4 mil.), Ireland (1.6 mil.) and The Netherlands (1.2 mil.).

Table 7.1 Visits abroad by UK residents, by main purpose (1000s), 1993

	Holidays	Business	Visits to friends and relations	Other
Austria	551	74	29	194
Belgium/Lux.	500	367	137	53
Denmark	91	75	38	4
Finland	15	32	15	2
France	5319	956	456	1085
Germany	555	747	446	76
Greece	1897	38	60	14
Ireland	685	515	970	162
Italy	757	244	164	49
Netherlands	627	444	187	52
Portugal	970	65	47	14
Spain	5948	217	230	46
Sweden	40	95	31	–
Total	**17955**	**3869**	**2810**	**1751**

Source: Adapted from *The Digest of Tourist Statistics* (BTA)

Figure 7.1 shows where the 20.579 million visitors to Portugal came from, and again shows that the movement of people is usually dominated by which countries happen to be closest.

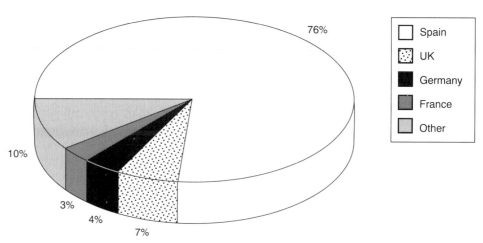

Fig 7.1 Visitors to Portugal by country of origin, 1993
Source: Adapted from EUROSTAT

The right to freedom of movement of people will affect work practices in all of the following ways:

→ Employment is now potentially international for all EU firms and individuals. Over five million EU citizens now live in countries other than their own.

→ Potential workers can be recruited from any EU country and, where the ability to speak another language is important, that clearly gives an edge to workers from other countries.

→ It is now far more common to find nationals from other EU countries coming to buy goods and services and this will mean that businesses and staff will have to be prepared for this. Counter staff will have to be able to speak other languages and advertisements and instructions may have to be in more than one language.

> **Bilingual German Secretary – Flexitime**
>
> Up to £17,000
> A German interior designer is looking for a bilingual secretary/administrator, who will be responsible for English and German correspondence and office administration. The London-based role requires a mature, flexible person. You must have a minimum of two years' UK work experience and good secretarial skills (min. 55 wpm typing, W4W and Spreadsheets).

■ The free movement of goods and services

Many of the freedoms of movement mentioned above, such as Schengen and the removal of taxes, also apply to the free movement of goods and services. EU firms may buy raw materials, stocks and services from anywhere in the EU and sell their own goods and services in other EU countries. The EU is now the major trading partner of every EU country (*see* Figure 7.2).

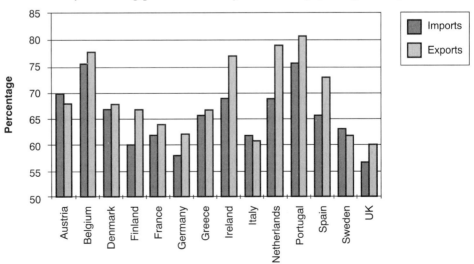

Fig 7.2 Percentage of imports and exports with other EU countries, 1992
Source: Adapted from EUROSTAT

The free movement of goods has also been helped by the removal of non-tariff barriers. This has been achieved by:

➡ creating common technical and safety regulation on products.

➡ banning discriminatory taxes on imported products.

➡ ensuring that all public bodies have an open purchasing policy, i.e. they will buy their products, raw materials, etc., from any EU firm and not just from firms in their own countries.

➡ ensuring that state monopolies treat all EU firms in the same way that they treat their own national firms.

➡ removing customs checks, except random ones. This is expected to reduce delivery times by up to 20 per cent.

➡ removing the need for separate documentation for transporting goods within the EU.

➡ creating trademarks and patent protection that will apply to the whole EU.

 Filing a single application in English, French or German with the European Patent Office will give a twenty-year patent cover in eighteen European states. These are the fifteen EU states and Liechtenstein, Monaco and Switzerland.

In the service sector, various rules and directives have been put in place which have opened up trade in specific services areas:

➡ Banking, insurance and investment firms can now sell their services anywhere within the EU.

➡ Telecommunication firms can compete for business and set up branches and companies in any EU country.

➡ Transport services can now be offered to any EU country on the same basis as national firms.

➡ Firms offering professional services, such as architects and lawyers, can now practise in any EU country that they wish to.

■ The free movement of capital

It is now possible to move capital freely from one EU country to another. This is vital if firms are to not only sell in other countries but also produce there. The firms will have to obey the national rules on setting up business, and these vary considerably from country to country, but they cannot be prevented from setting up simply because they are non-national firms. Businesses can now:

- operate as self-employed people in any EU country
- set up new firms in any EU country
- set up branches of existing firms in any EU country

 The setting up of a local branch office or subsidiary confirms a company's commitment to the European market, and becomes a visible sign of its presence. This is good both for internal company morale and is also an indication to the market that you are there to stay. It also enables the direct employment of local managers and salesmen, as opposed to relying on the part-time services of an agent. Head office decisions can be more easily communicated and implemented, enabling tighter controls of budgets, marketing and promotion policies.

Source: Profiting from Europe by Peter Danton de Rouffignac and Paul Gregg

The free movement of capital throughout the EU also means that EU firms can raise finance from a much wider range of sources. It is important to note, however, that different countries have different regulations on loans. Dutch banks can only lend for up to 30 years. In Spain overdrafts have a limit of only fifteen days and many loans, although renewable, are only offered for six months.

The right to reside in the EU country of one's choice

It has always been possible to live in other EU countries, but EU citizens did not have an automatic right to live where they wanted to until Maastricht. Under the Treaty on European Union, EU citizens now have an **automatic right** to live in whichever EU country they want, as long as they can show that they are capable of supporting themselves, and have not broken any serious national laws.

A growing number of EU citizens now live in other member countries. Many live abroad because they have jobs there. Others own property abroad and eventually take up temporary or permanent residence. Yet others decide that they have had enough of whatever annoys them about their own country and – when it comes to retirement – they sell up and move out. All of them – workers, holidaymakers and people looking for comfortable places to retire – now have the right to reside in the country of their choice. And they may stay there for as long as they wish, provided they are not a financial burden on the host nation and that they do not break national laws. In June 1990 three EC directives extended this right of abode to the following groups of people:

- **Students**, who have an automatic right to reside if they are following an educational course in another EU country. Permission does, however, have to be renewed each year. A student's husband or wife, and dependent children, also have an automatic right to reside during the student's period of study.

- **Retired workers**, who may reside in any country they choose, as long as their pensions and health provision will cover their needs so that they are not a burden on the host nation. Permits are granted for five years and can then be renewed as of right.

- **Unemployed people**, who may reside in any country, with their families, on condition that they have sufficient resources so that they are not a burden on the host nation. As above, this permit is valid for five years and may be renewed.

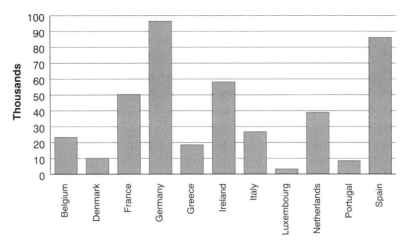

Fig 7.3 UK citizens living in other EU countries, 1991
Source: DTI

On the face of it, it does sound as though EU citizens can now live wherever they want within the Community, with no more trouble than a UK national would experience in moving from, say, Manchester to London. If, however, you want to live in another EU country there are additional requirements that would not be necessary when moving within your own country:

➡ A residence permit. This is required in all EU countries.

➡ A health clearance certificate to show that you are not suffering from notifiable diseases, such as tuberculosis.

➡ Proof that you are able to support yourself through employment or savings and will not be a burden on the host nation.

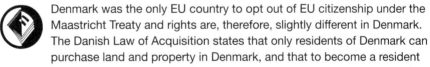

Denmark was the only EU country to opt out of EU citizenship under the Maastricht Treaty and rights are, therefore, slightly different in Denmark. The Danish Law of Acquisition states that only residents of Denmark can purchase land and property in Denmark, and that to become a resident you must have resided there for five years. EU citizens may buy property if it is for their own use and is their principal residence, and if they are employed or self-employed in Denmark. Holiday homes, or homes which are not for residence, cannot be purchased.

The general right to live in any EU country of one's choice will open up a whole new range of working conditions. Although the Community does lay down certain general rules on working practices, the vast majority are decided by national laws and custom.

The right to work in the EU country of one's choice

In principle, EU citizens now have the right to work in any EU country that they wish to work in. There are limitations, as explained below, but working in other EU countries is now significantly easier than it was even a decade ago. The changes that have been introduced since 1986 (and the Single European Act) should have the effect of increasing the potential job market for both the unemployed and for those who simply wish to change their jobs. Those people most likely to benefit, however, will be those with a working knowledge of foreign languages.

Job seekers have an **automatic** right to reside for **three** months in another EU country, as long as they are **self-sufficient**. If a person finds a job, he/she will then have automatic entitlement to a residence permit, assuming that the correct application procedure has been followed. People may, of course, have already agreed a job with their new employers before they arrive. In both cases they will generally have to show the authorities in the local area their passports and proof of employment before they will be granted residence permits. The permits will be renewable every five years.

Quick Quiz No. 5

EU workers working in countries other than their own will require a residence permit. In which countries is this permit called:

a) authorização de residência?

b) carta di soggiorno?

c) the blue card (when translated)?

The answers are given on page 153.

Limitations

Despite the right to work in any EU country, there are still important limitations imposed by national governments and by social and economic conditions. Some of these are given below:

➡ In all EU countries, some jobs in public service employment (such as the police force and army) can only be filled by the country's own nationals.

➡ Although it has been agreed that qualifications for specific professions, e.g. teaching and engineering, should be harmonised across the EU, only a few professions have achieved full harmonisation (so far).

➤ All jobs will have a list of requirements that the applicants are expected to meet, and many will specify that applicants must have particular qualifications and/or experience. It will, therefore, frequently occur that, although UK nationals want to work abroad, they will not be employed because they do not fit the job specification. The most obvious shortcoming will be that they do not speak the language. Even if they do, some jobs will require different knowledge and skills than those needed in the home country.

> **Court ruling opens door to jobless**
>
> Opportunities for Europeans to apply for millions of jobs in teaching, hospitals, public utilities and even the Athens opera have been opened up as the result of a European Court of Justice judgement this week.
>
> The court found Belgium, Greece and Luxembourg guilty of breaking the single market principle of the free movement of workers following complaints from the European Commission. The ruling caps a five-year campaign by the Commission to break down national barriers to foreigners imposed by all member states.

Source: The European (July 1996)

Despite these restrictions, the basic principle remains: '*No EU citizen can be refused a job in another member country simply because they are not a national of that country.*'

Workers' rights

Workers' rights have been laid down by a wide range of Community legislation. Many have been mentioned above, such as freedom of movement, and the right to reside and work in other EU countries. Others relate more specifically to working conditions, and these are the ones that will be considered in this section.

■ The Social Charter

In May 1989 the European Commission approved the **Community Charter of the Fundamental Social Rights of Workers** (now commonly referred to as the Social Charter). The Council of Ministers, with the exception of the UK, adopted the Charter in December 1989. These are the main points agreed to in the charter:

1 The right to work in the EU country of one's choice.

2 The right to a fair wage.

3 The right to continuing improvements in living and working conditions.

4   The right to adequate social protection (generally as social security benefits).

5   The right to belong to a professional organisation or a trade union, and the right to be represented in collective bargaining.

6   The right to receive vocational training throughout one's working life.

7   A guarantee that men and women will be treated equally in the workplace.

8   A guarantee that workers will be consulted, provided with relevant information and be allowed to participate in decisions of firms, where appropriate.

9   The right to satisfactory health protection and safe working conditions.

10 A guarantee to protect children and adolescents, to include a minimum working age of fifteen years, fair pay, and reasonable hours.

11 A guarantee of a minimum decent standard of living for the elderly.

12 A guarantee to bring about changes that will make it easier for disabled people to become part of the workforce.

Although the UK opted out of the Charter, it does in fact recognise and approve of most of the conditions. What the UK government objected to was having conditions such as a minimum wage and maximum hours dictated to it by the Community. In reality some of these measures are being introduced under the health and safety regulations (such as maximum working hours) and not under the Charter.

In addition to these main objectives, the European Community has been developing a series of directives that either extend these objectives or are related to them. In June 1990, a draft directive extended all rights that applied to full-time employees to part-time employees and temporary workers as well. This directive is now in force (except in the UK).

New rights for workers and responsibilities for businesses are being created all the time. Details, therefore, go out of date very quickly. But the main objectives remain those laid down in the twelve points of the Social Charter given above.

Additional social objectives are achieved through the European Social Fund (see page 145).

> **Working hours**
>
> The European Court's advocate general has ruled that the European Commission acted correctly in its decision to treat the working time directive as a health and safety measure, requiring a majority vote by the EU member states. The legislation, adopted in November 1993, sets a maximum 48-hour working week and covers aspects of night and shift work.

Source: European Focus (May 1996), KPMG

Equal opportunities and equality for women

Article 119 of the Treaty of Rome (1957) stated that, '*Each member state shall . . . ensure and . . . maintain the application of the principle that men and women should receive equal pay for equal work.*' This applies to both piece-rate and time-rate. All member nations therefore have laws which ensure that there is no discrimination on the basis of sex in terms of pay.

The fact that women still receive significantly lower pay than men shows how difficult it is in reality to enforce this law. If, for example, an employer only employs women, he cannot be accused of paying them unfairly on the basis of sex. If an employer makes certain that the work that men and women are doing is fundamentally different, he cannot be found guilty of breaking the law, unless he prevents equally qualified women from doing the jobs that the men were doing.

Pensions were not covered under this article, but it has since been agreed that women will have the right to retire at the same age as men if they wish to. Strangely, the right for men to retire earlier, i.e. when women can retire, has not been agreed.

Other directives have insisted that member states must ensure that there is equal treatment for men and women in terms of:

➡ working conditions, access to employment, training and promotion

➡ social security provision covering illness, disability, old age, unemployment, etc.

➡ occupational pension schemes

➡ opportunities provided in education

Despite all of the measures outlined above there is still discrimination. Individual nations can still prevent women from taking up certain jobs, such as in the armed forces. Sometimes nations purposely discriminate against women. In Belgium, for example, women are not allowed to work at night (except in the case of nurses and barmaids). In other countries women are given equal status with men. In The Netherlands women have the same rights as men, and are treated the same, even in the armed forces.

The defence minister himself, Volker Rühe, ringingly proclaimed that women in combat units was completely out of the question.

'Women will never drive tanks,' he said.

Yet they can and do in Denmark, Norway, Belgium, The Netherlands, France, Canada, the United States and Israel.

Only a few countries completely reject the idea of women brandishing guns on the front line, notably Germany, the United Kingdom, Italy, Greece and Portugal.

In the UK, women have served in the British forces as nurses, drivers, cooks and clerks for the past 100 years.

Source: The European (July 1996)

However, even here, only men *have* to do military service.

Equal opportunities are also covered by the rights of EU citizens to live and work in any EU country that they wish to work in, and by such measures as the mutual recognition of qualifications across the EU. Readers should check the relevant sections of this book for details.

Women's rights have been generally well protected by both Community and national law. There are, however, other areas of discrimination that have less protection. International law, to which the EU is signed up, does legislate against discrimination on the basis of race and colour, but the basic laws come at national level, and are frequently not very successful. The real problem is one of proving that racial discrimination has taken place.

The Commission has proposed that 1997 should be the **European Year against Racism**. It has also outlined three main areas of action which it feels the Union should take to reduce racial discrimination:

➡ Promoting greater integration of races and equal opportunities.

➡ Raising public awareness of the level of racial discrimination and taking positive actions to combat racial prejudice.

➡ Taking positive actions to prevent racist behaviour both in the workplace and in society in general.

■ Health and safety

Quick Quiz No. 6

The worst industrial disaster in the EU was in 1967 in Brussels when 322 people were killed. The worst UK industrial disaster was in 1988 when 173 people were killed. What was

a) the disaster in Belgium in 1967?

b) the disaster in the UK in 1988?

The answers are given on page 153.

Article 118a of the Treaty of Rome stated:

> *Member states shall pay particular attention to encouraging improvements, especially in the working environment, as regards the health and safety of workers and shall set as their objective the harmonisation of conditions in this area, while maintaining the improvements made.*

This fairly vague wording is what has allowed the Commission to introduce directives on such working conditions as the length of the working week, under the heading of health and safety. The health and safety requirements have been brought in through a series of directives, and include specifications for:

➡ the minimum requirements for health and safety in the workplace

➡ the safe use of work equipment and personal protective equipment

➡ the handling of heavy loads

➡ work with visual display units

➡ exposure to substances that cause cancer or are biologically harmful

➡ work on temporary or mobile construction sites

➡ health signs in the workplace

➡ working conditions for workers extracting minerals and working on vessels

➡ working with a wide range of different types of machinery

 The major emphasis has been on safety and health in the workplace, where more than 100,000 people are killed in accidents each year and millions injured. The ECSC was involved from the outset. It established the Mines Safety and Health Commission, a body composed of government representatives, employers and workers, to help prepare proposals for coal mines and other industries. A similar body with a more general remit, the Advisory Committee on Safety, Hygiene and Health Protection at Work, was set up in 1974.

In its second action programme on work safety, adopted in 1984, the EC has concentrated on:

● rules for the use of dangerous substances;
● ergonomic measures and principles for preventing accidents and dangerous situations;
● improvements in organisation, training and information;
● problems posed by new technologies.

Source: The Economist Guide to the European Community by Dick Leonard

8 Differing work practices in EU member states

Employment conditions in EU countries

Although there is now a basic right that allows Community citizens to work in any other member country that they wish to work in, the conditions of work are only partially regulated by Community law. Each country still has its own employment laws which will regulate such conditions as trade unions, taxation and contracts of employment.

Some conditions are dictated by the Community, e.g. that women are allowed to retire at the same age as men and that part-time workers must be treated, pro-rata, the same as full-time workers. Some conditions are dictated by national government, e.g. what the retirement age should be, the role women may have in the armed forces, or how quickly foreign workers must apply for residence permits. For EU citizens who wish to work outside their own country, considerable confusion may well arise as to how these conditions vary. Details of differing conditions can be found by contacting national embassies or consulates (*see* page 261), but also through:

- The Employment Service, Overseas Placing Unit, Rockingham House, 123 West Street, Sheffield, S1 4ER
- The Department of Social Security, Overseas Branch, Longbenton, Newcastle Upon Tyne, NE98 1YX
- Employment Conditions Abroad Ltd, Anchor House, 10 Britten Street, London, SW3 3TY. Tel: (0171) 351 7151
- The Department of Trade and Industry, European Division, Ashdown House, 6th Floor, 123 Victoria Street, London, SW1E 6RB. Tel: (0171) 215 5000

Overseas workers checklist for the EU

Before you take up employment ensure that:

- you have a valid full UK/EU passport/National Identity Card; a visitor's passport is not sufficient.
- you understand the terms and conditions of the contract, including method/frequency of pay.
- you know what travel arrangements need to be made and who is liable to pay for them (you or the employer).
- you have arranged accommodation.
- you have investigated the area of health insurance.
- you have adequate money to last until you are paid or to cover the cost of returning home if you need to.

Source: The Employment Service, Overseas Placing Unit

■ Holidays, working hours and taxation

Tables 8.1 and 8.2 show the wide range of conditions with which workers in different countries will be faced. These figures indicate only the standard conditions in each country. Different jobs may have different rights and conditions, especially when it comes to holiday entitlements and hours of work. In 1994 the Commission agreed to set a maximum to the number of hours that could be worked in a week, but this has been very strongly resisted by the UK.

The statutory maximum length of the working week applies to normal working. It is possible to work longer (again to the specified limits), but then overtime rates must be paid. This raises costs for the firm and is one of the reasons why the UK opposed the EU maximum limit of 48 hours.

Table 8.1 Holiday entitlement, average working hours and income taxation in the EU

	No. of days of holiday per year	Public holidays	Average normal working week (hours)	Income tax range (%)
Austria	20	13	38	16–33
Belgium	28	12	40	25–72
Denmark	30	11	37	28–78
France	25	11	39	5–56
Germany	24/42	16	40	19.5–56
Greece	21	14	44	8–50
Ireland	15	11	40	35–58
Italy	20/30	11	44	10–65
Luxembourg	25	10	40	10–56
Netherlands	14/21	9	38	14–72
Portugal	28	14	38	4–60
Spain	21	17	40	8–56
Sweden	35	12	40	30–70
UK	25	9	40	20–40

Source: Various

Table 8.2 Time regulations on the working week in different EU countries

	Statutory working week (hrs)	Permitted overtime
Belgium	40	65 hours in 3 months
Denmark	None stated	Decided by collective bargaining
France	39	9 hours/week, yearly maximum 130 hours
Germany	48	2 hours/day, yearly maximum 60 hours
Greece	5-day week	Set up by Ministry of Labour
Ireland	48	2 hours/day, yearly maximum 240 hours
Italy	40	No statutory limit
Luxembourg	40	2 hours/day
Netherlands	48	3.5 hours per day
Portugal	44	2 hour/day, yearly maximum 200 hours
Spain	40	80 hours/year
UK	None stated	No statutory limit

Source: Adapted from Eurostat

Overtime is never compulsory in Spain and can't exceed 80 hours a year. It must be paid at a premium of not less than 75 per cent of the normal hourly rate, i.e. normal rate plus 75 per cent. Employees can't be obliged to work on Sundays unless collective agreements state otherwise, although when an employee agrees to work on a Sunday, normal overtime rates are applicable. Overtime may be compensated for by extra free time rather than extra pay, providing there's a written agreement to that effect. Employees are entitled to a minimum of one and a half days (including Sundays) free each week plus public holidays.

Source: Living and Working in Spain by David Hampshire

As shown in Table 8.1, most EU countries have a lower starting rate of income tax than in the UK, and working and living in another country may, therefore, seem attractive. But moving to another tax system is not immediate. Before you will be allowed to stop paying UK income tax, you will have to meet the following conditions:

1 You must be based abroad for a full year.
2 You must not return to the UK for more than three months in any one year.
3 You must not have property for your own use in the UK.
4 All of your main work must be carried out outside of the UK.

Quick Quiz No. 7

In Portugal income and capital gains are both counted as part of income and are subject to income tax. In the mid-1990s the tax bands were as follows:

a) Income up to 970,000 escudos

b) Income from 970,000 to 2,260,000 escudos

c) Income from 2,260,000 to 5,790,000 escudos

d) Income over 5,790,000 escudos

What percentage rates of tax were applied to each band?

The answers are given on page 153.

■ Welfare provision

Countries' attitudes to their workers are also shown by what provisions they make for their welfare at work and how well they are protected financially if they become unemployed, or retire, or fall sick, or suffer injury at the workplace. In order to help pay for this cover, governments charge National Insurance Contributions (NICs), which are deducted from workers' pay packets. It is now agreed that these contributions can be transferred from one national system to another. This means that when a person has paid NICs in one country, and then moves to another EU country, he or she will not lose his or her entitlements.

Directive on social protection

Directive (92/442/EEC) was agreed in July 1992 to ensure that all EC countries should provide a social security system that would:

a) guarantee that any EU citizen legally residing in a member state has a level of income in keeping with basic human dignity and is given access to the state health care system in the host country.

b) guarantee to help any EU citizen seeking employment to find it.

c) guarantee to provide a reasonable standard of living for those who are unable to work through sickness, accidents at work, maternity and disability.

Source: Social Protection in Europe (1993, Commission of the European Community)

Figures 8.1 and 8.2 show that there is a wide variation in the support offered in different EU countries, but all countries provide a basic level of support through each of the following:

➡ Unemployment benefits

➡ Pensions

➡ Cover for accidents at work

➡ Health cover

➡ Maternity benefits

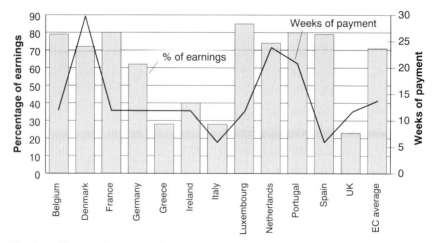

Fig 8.1 Unemployment benefits as a percentage of earnings and duration of payment, August 1992
Source: Adapted from Eurostat

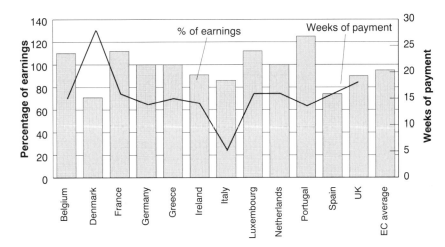

Fig 8.2 Maternity benefits as a percentage of earnings and duration of payment, August 1992
Source: Adapted from Eurostat

Figures 8.1 and 8.2 give only part of the total picture of social benefit provision in EU countries, and adjustments are being made all the time. Levels of provision are in fact much more complicated. The examples show only the basic provision, and only the first levels of support. Most countries continue unemployment support beyond the stated number of weeks, but at considerably reduced levels. Greece and Italy provide no unemployment benefit beyond the stated time. In France there are five rates of support, dropping from 80 per cent to 67 per cent, to 46 per cent, to 38 per cent, to 33 per cent across a period of weeks, and it then becomes indefinite.

Figure 8.3 shows how EU countries compare against the EU average in the provision of all basic social benefits. These include benefits and insurance to cover old age, sickness, child bearing and family commitments, disability, unemployment, etc. In Figure 8.3, the graph is shown with the EU average on the vertical axis, and each country's position given by how many percentage points it is above or below the average. There appears to be no figure for Italy because it happens to match, exactly, the EU average.

■ **Part-time workers**

Working practices in most EU countries have changed considerably in recent years, reflecting not just the changes in the labour market but also the needs of the employees and our changing lifestyles. Part of this change has been the move from full-time jobs for life to part-time temporary jobs. Details of these changes are given on page 196.

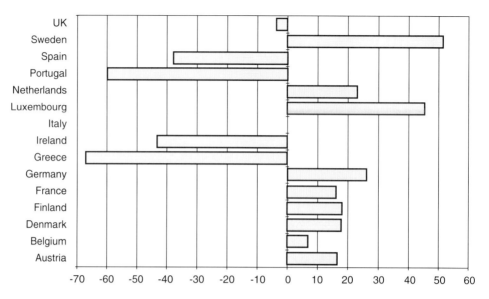

Fig 8.3 Social protection and benefits provided by EU member states, 1993 (EU average = 0)
Source: Adapted from EUROSTAT

Contracts of employment

Definition

A **contract of employment** is an agreement between an employer and an employee stating the terms on which the employee will work and the terms on which the employer will reward the employee. The contract is enforceable by law.

From July 1993, all member states have been required to insist that employees have a **contract of employment**, or a declaration stating the main terms of employment. This was laid down by the **Proof of Employment Contract Directive 91/533/EEC**. Member states can decide individually if these rules are applied to employees who work less than eight hours per week, who are employed for less than a month, or who work on a casual basis.

The directive insisted that all of the following details are included in the contract:

➡ The name of the employer and employee.

➡ The place of work, or a statement that this may be variable.

➡ The start date, and length of contract if it is temporary.

➡ The title, duties and responsibilities of the job.

➡ The basic hours of work per day or week.

➡ The rates of pay and conditions of pay, e.g. time-and-a-half for overtime.

➡ Holiday entitlement.

➡ Social security and pension provisions.

➡ The notice required by both employee and employer.

➡ Reference to collective agreements where these apply.

Because these rules were given as a directive it has been up to the national governments as to how exactly the law should be written. There are, therefore, distinct differences in the way that contracts must be drawn up across the EU. The examples given below show how and why contracts are different.

In the **United Kingdom**, any employee who works for sixteen hours or more must be given a contract of employment within two months of starting work. The Employment Protection (Consolidation) Act 1978 and the Trade Union Reform and Employment Rights Act 1993 also lay down minimum details which must be included in every contract. These are essentially the points given above but include the requirement to provide details of pension schemes, and of where employees can read the grounds on which summary dismissal is allowed.

In **Belgium**, contracts are usually written and must be in French or Dutch. A trial period of up to one year is common and in that period only one week's notice is required. After the year, at least three months' notice must be given and this rises as the status of the worker becomes more important. Employees only need to give six weeks' notice. Most employees are entitled to a thirteenth month of pay (a bonus payment). Temporary work in the construction industry is prevented by law.

In **Denmark**, periods of notice are set down by the Employees Act and depend on length of employment.

Length of employment	Notice required (months)
Up to five months	1
5 months – 2 years 5 months	3
2 years 5 months – 5 years 8 months	4
5 years 8 months – 8 years 7 months	5
Over 8 years 7 months	6

These periods apply to all employees who are paid by the day, week or month. Employees who are paid by the hour have no minimum notice period laid down by law, but there is usually a minimum agreed through collective bargaining with the unions.

In **Finland**, Employment Contract Law and Work Safety Law protect employees. Terms and conditions of work are normally dictated by collective bargaining between unions and employers. Managerial and professional staff tend to have individual contracts. Termination of employment requires a minimum of two months' notice and employers cannot terminate on the basis of illness, pregnancy, religion, politics or trade union action. If there is a shortage of work in the area employers must first try to place employees in another job.

In **France**, dismissal procedures are complex and lengthy. Firms, therefore, prefer to take employees on for a three-month trial period. During this time there is no written contract and either side can terminate the employment without any period of notice. After three months a written contract will be drawn up and notice periods will come into force. France has a minimum wage which is currently over £5.00 per hour.

Some of the main considerations for the employer, whether addressing the EC or non-EC area, are as follows:

Working hours: Vary from 37 – 44 hours.

Holiday entitlement: Varies from 14 – 35 days, and can vary with length of service. In many countries more than the statutory minimum is expected as a recruitment incentive.

Overtime: Limited in many countries, or has to be approved by the labour inspector or works council.

Pay: Minimum pay rates exist in several countries. In some, profit-sharing schemes and a thirteenth-month bonus are mandatory.

Dismissal terms: May exceed the one week or one month customary in the UK. Employee notice is frequently much shorter than employer notice period.

Redundancy: Settlement terms are frequently more onerous on the employer than in the UK.

Trade union membership: Single union and no-strike deals are becoming popular, but governed by local law.

Works councils: Must be formed in many countries by companies with more than a nominal number of employees. (In Germany, all companies with over five employees are required to form a *Betriebsrat*.)

Company officers: In some countries companies must appoint an officer (or committee, with worker participation) to oversee affairs such as health and safety, training, sex and race discrimination and equal opportunities for disabled people.

The black economy: This is an essential part of the workforce in some countries, especially Greece, Spain and Italy.

Source: Your Own Business in Europe by Mark Hempshell

In **Spain**, most contracts are in writing. Many general agreements are made with unions and the details are then considered legally binding on the industry, acting as the minimum conditions of the contract. There are two main types of contract in Spain – long term and short term. There are high costs of dismissing labour if they have been working for three years on one contract. It is therefore common practice to employ workers on yearly short-term contracts and then renew them. By law this is only allowed to be done three times for one employee, and then a long-term contract must be given. The fact that 75 per cent of contracts were short term in 1991 suggests that this law was not being followed.

Trade unions

Definition

A **trade union** is an organisation of workers, or employers, which is formed to achieve common objectives that will improve the working conditions of those involved.

A **works council** is an organisation of employee and employer representatives who discuss and decide matters relating to the working conditions.

The Social Charter confirmed the right of all workers to belong to a professional organisation or **trade union**. Even in the UK, which opted out of the Social Charter, the right to be a member of a trade union is recognised. All EU countries have some trade unions, but the level of representation differs considerably from country to country. The list below gives basic details for each country.

Austria has only one trade union which represents all industries. Membership is voluntary, but the agreements made through the union are binding on all workers. Strikes are rare.

In **Belgium**, firms are obliged to establish a system of consultation between workers and employers. Industrial relations are good. Working conditions, lengths of working days and weeks and overtime are all regulated by Royal Decree, and are not subject to individual agreements. Companies with over 100 employees must have a works council.

At industry level, collective bargaining takes place between senior trade union officials and representatives of all the employers' organisations in that industry. Agreements are then made for the whole industry. There is also a National Labour Council (*Conseil National de Travail*) composed equally of trade union and employer representatives. This council discusses major employment conditions and makes recommendations to the government.

In **Denmark**, more than 80 per cent of employees are members of unions and they take an active part in negotiating working conditions. Strikes are, however, rare. Wages and conditions are negotiated every four years. The main trade union confederation, the *Landsorganisation I Danmark (LO)*, represents over 50 per cent of all union members.

Finland is one of the most highly unionised countries in the world, with over 80 per cent of workers in unions. Over 60 per cent of trade union members are affiliated to the Central Organisation of Finnish Trade Unions. Unions tend to be industrial, with only one union in each workplace. The basic framework of conditions on pay, tax and working conditions is usually decided between representatives of the union confederations and employer confederations. The details are then left to collective bargaining between individual unions and firms.

In **France**, trade union membership is sharply divided between private and state-owned firms, with about ten per cent membership in the private sector and up to 50 per

> Strikers at Nice Airport voted yesterday to continue a protest that halted flights by Air France.

Source: The Financial Times (August 1996)

cent membership in some parts of the state sector. All firms with over 50 employees have works councils and representatives can attend company board meetings.

Definition
A **closed shop** occurs when potential workers are unable to work in the firm unless they are members of the trade union.

In **Germany**, there are few trade unions but they tend to be large, with one union for each industry. About 40 per cent of workers are in unions. About 90 per cent of employers belong to employers' associations. There are no **closed shops**. Salaries and wages are usually agreed for all workers once a year and at the same time. This prevents unions trying to outbid each other. Working conditions are usually decided for a number of years. A 75 per cent vote is needed for strike action. Companies with over five workers must have a works council. The effect of all these measures is that Germany has few labour disputes.

In **Greece**, small firms do not tend to have unions but in large firms membership is high. Works councils are compulsory for companies with more than 50 employees (twenty employees if there is no union representation). Legal minimum wages are set under collective labour agreements. Industrial disputes appear to be very common but that is because a day of dispute is recorded even if work is stopped for only one hour.

In **Ireland**, membership is variable, with up to 70 per cent in some industries but averaging out at about 40 per cent. There are many individual unions, organised along craft, industrial and general lines. There is only one confederation, the Irish Congress of Trade Unions (ICTU), to which most unions are affiliated.

Quick Quiz No. 8

The ICTU has a unique position in the EU. It also represents unions from another EU country. Which country is that?

The answer is given on page 153.

In **Italy**, trade union activity is very high. There are five main unions and a wide range of smaller ones. National collective agreements are made every three years for each of the major industries. These are agreed by consultation between trade union and employer representatives. Works councils must be set up in all companies with more than fifteen employees, if the workers want them.

In **Luxembourg**, trade union membership is around 60 per cent. Companies with more than fifteen employees must have an employee representative. Works councils are required for companies employing more than 150 employees.

In **The Netherlands**, about 30 per cent of workers are union members. Industrial disputes are relatively rare. Minimum wages, income agreements, and some of the working conditions are laid down by government so relations between workers and employers tend to be good. Wage agreements are usually decided for the whole industry concerned.

In **Portugal**, the state has provided considerable protection for the workers, e.g. giving them the right to strike, setting a minimum wage, making employer lock-outs illegal, protecting workers against unfair dismissal and setting up works councils in larger firms. Trade union activity therefore tends to be fairly limited.

Train drivers are on strike in Portugal complaining over their nine-hour day and the lack of consultation with management. Initially this is a five-day strike but it will still stop 20 per cent of commuter traffic and 50 per cent of long-distance services.

(August 1996)

In **Spain**, there is relatively low unionisation – only just over 10 per cent. Minimum wages are set by government. Collective bargaining for wage levels and conditions occurs in some industries. The conditions then tend to be accepted as the norm in non-unionised firms.

In **Sweden**, union representation is encouraged and employees' views are well respected. Consequently, employee/employer relations tend to be good. Collective agreements are fairly common and dictate wage levels and working conditions.

In the **United Kingdom**, trade union power has fallen considerably since 1979. A series of employment acts have stopped secondary picketing, made secret ballots compulsory, essentially removed the closed shop, and taken away many other rights that unions used to have. Membership has now fallen from over 50 per cent to less than 40 per cent. Many industries tend to have a number of unions, and this may occur even within one firm. This makes negotiations complicated. In the older, secondary industries, working conditions and rates of pay are mainly decided through negotiations with unions, rather than by government.

Hotel workers may strike in the Balearics

Hotel workers in Mallorca, Menorca and Ibiza have been urged to take strike action on nine days in late June and early July by their trade unions.

The country's two largest unions, the Workers' Commission (CCOO) and the General Workers' Union (UGT), asked 60,000 hotel staff in the Balearic Islands to stop work in protest at the collapse of collective wage talks, suspended after two months of fruitless negotiations.

Source: *The European* (June 1996)

Industrial action virtually shut down the Underground system on strike days, leading to severe traffic congestion and misery for commuters.

It was started by Aslef, which represents 2300 drivers, the majority on the Tube network, after the two unions rejected a 2.7 per cent pay offer in May. RMT joined the action in July.

Source: *The Daily Telegraph* (August 1996)

Throughout the EU the importance of trade unions is declining, as is overall membership. Many of the rights that trade unions traditionally fought for, such as better and safer working conditions, financial protection on losing a job, and minimum rates of pay, are now guaranteed by governments. Trade unions are still mainly associated with older industries. The new high-tech industries, which tend to be the growth industries, always offered good rates of pay and good conditions. Here unions are not required and have very rarely developed.

Despite the decline in levels of trade union membership, unions can still have a considerable effect on the economy. This is shown by the insets from newspapers (opposite) and the details on days lost through strikes given in Tables 8.3 (a) and (b).

Table 8.3 (a) Total number (000s) of days lost through industrial disputes (1992 to 1995)

	Finland	France	Italy	Spain	UK
1992	76	362	19,159	521	518
1993	17	517	23,798	168	649
1994	524	372	23,359	521	277
1995*	998	743	6,041	105	411

*Figures for 1995 include an estimate for the last quarter.
Source: Adapted from Main Economic Indicators (OECD)

Table 8.3 (b) Total number of days per 1000 employees lost through industrial disputes (1992 to 1995)

	Finland	France	Italy	Spain	UK
1992	35	16	891	42	20
1993	8	23	1107	14	25
1994	238	17	1097	42	11
1995	454	33	281	8	16

Source: Adapted from Main Economic Indicators (OECD)

Table 8.3 (a) shows the number of days lost through industrial disputes in five EU countries. It show that disputes fluctuate considerably from year to year, especially in Finland. A real comparison is, however, only possible if the size of the working population is also taken into account. This has been done in Table 8.3 (b), where the number of days lost for every 1000 employees is shown. This shows how prone Italy is to industrial disputes. France and the UK both fare well, but in both cases 1996 was a bad year, with strikes in railways, the Underground and the post office in the UK, and strikes in many public sector industries in France.

Table 8.4 shows two periods of five years, 1985 to 1989 and 1990 to 1994, where the average number of disputes per 1000 employees is given. This clearly identifies the countries with good and bad industrial relations. The figures must, however, be taken with a large pinch of salt. The very high Greek figure is caused by defining a lost day as any stoppage of work for more than an hour. For the UK, in contrast, only disputes which last for more than ten days are included.

Table 8.4 Working days lost per year through industrial disputes per 1000 employees (1985 to 1989 and 1990 to 1994)

	1985 to 1989		*1990 to 1994*
Greece	3976	Greece	3500
Spain	647	Spain	492
Finland	337	Italy	240
Italy	300	Finland	218
Ireland	292	Ireland	135
Denmark	235	Sweden	57
United Kingdom	180	Belgium	57
Sweden	121	Portugal	39
Portugal	94	Denmark	37
France	57	United Kingdom	37
Belgium	52	France	30
Netherlands	9	Germany	23
Germany	2	Netherlands	16
Austria	2	Austria	7
EU Average[1]	324	EU Average[1]	231

[1]The EU average has been calculated by taking account of the size of each country's employed workforce
Source: Adapted from the Labour Force Survey

The overall figures may not seem very high, averaging out at 0.3 and 0.2 days lost per worker per year through industrial disputes, but when this is multiplied by the number of workers that there are in the EU, we are talking about nearly 40 million days being lost per year between 1985 and 1989, and nearly 30 million days being lost between 1990 and 1994. As practically all of these disputes arise from trade union activity, this suggests that trade unions are still a powerful force in the EU economy.

9 Education and training practices in EU states

The provision of education in each member state remains the responsibility of the individual national government. There have been general EU initiatives which have tried to create some uniformity between the different systems, but the nature, content and delivery of education are actually decided by each country acting separately. Nevertheless, a general community programme was adopted in 1976 by the Council of Ministers. Its stated objectives were to:

➡ improve cultural and vocational training for migrant workers and their children.

➡ encourage better understanding of the education systems in other member countries.

➡ collect and publish basic statistics on the EU countries so that general information was available to all. This is carried out by EUROSTAT, the Statistical Office of the European Communities.

➡ encourage co-operation at higher education level, supporting opportunities for students to study in countries other than their own (see page 150).

➡ set a priority on a greater level of foreign-language teaching, especially at secondary school level.

➡ ensure equality of opportunity in education for all students.

In most EU countries, the state is the main provider of education at primary and secondary level, either directly or through grants to private schools. In Belgium and The Netherlands over half of the school places are in private education, although heavily funded by the state. In all other EU countries, compulsory education is predominantly provided by the state. In Ireland and Spain this is around 70 per cent, and in the other eleven states, over 90 per cent.

The state dictates the age at which children must attend school (*see* Figure 9.1). The state also decides what subjects must be studied. Some schools, as in

France, are very closely controlled in terms of what must be taught and how it must be taught. In the UK, there is more freedom in terms of how subjects should be taught, but schools (other than private schools) are forced to follow the National Curriculum.

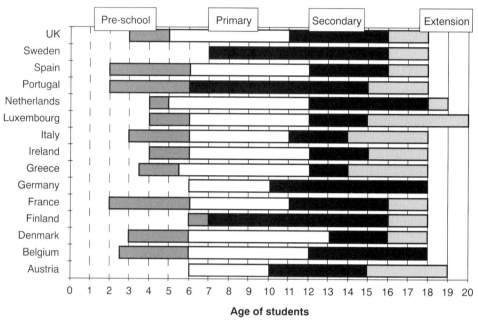

Fig 9.1 Years of pre-higher education in EU member states
Sources: Various

Figure 9.1 shows the basic education structure (at the time of writing) for state or state-funded education up to the end of normal schooling. The graph shows the years of compulsory education under the headings of 'primary' and 'secondary'. The 'pre-school' education is used by most parents, but it is not compulsory. The extension period generally takes place in the secondary schools, although many countries have specialist vocational schools as well. In the UK, for example, seventeen- and eighteen-year-olds may continue their studies at their secondary school, move to a sixth-form college or college of further education, study at a college of technology, or study at a specialist art school or agricultural college, etc. The use of the term 'extension' simply means that study is being carried on at a secondary level and is not compulsory.

The graph does, however, only give a very rough guide as to what actually happens in member countries. Even in the UK, there is no set age pattern with some secondary schools starting at the age of ten, some at eleven, and some counties still operating middle schools. In the rest of Europe similar problems of classification occur, with splits between upper and lower secondary, and with many countries making a division between academic schools and vocational schools, which tend to operate at different ages.

To fully understand any country's educational system, it is necessary to consult the right sources of information. Some sources are given at the end of this book, and details of some educational systems are given, as examples, below. Countries are also regularly amending how their education systems operate and readers are strongly advised to check the latest data from the appropriate source.

Examples of educational systems in different EU states

■ Denmark

In Denmark most children start their education at pre-school *kindergartens* between the ages of three and six. Three-quarters of all children attend specific one year pre-school training, preparing them for when they go to the *folkeskole* at the age of six. From the age of six to sixteen they attend the *folkeskole*. Special schools are available for slow learners and those with learning difficulties.

> **Quick Quiz No. 9**
>
> The word *education* is much the same in Italian (*educazione*), French (*éducation*) and Spanish (*educación*), because each word comes from the same Latin stem – **educo**.
>
> What does the word **educo** mean when translated exactly?
>
> *The answer is given on page 154.*

At the age of sixteen, students decide on three career routes:

➡ The **academic route** (taken by about 33 per cent of students). Students will study at the *gymnasium* for three years and sit the **studentereksamen**, which is the entrance qualification for university.

➡ The **vocational route** (taken by over 50 per cent of students). These courses are taken at specialist colleges, offering skills in technology, commerce, health care, etc. They provide theoretical and on-the-job training, and last for between two and four years. Qualifications gained here can lead to further technical and commercial courses at a higher level – in production, marketing, etc. These higher courses last for one to three years.

→ Going straight to **work** (taken by the rest, although youth unemployment in Denmark is relatively high). This does not usually end the education process because Denmark operates a very active programme of on-the-job training and retraining (*see* page 146).

About 15 per cent of students go on to higher education, either to the five academic universities or to colleges of professional training, such as the Royal Dental College of Copenhagen or the School of Architecture in Aarhus. All lectures at university and higher education are open and free for the public to attend if there is space.

The Danes are keen learners and many people attend *folkehøjskoler*, the general adult education school. These are free and provide a wide range of courses for adults, both academic and for pleasure.

■ Italy

In Italy, schooling is compulsory from the age of six to fourteen, but it is available from the age of three to the age of sixteen to nineteen. The schools are separated into four age groups:

→ *Scuola materna* (nursery school) for students aged three to five. These are provided by the state in all towns and cities. It is not compulsory and is generally used by working parents as an alternative to child minders. Students are, however, given basic education.

→ *Scuola elementare* (elementary school) for students aged six to ten. These state schools have regular careful assessment and testing of the students, and if they fail they are made to retake the year.

→ *Scuola media* (middle school) for students aged eleven to fourteen. Students have yearly assessments and a final examination. A pass in the final examination is the entry requirement for continuing on to upper school.

→ *Scuola secondaria di II grado* (upper secondary school) for students aged fifteen to twenty, depending on the course taken. Students follow courses at one of five different types of school:

- *Liceo classico*, which provides a five-year course for students specialising in humanities and languages. The first two years are taken at the *ginnasio* and the next three years at the *liceo*.

PM decrees last days for old system

The new minister [of education in Italy] will have to steer through parliament the raising of the school-leaving age from 14 to 16, with the inevitable shake-up of the secondary system, which at present is divided into two rigidly separate units, *scuola media* (11 to 14 year olds) and *scuola superiore* (15 to 19).

Numerous previous attempts to achieve this have failed. The novelty this time is that the new education minister has been given a deadline. 'This is the last year of the old system,' the prime minister has promised.

Source: *Times Educational Supplement* (June 1996)

- *Liceo scientifico*, which provides a five-year course for students specialising in sciences.
- *Liceo artistico*, which provides a four-year foundation course in art.
- *Instituto tecnico*, which offers three- and five-year courses in technical subjects such as commerce, agriculture and navigation.
- *Instituto professionale*, which offers two- and three-year practical vocational courses.

■ Spain

Prescuelar (pre-school) institutions are available between the ages of two and five, although most parents do not send their children until they are four years old. At this age, 90 per cent of children attend.

Escuela primaria (primary school) is for children aged six to eleven. A wide range of compulsory subjects are taught, including a foreign language. A final examination determines whether students go on to higher secondary school, where they study for an academic *baccalaureate*, or to a vocational school and a vocational *baccalaureate*. In secondary schools, most subjects are compulsory but there are also options available. In both primary and secondary schools exams are taken, and if students do not pass they can be kept down.

■ General

All member states provide students with courses in basic subjects such as maths, their own language, science and humanities. The emphasis put on these core subjects in terms of time, the need to pass examinations, etc., varies from country to country. The time set aside for teaching subjects such as information technology, religious studies, art and music varies even more, and may not form part of compulsory school subjects in some countries.

In 1984 the Council of Ministers agreed to introduce changes in the delivery of foreign languages so that students would have a working knowledge of two foreign languages by the end of their period of compulsory education. Many nations have been slow to move towards this. The UK, for example, has only just made it compulsory for all secondary students to study at least one foreign language. Figure 9.2 shows which languages are most popular out of English, French and German in different countries, and the levels of uptake in secondary schools. The figures are for 1992 and generally the study of a foreign language is far more comprehensive today.

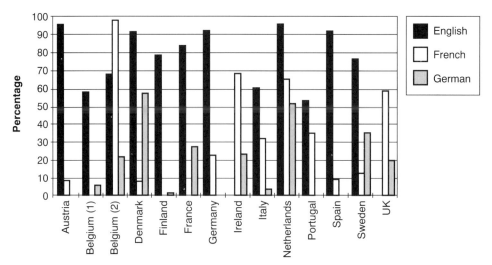

Fig 9.2 Percentage of pupils in general secondary education learning English, French or German as a second language, 1992
(Belgium (1) refers to French-speaking Belgians and Belgium (2) to Flemish-speaking Belgians.)
Source: Adapted from *Europe in Figures* (Eurostat)

Figure 9.2 must be carefully interpreted. Some countries do not appear to study the three listed languages as foreign languages because they are in fact the country's first language (*see* page 182). In Austria, German is the first language. In Ireland (Eire), English, not Gaelic, is the official language. In other countries the major foreign language that is studied has not been listed. For example, in Portugal there are more people who speak Spanish than any other foreign language, and in Finland Swedish is an official language. All the same, English does come out as the most studied language in the EU.

Higher education

All EU countries offer a range of higher education opportunities to students. These include universities, which historically have catered for academic studies, and polytechnics, which have specialised in vocational courses. Today much of the distinction is artificial and the UK perhaps has the best approach, which is to call both institutions 'universities'.

There are also numerous specialist colleges which train and examine students for specific professions, such as medicine, agriculture, and arts and crafts. Details of the forms of higher education available in different EU countries are available in most good public libraries. Some examples are given below. Details of teacher training courses, and qualifications, are given in Part 4, on page 253.

Greece

Greece makes a clear distinction between universities and technological educational institutions (TEIs). There are seventeen universities and thirteen TEIs which take about 200,000 students on an approximately 60/40 split. Both types of institution are self-governing public bodies, financed and controlled by the state.

University courses are primarily academic and generally last for four years. Agriculture, engineering, veterinary medicine, dentistry and fine arts are five-year courses and pure medicine is a six-year course.

TEI courses generally last for four years, but include six months of practical training in the relevant industry. Courses specialise in technology, agriculture and food technology, health and caring, administration and economics, and graphics and fine arts.

Places in higher education in Greece are limited. Students must qualify for a place by taking a competitive general examination. One per cent of places are set aside for foreign students, most of whom actually come from Cyprus.

> ### New exams planned
>
> Nationwide university entrance exams will be a thing of the past from 1999. For the first time Greek students who want to go to university will be selected on the basis of their grades in a new national certificate of education and on their performance in the last two years of senior high school.

Source: *Times Educational Supplement* (June 1996)

Portugal

Higher education is offered by both public and private universities and polytechnics. The basic entry qualification is the certificate of secondary education. Portugal runs a quota system for places so students have to bid for enrolment against other hopefuls in a national entrance examination. Students over 25 do not have to sit the examination but are still bound by the quotas.

The thirteen universities offer four-to-six-year courses of study in the usual academic studies leading to the *licenciado*. A further two years of successful study leads to the *mestre* (masters) qualification.

Polytechnics provide courses in technical studies, fine arts, management and educational studies. They are essentially practical in nature with a three-year course leading to the *bacherel* and a one-to-two-year course leading to the *diploma*.

Vocational education systems

All EU countries have some form of vocational education, both inside the basic educational programme and through specialist vocational and technical schools and colleges. In the UK, we teach technology and information technology to all students in state schools as part of the compulsory national curriculum. We also offer students the opportunity to study music, art and now a wide range of GNVQs (and NVQs) within the state secondary education system.

Quick Quiz No. 10

Business GNVQ is one area of vocational study that is available in schools and colleges. What other GNVQ courses are available?

The answers are given on page 154.

In addition to vocational training, within the school system students can attend specialist colleges. Some examples are given below.

■ Austria

Austria has three main types of technical and vocational schools:

Berufsbildende pflichtschulen

Young apprentices in industry are required to attend part-time courses at these schools as part of their training. This is done with day release or block release and takes between two and four years to complete. Courses are offered for apprentices in trade, industry, commerce, agriculture and forestry. The final examination (*lehrabschlussprüfung*) completes the period of apprenticeship.

Berufsbildende mittlere schulen

These schools provide basic skills training for employment in a wide range of industries, such as agriculture, arts and crafts, catering, commerce, technology, tourism and social work. The courses are generally full-time and last for one to four years depending on what is being studied. Each school is usually dedicated to one profession; for example, those wishing to take up a career in forestry attend a one-year course at the *förstliche fachschule* and those wishing to take up data processing attend a one-, two- or three-year course at the *schule für datenverarbeitungskaufleute*.

Berufsbildende höhere schulen

These are the higher vocational schools and courses that generally last up to five years offering students skills and management training. Successful students, having passed the *reifeprüng* (or *matura*), would be expected to leave to take up posts in middle management. Again the schools tend to specialise in specific types of training, e.g. technical and engineering trades are catered for in the *höhere technische und gewerbliche lehranstalt*.

■ Finland

Vocational and professional training in Finland is provided at the end of the comprehensive schools (when students are aged sixteen) or at the end of the upper secondary school (when students are aged nineteen). Vocational education is provided in specialist colleges, with 25 main areas of study covered in twelve types of vocational college. The colleges give training in groups of related vocational areas so that students can choose between a range of jobs when they qualify. Examples of the range offered are:

➡ *Maatalousalan oppilaitokset/läranstalter inom lantbruksbrachen* (agricultural colleges) offer courses in agriculture, horticulture, dairying and fishery.

➡ *Teknilliset oppilaitokset/tekniska läroanstalter* (technical colleges) offer training in engineering, construction and vehicle construction and maintenance. Technicians train for three years and engineers for four years.

■ Spain

Spain offers vocational training in a wide range of skills and professions. What is unusual about Spain is that the training starts at many different ages. The basic division is between:

➡ the first grade (*primer grado*), which is for students of school age

➡ the second grade (*segundo grado*), which is for students aged sixteen to seventeen and takes place in further education colleges

➡ the third grade (*tercer grado*), which is for students aged eighteen and over and takes place in higher education establishments

In the *primer grado* a variety of specialisms are offered, such as agriculture, art and catering. Students generally start at thirteen years of age, but art schools (*escuelas de arte y oficios artistico*) will take students at eleven on their five-year course. Commercial schools (*escuelas periciales de comercio*) offer three-year courses to students aged at least fourteen.

Table 9.1 Standard academic year in EU countries

	Academic year		Academic year
Austria	Oct. to June	Italy	Nov. to May
Belgium	Oct. to July	Netherlands	Oct. to June
Denmark	Sept. to June	Luxembourg	Oct. to July
Finland	Sept. to May	Portugal	Oct. to July
France	Oct. to June	Spain	Oct. to May
Germany	Oct. to April	Sweden*	Aug. to June
Greece	Oct. to June	United Kingdom	Sept. to July

*Sweden has two semesters, separated by a long winter break.
Source: From *How to Study Abroad* by Teresa Tinsley

■ France – an example of specialisation in the timber industry

More than a quarter of France is forest and the area is increasing. Very little of it is commercially exploited. There is now, however, a scheme to train specialists in the timber industry, creating *'ingénieurs du bois'*, who should know everything about trees, from cultivation to furniture, carpentry and retailing of wooden products. Students will train in one of three colleges:

➡ *L'école supérieure du bois de Nantes (ESB)*, founded in 1934. This college takes 50 students each year and includes such projects as building a yacht out of cedar, pine and ash, with instruction from a shipbuilder.

➡ *L'école nationale supérieure des technologies et industries du bois d'Epinal (ENSTIB)*, founded in 1984. This college takes 40 students each year and is currently working on such projects as building an entire amphitheatre out of wood.

➡ *L'école nationale d'arts et métiers de Cluny (ENSAM)* at Saône and Loire, founded in 1985. This college takes about 24 students each year.

Many of the students who qualify in these colleges go directly into timber-related professions, but the general nature of the training also allows them to take up a range of other careers in manufacturing and research.

One of the leading carpentry firms in Europe is Lapeyre, and it takes on five or six *ingénieurs du bois* each year. They are then trained on the job. They work alongside the firm's experienced staff for six months, experiencing all aspects of the firm's work. They then have to complete one or two pieces of research. If they successfully complete all this they are made shop-floor managers, responsible for 40 to 60 people.

Training practices

The days when students left school or higher education, joined a firm and had a job for life have essentially gone. The vast majority of EU citizens move from one job to another during their working life, and many of them will have to learn new skills either in their existing jobs or in order to move to new jobs. This changing condition of employment is well understood by governments and all have schemes already in place to encourage the development of new skills and retraining.

 The EC enthusiastically encourages vocational training, although this is not, as yet, an area much affected by legislation. Generally, every European country, by convention rather than law, places more emphasis on vocational training, and injects more finance into it, than in the UK.

Few school leavers in Europe leave without having undertaken some vocational training. The offer of a well-structured training programme throughout a career is found necessary by most employers as a recruitment tool. Larger employers conduct most training in-house, whilst smaller companies can hire in the services of training consultants – a common practice in France, Germany, Benelux and Scandinavia. In many countries paid leave to undertake paid-for training is customary, or even legally required.

Source: Your Own Business in Europe by Mark Hempshell (1994)

Training schemes are also encouraged and supported by the **European Social Fund** (ESF) of the European Union. Despite its title, the ESF is primarily concerned with training, retraining, resettlement and job creation. Since 1990 the ESF has been particularly concerned with measures to help the long-term unemployed and set up on-the-job training for young unemployed. Seventy-five per cent of the ESF budget must be spent on training and employment of the under 25s. Specific areas of the EU tend to be targeted, including the whole of Greece, Ireland and Portugal. Specific regions include Mezzogiorno in Italy, Extremadura, Galicia and Murcia in Spain and Northern Ireland in the UK.

Adults are given aid through the ESF if they are:

- long-term unemployed, i.e. unemployed for over one year (*see* Figure 12.12)
- women wishing to return to work
- disabled people who could work if the right job was offered
- potential workers who are moving from one country to another
- employees who need to be retrained after the introduction of new technology
- employees who have lost their jobs when coal, iron or steel firms closed

Many of the training facilities that are on offer involve employees, or the unemployed, going back to college, either full-time or part-time. These educational routes have been covered above under the heading of vocational education. The examples given below are a mixture of schemes that require on-the-job training and training in educational institutions. In both cases, the role of the employer in supporting these training programmes is a major factor in their success.

■ Belgium

In Belgium the government insists that 0.25 per cent of all wage bills must be devoted to employee training.

■ France

If firms do not spend 1.5 per cent of their pay roll on adult training this sum will be taken as tax by the government. Firms that employ more than ten people are required to provide job-related training (*formation continuée*) to all employees who want it.

■ Denmark

Anyone between the ages of sixteen and eighteen who takes up skilled work must become a registered apprentice. They must then complete a two-to-four-year training period, including training in the theory of the job, at a technical school. The length of training and whether or not they are required to take examinations depend on the trade that is being followed. Shop and office apprentices, for example, attend specialist schools for two years, part-time, and must pass the *handelsmedhjaelpereksamen* (shop and office assistants' examination).

General courses in vocational education at technical schools are also available in Denmark for people who have not made up their minds what job they wish to do. The general course then allows specialisation. The courses combine teaching with periods of time training in work. The courses are usually about three years long and the final certificate is equivalent to the apprenticeship qualification.

General training is actively encouraged for all workers. Courses in new technologies receive 80 per cent funding by the state, the other 20 per cent being paid by the worker or the employer. Educational grants are provided to people over the age of eighteen who attend work-related courses.

The mutual recognition of qualifications

It has been a long-term objective of the Union that the qualifications gained in one member country should be recognised in all other member countries. This is necessary if labour is to be truly mobile. There have been three main areas in which this mutual recognition has been developed.

- Qualifications for **professions** which require at least three years of degree-level training, or three years of on-the-job training, are now, generally, recognised across the EU. These include qualifications for doctors, accountants, teachers, vets and nurses.

- More general **skills-based experience** is recognised through a *Certificate of Experience*, which will be awarded if the applicant has several years of experience and has reached certain agreed standards. These are currently recognised across the EU in a wide range of occupations, including insurance, hairdressing, travel agents and postal workers, but there are many areas still to be recognised.

France is violating the rules by insisting that qualified teachers from other countries must participate in a national competition and go on a French training course.

Complaints have also poured in against Germany provoked by 'the apparent refusal to recognise teaching qualifications from non-university higher education establishments'.

Access to the teaching profession falls within the jurisdiction of the *Länder* or districts. It is more than five years since the European Union rules came into force. Yet six *Länder* have still to bring their laws into line with the single market.

Further problems, now being examined by the Commission, arise from the requirement for all teachers in Germany to be capable of teaching two subjects.

Last year, Belgium and Greece were condemned by the European Court of Justice for failing to implement the directive.

Source: The Times Educational Supplement (March 1996)

- Qualifications for **other occupations** not covered above. These include hotel and catering, textiles and clothing, and clerical.

CEDOFOP (Centre Européen pour le development de la formation professionelle) is the institution that has been given the difficult task of getting the member nations to agree on how all the various national qualifications equate. The individual countries have, as we have seen above, different education and training systems, and the content of courses, examinations and skills assessments are different. For many skills it remains difficult to get initial agreement and even when this is agreed many nations then put additional barriers in the way of full mutual recognition.

The latest information on which occupations have been recognised can be found from:

The Public Inquiry Unit
Department for Education & Employment
Sanctuary Buildings
Great Smith Street
London SW1P 3BT
Tel: 0171 925 5555

Table 9.2   Entry requirements for UK students wanting to study a first degree in other EU countries

	Basic requirements	*Additional requirements*
Austria	Evidence of having been offered a place at a UK university	A pass in an entrance examination for German
Belgium (Flemish)	'A' levels or equivalent	Certificate of proficiency in French
Belgium (Dutch)	Decided by the university	
Denmark	2 'A' levels	Working knowledge of Danish
Finland	2 or 3 'A' levels and 3 GSCEs	Knowledge of Finnish or Swedish
France	2 'A' levels and 3 GCSEs	Working knowledge of French
Germany	'A' levels	Good knowledge of German
Greece	'A' levels	Knowledge of Greek may be tested
Netherlands	3 'A' levels	Good knowledge of Dutch
Ireland	2 'A' levels	GCSE in English, maths and another language
Italy	2 'A' levels and 4 GCSEs	GCSE in Italian and a pass in the university's entrance examination
Luxembourg	Full secondary education	Working knowledge of French
Portugal	'A' levels	Good knowledge of Portuguese. Pass in entrance examination
Spain	2 'A' levels and 5 GCSEs	Entrance examination with three subjects (one being Spanish)
Sweden	11 years of schooling	Knowledge of Swedish and a residence permit

Source: Various

Under the Treaty on European Union (Maastricht) in 1992, the countries of the Union agreed in principle to make their education systems more uniform. There has been little progress on this, but they do now recognise student qualifications for entry to higher education. EU students may now study for first degrees and post-graduate degrees in any EU country, as long as they have high enough qualifications. Table 9.2 shows the basic requirements for UK students who wish to take first degrees in other EU countries.

Some qualifications, that are available in certain schools in the UK and in other EU countries, are accepted more generally. The **international baccalaureate** is a qualification that is accepted for degree-level entry in many countries in the world, and the new **European baccalaureate** provides an accepted qualification for degree-level entry in EU countries.

The right to education for your children

EU citizens have the right to send their children to state schools in any EU country where they are living. At primary and secondary level, education is provided free and this right is extended to EU foreigners who are living in the country. These schools will deliver education in the national language.

There are now many schemes that encourage students to study all, or part, of their courses abroad, usually with the very valuable benefit that they become fluent in a second language.

Erasmus is the best known of these schemes. This provides grants for students to spend part of their degree courses at foreign universities, mainly in the EU, on an exchange basis. It is expected that 180,000 students will have taken up exchanges on this programme between 1992 and 1994. Other schemes include:

➡ **Youth for Europe**, which provides exchanges for 15 to 25 year olds

➡ **Lingua**, which arranges specific language training programmes

➡ **PETRA**, which offers vocational training for young people in other countries

➡ **FORCE**, which offers opportunities for in-service training in other countries

SOCRATES

This is the EU's new education programme for 1995 to 1999 building on the success of ERASMUS and LINGUA. It will improve the current programmes in three ways:

(a) It will promote even greater mobility of students and teachers at higher education level by making certain that credits gained in one country's universities and polytechnics are recognised in other countries' higher education establishments.

(b) It will provide funds (under the heading of COMENIUS) for partnerships between schools where three or more countries are involved, and where international projects are developed to help children from migrant and gypsy families.

(c) It will add to the LINGUA programme by encouraging training in minority European languages, such as Danish and Portuguese.

Youth for Europe III

The Youth for Europe programme will be extended to 1999 with the continued objectives of:

(a) promoting exchanges within the EU for people aged 15 to 24
(b) supporting youth projects
(c) providing assistance for the training of youth leaders
(d) promoting exchanges with young people from non-EU countries

ASSIGNMENT 2
Investigate the impact of European legislation on employment practices

Working in pairs, select two EU states, one of which may be the United Kingdom. Read the tasks below and decide on how each task should be divided. NB Each student should be contributing to all of the tasks.

For each task you must produce summary notes. Make it clear who has carried out the research and written up each part, and where it has been a joint effort.

TASK 1

➡ Select **two** items from the range **education and training practices**. Research the details for the chosen countries and compare them.

TASK 2

➡ Describe how key parts of European legislation have affected the mobility of people and goods in the EU. This should be done by considering the effects on mobility between each of the countries you have chosen and two other EU member states.

TASK 3

➡ Outline the main effects of European legislation on employment practices in the two chosen states. Evaluate the effects in terms of benefits and constraints.

TASK 4

➡ Each student should select one occupational area to study. For each of the two states you must explain how social and legal policies have affected that occupational area.

NB The effects of European legislation can only really be assessed if one knows what the national and local laws and customs are (and were), so it is appropriate to include these in your summaries.

Sources of information

This textbook, details of the listed laws and social policies, local and foreign firms, government and European Commission publications on the EU, consulates, chambers of commerce.

Key skills available for testing

- **Application of Number**: Some data may be presented numerically but generally there is little opportunity for gaining Application of Number skills here.
- **Communication:** Elements 3.2 and 3.4 will form major parts of your work here. You will be working in pairs and you will be contacting other people so Element 3.1 should be covered. There are also opportunities to use images, which will help to make your summaries more interesting.
- **Information Technology:** Information technology can be used to support all of the tasks in the assignment, and will cover Elements 3.1, 3.2 and 3.3.

Answers to Quick Quizzes

No. 1

a) The *Cortes* is the parliament of Spain.
b) The *Eduskunta* is the parliament of Finland.

No. 2

The European Court of Justice is based in Luxembourg City.

No. 3

Maastricht is in the very south-east tip of The Netherlands.

No. 4

The three other EFTA countries are Liechtenstein (which is trying to join the EU), Iceland and Norway. Together with the EU countries, they have an agreement where they accept most of the rules of the EU and receive most of the benefits such as the freedom of movement, and no tax and tariff barriers. Together the EU and EFTA have formed the European Economic Area (EEA).

No. 5

a) The *autorização de residência* is the Portuguese residence permit.
b) The *carta di soggiorno* is the Italian residence permit.
c) The *blue card* is found in Greece.

No. 6

a) In 1967 L'Innovation, a store in Brussels, caught fire.
b) In 1988 the Piper Alpha oil rig in the North Sea exploded and caught fire.

No. 7

Tax rates for the given bands were:
a)	Up to 970,000 escudos	15% tax
b)	975,000 – 2,260,000 escudos	25% tax
c)	2,260,000 – 5,790,000 escudos	35% tax
d)	Above 5,790,000 escudos	40% tax

No. 8

The ICTU also allows unions from Northern Ireland, which is part of the United Kingdom, to be affiliated, and supports their interests as well as those of unions in Southern Ireland.

No. 9

The Latin word 'educo' literally means 'I lead out'. It was also used to mean 'I bring up'. Together, these two meanings pretty well cover the objective of modern-day education.

No. 10

Currently GNVQs are offered in all of the following subject areas:

Art and design

Construction and the built environment

Health and social care

Information technology

Leisure and tourism

Media: communication and production

Performing arts and entertainment industries

Retail and distributive services

Business

Engineering

Hospitality and catering

Land-based and environmental studies

Management studies

Manufacturing

Science

PART THREE

Element 16.3
Examine customs and cultures in the European Union

PERFORMANCE CRITERIA

A student must:

1 outline **customs** in European member states

2 outline **cultures** in European member states

3 **compare** the **effects** of **customs and cultures** on **working conditions** in the UK and one other member state

4 **compare** the **effects** of **customs and cultures** on lifestyle in the UK and one other member state

10 Customs and cultures in EU member states

Part 2 dealt with the main Community laws that affect the working and trading environments of the EU. It also considered some national laws and how working conditions, training, education and benefits vary from country to country. However, many of the differences that exist between countries come not from laws but from customs passed down through the generations and from the culture that has been built up over generations.

Part 3 will consider what the main elements of custom and culture are:

→ What the terms custom and culture include.

→ How and why customs and cultures differ across the EU countries.

→ How these differences affect the ways in which people work and the conditions in which they work.

→ The general lifestyle to be found in different countries and how this has been affected by customs and cultures.

Customs and cultures

Definitions
Customs are ways of behaving that have become so well accepted in a society that people in that society are expected to behave in that way all the time.

Culture reflects the intellectual side of society and shows how tastes, manners, behaviour, etc., have developed.

It is difficult to separate the words **custom** and **culture**, mainly because each one relies very heavily on the other. In the UK, it is the custom for many people to queue when they are shopping, but this has really developed out of a culture which believes that this is a fair way of deciding who will be served first. In many schools, on the other hand, the culture is one where staff are considered (usually by themselves) to be superior to their students and because of this they feel that it is acceptable to go to the front of the lunch queue to get served first.

Culture also develops from custom. For example, our language is part of our culture, but it is constantly changing because words that we use frequently, as custom, eventually get adopted as part of accepted language. Some dictionaries produced in 1996 have ceased making a distinction between the words 'infer' and 'imply', although they mean (or used to mean) completely different things. The reason given for this change is that most people do not know the difference and use them to mean the same thing. The dictionaries' editors have, therefore, concluded that there is no point in separating the words.

Quick Quiz No. 1

Many words used in the English language come from other languages. Which language do each of the following words come from?

a) Employ, employer, employee

b) Kindergarten

c) Hurricane

d) Panorama

The answers are given on page 224.

Customs and culture, even more than laws, dictate how we live our lives. They explain why most people work on only five days of the week, why employees expect to be paid weekly or monthly rather than each day, what we eat and drink, what music we listen to, where we take our holidays, etc. Customs and culture influence every aspect of our lives from when we get up to when we go to bed.

➡ While still in bed, customs and culture influence where we sleep, what we sleep on and what we sleep under. Many people in the UK will be sleeping under blankets, whereas on the Continent, and increasingly in the UK as well, people sleep under duvets (from the French for the first feathers on a young bird, or down).

➡ When we get up, customs and culture will influence what we eat for breakfast. Many people in the UK still eat a cooked breakfast or cereals. In France they will have coffee (from the Arabic *qahwah*) and light food such as croissants (from the French, meaning a crescent). In Germany they will have bread with cheese, jam or cold meats.

➡ When we go to work, customs and culture will influence what we wear. In the UK people dress for work in distinctly different types of clothes depending on where they work and what job they have. Many workers in the City still dress in suits (from the Latin *sequita*, meaning follow) and many school students are expected to dress in school uniform (also from the Latin, *uni forma*, meaning of one form or type).

And, as the day progresses, more and more examples of the influence of customs and culture can be found.

 Italy is renowned for its laissez-faire attitude and organised chaos. However, this is largely an unfair image. Italian businessmen and women are generally single-minded and determined and exhibit an imaginative flair – often interpreted as rule-bending by more authoritarian Europeans.

Matters such as etiquette, dress and entertaining are all essential tools in Italian business; so much business goes to a friend-of-a-friend. However, unlike the French, the Italians are not apt to be xenophobic and welcome foreigners into their social and business circles once they have proved themselves.

Business attitudes in Portugal are quite distinct from those in Spain – and in no circumstances should the two be confused. Portuguese executives tend to be less relaxed, certainly more formal and, where local conditions permit, reasonably efficient. It is easy to forget that Portugal is not a Mediterranean country, and so does not share a Mediterranean outlook.

Source: Your Own Business in Europe by Mark Hempshell

Customs and culture reflect people's behaviour and way of thinking, and they therefore also reflect how these people expect other people to behave. With time they build up to provide quite distinct patterns of behaviour that often take years or even centuries to replace. Even in the simple process of shopping, clear differences in behaviour can be seen, reflecting the influences of customs and culture:

➡ In the UK we tend to form queues and wait to be served, whereas in many EU countries the custom appears to be 'all push together and the loudest and strongest will be served first'.

➡ In the UK we generally accept the price given by street market sellers, whereas in countries like France, Greece, Spain and Italy customers will often bargain with the seller.

➡ In the UK most people treat shopkeepers and staff as though they are just there to serve. In many EU countries shopkeepers are respected members of the local community and are seen as equals with whom it is common courtesy to pass the time of day before you start buying.

➡ In the UK the main weekly shop is done in the supermarket. In some EU countries, e.g. Greece and The Netherlands, much of the shopping is still done in specialist retailers such as fishmongers, greengrocers, bakers, etc. (*see* page 196).

- In the UK it is normal to pay for products in bars and cafés when you order them. For most EU countries you will be expected to pay for products in bars and cafés when you leave.
- The types of food on offer and wanted by the consumers differ significantly from one EU country to another.

The examples given above are designed to show how wide the influences of customs and culture are, but also to show how easy it is to find examples of how they influence our lives and the lives of people in other EU countries. Anyone who has spent time abroad should have a wealth of potential examples

> In Italy also, the one-month national evacuation to the seaside has changed. Italians are behaving more like Americans, taking shorter breaks and making more use of long weekends. The average Italian vacationer now goes away for 17 days, travels by car and prefers to make his or her own arrangements.

Source: Time (September 1996)

that can be used to support any points and comparisons that are being made. Newspapers, magazines, the television, guide books, travel brochures from travel agents, friends and relations, etc., all provide constantly updated sources of information, as does the Internet.

Customs and cultures in the EU

Customs and cultures across the EU are a mixture of similarities and differences. The people of Europe have lived, worked and travelled in each other's countries for a very long time and many customs and cultures have been adopted across national borders. At the same time there are still distinct characteristics that separate countries, and even regions within countries.

■ International customs and cultures

Definition
Pan-European means relating to the whole of Europe.

Customs and cultures can range from being almost universal to the whole of Europe, to only being found in one town or village, or even in only one part of a town. **Pan-European** customs and cultures will be found as the norm in all EU countries, but they will not necessarily apply to everyone who lives in the country, because all EU countries are, to some extent, multicultural (*see* page 185). Examples of pan-European customs and cultures include all of the following:

- Using hand shaking as one form of greeting people.
- Taking Sunday as the official day of rest.
- The provision of education primarily by the state.
- The division of society into some kind of class structure.

- The keeping of dogs as pets.
- Celebrating birthdays.

These examples all arise because Europe has had a very similar history in terms of how each society has developed. The custom of shaking hands was done to show that a person was not holding a sword or concealing a knife, and at some stage all European countries have had people armed with these weapons. Other customs have become pan-European because countries tend to import customs and cultures from each other. Examples include:

- The playing of football and golf
- The drinking of tea and coffee
- The wearing of suits by businessmen
- The use of credit and debit cards
- Santa Claus

Quick Quiz No. 2

In which EU countries did the modern games of

    a) football

and **b)** golf

originate?

The answers are given on page 224.

■ National customs and cultures

Many customs and cultures relate to whole countries, and may or may not be shared by their neighbours. Most citizens are nationalistic and feel proud to be citizens of a particular country. They will tend to fight hard to preserve customs and cultures that set them apart from other people and in doing this they help to create unique features that often only apply to them. The examples given below inevitably lead to some stereotyping (*see* page 169) but they are true in general terms:

- The UK, and more specifically, England, is the only major EU country where cricket is played.
- Spain is the main country where bull-fighting occurs, although it is also to be found in southern France.
- Language is often unique to individual countries, especially Greece and Italy (although Italian is also spoken in Corsica).

Other customs and cultures spread across neighbouring countries or areas of Europe and often reflect different climates:

- The building of wooden houses is common in the Scandinavian countries of Finland and Sweden, where there are very high acreages of forest.
- The speaking of French and Dutch meet in Belgium, where both are spoken.
- The three- to four-hour lunch break is a feature of southern Europe, where midday temperatures are often too high for many types of work to be comfortable.

Queens of the light

Every December Swedish girls dispel midwinter gloom by placing small electric candles in their hair to honour St Lucia, the patron saint of light. Long white dresses, scarlet sashes and evergreen garlands complete their costumes, and communities throughout Sweden elect their own St Lucias, or Queens of the Light. Candles are burnt in homes, shops and offices during the day and special saffron buns – shaped like cats for luck – are eaten.

Source: Reader's Digest Book of Facts

■ Regional customs and cultures

Other customs are regional in nature and are found in only certain parts of a country. Sometimes these regions span national borders as with the Basque culture on either side of the west Pyrénées. Regional variations in lifestyle, customs and culture are very common, as is shown in the UK by the split between rugby union in the south of England and rugby league in the north, the speaking of Welsh and Scottish Gaelic, the distinction between the Scottish and Northumberland bagpipes, the eating of black pudding in the north of England, the distinction between church and chapel in Wales, and so on. Regional differences in the EU are equally common, as the careful study of any EU country will reveal. Examples include the following:

- In Brittany and Normandy, the making of cider is common but in many other regions of France wine is the main alcoholic beverage produced.
- In Galicia in Spain, the influence of a Celtic history is very strong and the traditional musical instrument is a bagpipe.
- In Sicily, the Mafia – who were originally employed by absentee landlords to collect their rents for them – have become the unofficial rulers of the country, creating a unique black market culture.

Except for its coastal plain and a few small towns in the interior, Sardinia is a barren, windswept land with nothing but rocks and meadows on which little will grow except grass . . . The shepherds who roam the mountains, hills and plains with their flocks looking for grass lead an unenviably harsh and lonely life. Away from their homes and families for months on end, they live principally on the game they manage to capture, and the bread which they bring with them from their homes . . . Isolated in the mountains, the shepherds have learned to improvise their methods [of cooking], of which the roasting spit is the chief implement. Their usual dish is wild suckling pig, skewered and roasted beside an open fire of juniper, mastic and olive wood, whose aromatic properties impart a unique flavour to the meat.

Source: Italian Regional Cooking by Ada Boni

Local customs and cultures

Some customs are very local indeed and are only to be found in one town or village. In the UK:

➡ hymns are sung from the top of Magdalen College in Oxford on 1 May every year

➡ every four years in the Essex village of Dunmow a side of bacon is presented to any couple who 'will swear that they have not quarrelled nor repented of their marriage within a year and a day after its celebration'

➡ in 1981 the first London Marathon was run, and has now become a yearly custom with over 20,000 runners

In other EU countries there are just as many local customs, many of which reflect local cultures:

- On 23 January, every year, the villagers of Piornal, the highest village in Extremadura (Spain), 3891 feet above sea level, take part in a weird local custom that involves hurling swedes at a man dressed as a bear.

- At Roche-aux-fées in Brittany (France), 42 stones are set in a circle around a chamber. When there is a new moon, engaged couples walk around the stones in opposite directions, counting as they walk. If they have reached exactly the same number when they meet, the fairies will bless their wedding.

- Each year a 1000-egg omelette is cooked and eaten in Ponti (Italy) on the Friday before Lent.

The Tumultuous El Rocío Festival

Although the tradition of worshipping a feminine deity in these deserted lands is thought to date from before Roman times, ever since the thirteenth century this mad celebration has taken place seven weeks after Easter Sunday. Pilgrims come by the hundreds of thousands to the marshlands of Almonte – almost uninhabited the balance of the year – through the sands of Coto Doñana and by barge across the Guadalquivir. They come on horseback, in colourful carriages and carts, or by jeep (cars can't make it through the sand), dressed in flamenco style and already in a partying mood, dancing and drinking the days and nights away.

The culmination comes when the Virgin of the Dew (Rocío) is brought out of her sanctuary on a float and is treated in the most unmannerly fashion by her delirious young male admirers from Almonte, who struggle to keep all other hands away from her. Mêlées erupt, and the Virgin sways precariously, as everyone strives to at least touch her. It's a madhouse.

Source: Discovering Spain by Penelope Casas

All of these customs and cultures reflect history, because time and repetition are what create customs and culture. But they also reflect the physical conditions in which we live. These physical conditions are themselves determined by climate, weather, temperature and relief. These two major influences, history and the physical environment are dealt with briefly below.

The effects of history

Customs and cultures are, by their nature, a reflection of history. Where behaviour is seen as something that was done in the past and was acceptable, it frequently becomes the custom of the present. In the UK the eating of fish on Fridays was introduced because there was a shortage of other meat. This soon became associated with Christian religion and most people forgot the real reason for eating fish on Fridays. In the 1990s religion is far less important in the UK and today very few families make a special effort to eat fish on Fridays. History is now recording the effects of 'mad cow disease', salmonella in chickens, excess fat in pork and lamb, and giving us a new reason for eating fish.

Quick Quiz No. 3

The UK has been invaded on numerous occasions in its history, each time adding a new element to our customs and culture. All the invasions came from European countries, all but one of which are now in the EU. Which modern European countries did the following people(s) come from?

a) the Romans

b) the Saxons

c) the Vikings

d) King Canute

e) the Normans

The answers are given on page 224.

History will influence customs and culture in all of the following ways:

➡ As people move from one place to another they take their language with them and, if there are enough people migrating, they will slowly change the existing language. English is a mixture of Celtic, Latin, German, Norse and French.

➡ Many of the changes in people's rights and their way of life have come about through internal revolution. The French Revolution introduced the culture of *'liberty, fraternity and equality'* to France.

A spectacular island steeped in history

Sicily is unlike any other Italian island . . . Greeks, Romans, Normans, Saracens and Arabs all came here attracted by the climate, the incredibly fertile soil and sheltered harbours. The island absorbed all their cultures, subtly changing and adapting them to give a flavour that is wholly unique . . . Sicilian cuisine is one of the most interesting in Italy. It is richly flavoured with a particularly tasty use of fish and vegetables and has some strong Arabic influences; there is a Sicilian variety of couscous and pasta 'arrabbiata' is spiced with chillies and tomatoes.

Source: The Magic of Italy

➡ Many of the products that we eat are considered acceptable because that is what people ate in the past. In Scotland they eat *haggis* (minced sheep's offal cooked in a sheep's stomach), in France they eat *snails* and *frogs' legs*, and in Greece and Italy they eat *octopus*.

➡ What is considered an acceptable method of education usually reflects what form of education the parents had when they were children.

➡ Rules, regulations and laws are built up over years as governments feel that controls need to be imposed. Some laws continue to exist for years and even centuries after the reasons for introducing them have gone. The UK has only recently removed the law banning supermarkets, etc., from opening on Sundays.

> ### Abortion legal next week
>
> Abortion becomes legal in the Isle of Man next week. The battle to decriminalise abortion was hard fought, with the legislation coming under fire from pro-life organisations and the clergy. The Isle of Man will now be in line with most of the rest of the United Kingdom.

Source: Manx Independent (February 1996)

➡ The type of government that nations have develops over time. Usually this moves from control by the few (autocracy and monarchy) to control by everyone (democracy), though it sometimes moves in the other direction.

➡ Immigrants frequently come from countries that were once controlled by the host country. This is the case with West Indians and Hong Kong Chinese moving to the UK, and Algerians and West Africans going into France.

All of the above examples will affect lifestyle, although some of them, such as the law on working on Sundays, will also affect working conditions. Other historical effects on working conditions include:

➡ The historical place that women have had as mothers, wives and housekeepers in a male-dominated world. This outdated view of women explains why countries like Italy and Greece still have such low proportions of women in the workforce (*see* page 49).

➡ For most people the working day remains one based around the old nine-to-five day. This has its origins in the fact that these were the main daylight hours. We now have electricity, international markets that operate during our night-time and greater demand for 24-hour services from customers, and yet the basic working day, for the vast majority, remains the same.

➡ Part of the UK's history was one in which we were the major trading nation in the world, a time when we expected people to adopt our culture, and especially the speaking of English as the major trading language. Today many UK businesses still expect this and assume that trading with EU countries does not require specialist language skills.

→ Greece has a history of separate states, many small independent islands and a culture where laws and rules are only imposed where absolutely necessary. As a result many jobs are not declared for tax purposes and work is often offered on a casual basis, i.e. when the employer wants you.

 Finnish women have a long tradition of political and economic participation. They were the first in Europe to get the vote, in 1906, and the first in the world able to stand for parliament.

Source: The Nations of the World

Analysing any list of working conditions would show that practically all of them have some historical element.

The effects of the physical environment in which we live

Custom, culture and lifestyle will also be influenced by the physical environment in which we live, and as this is changed by better housing, better land management, new strains of crops, etc., our customs, cultures and lifestyles will change as well. Below are examples of how the natural environment will affect society:

→ Climate and temperature determine the kind of clothes people need and want to wear. And, when central heating and double glazing is used in houses, this will change what people choose to wear.

 In The Netherlands one million pairs of clogs are still sold each year to the Frisian people who find that they are better suited to the wetlands of Holland than are ordinary shoes.

→ Climate and vegetation will affect what types of food can be provided and will therefore affect our diet. Olives grow easily in Italy, Greece and Spain and cooking is therefore frequently done with olive oil. Now that many people travel to other countries for their holidays, the variety of foods that people want to eat is very much greater.

 Half the cherries eaten in Spain are grown in the Jerte Valley and from May to July all other life in the valley stops for the picking of the cherries.

- Physical relief will, among many other things, affect the kinds of sport that people are interested in. In Holland, where the land is very flat, cycling is very popular. In Austria, with its natural steep slopes and cold winters, skiing is a major local sport.

 In Sweden cross-country skiing is a national pastime with everyone in the country taking part – old, young and even babies in ski-borne cribs.

- Natural resources will tend to make one type of industry dominant in certain areas, as with fishing in Cornish villages and coal mining in the Ruhr district of Germany. Frequently the jobs will involve a certain way of life and this will become part of custom and culture.

 The Cornish custom of hanging Christmas lights on fishing boats, in house windows and shop fronts comes from the old custom of putting a candle in the window to guide seamen safely home.

Again, the examples given above generally affect lifestyle. Working conditions are also affected by the physical environment:

- All seasonal work, by definition, depends on the time of year, with grape picking being done first in Greece, Italy, Spain and Portugal, then in France, and finally in Germany and to a minor extent in the UK. Seasonal work will affect all of the following:
    - Recreation and sports such as skiing and cricket.
    - The holiday industry and tourism.
    - Agricultural products that rely on growing seasons.
    - Building work, which is difficult in cold and wet weather.
    - Education, which is structured into terms.
- The heat of the day will determine the need for air conditioning or heating. This changes dramatically from the north of Sweden to the south of Greece.
- The quantity of rainfall will determine what agriculture is possible, but also the type of industry that can operate. Most chemical processes, the dying of cloth and electricity generation require supplies of water on a large scale.

With each unique physical environment, slightly different work patterns evolve, creating their own customs and cultures.

Stereotyping

Stereotyping occurs when people are all classed together with the same characteristics, and the individual differences are not acknowledged. Sometimes this can be complimentary but often it is abusive, and generally it is inaccurate. The same is true when national characteristics are considered: the Scots are said to be mean, the Germans are loud and self-centred, the Spanish smell of garlic and the Swedes believe in free love. Undoubtedly there *are* mean Scots and free-loving Swedes, but to make sweeping generalisations like this is not just inaccurate, it is also foolish.

The problem with dismissing stereotyping out of hand is that there are many characteristics which *do* apply to large groups of people, and possibly even to whole nations. These are the customs and cultures, and here stereotyping may be both accurate and appropriate. When the characteristics become common in one country, or region, or even area or town, it is appropriate to use stereotyping, as long as one also recognises that there are likely to be important exceptions.

Quick Quiz No. 4

There is one EU nation where the men are so sure of their own attractiveness that they will get themselves wrapped up in huge Christmas gift boxes, and then ask their friends to deliver them to their girlfriends' houses as the ultimate Christmas present. In which EU country is this bizarre custom to be found?

The answer is given on page 224.

In many cases stereotyping is wildly inaccurate, but nevertheless it retains an extraordinarily forcible suggestive power. If the points being made, true or false, are repeated enough times, people will begin to believe them. Because this is a characteristic of the way that society, and business, operate, stereotyping has a significant impact upon both working conditions and lifestyle. The following are examples of where inaccurate stereotyping still affects working conditions:

- Few women are employed in engineering because it is assumed that jobs in engineering require physical strength.
- Northern businessmen often assume that all businesses in southern Europe close for three or four hours around midday so there is no point trying to do business with them at these times.

➡ Many countries assume that immigrant workers are less skilled than domestic workers and this explains, to some extent, why Algerian workers in France, Turkish workers in Germany, Bosnian workers in Austria and Afro-Caribbean workers in the UK receive lower average rates of pay than the national workers.

The carpet seller does not enjoy a good reputation in Provence and to describe a man as a *marchand de tapis* is to imply that he is at best shifty and at worst someone who would steal the corset from your grandmother. I had also been told that travelling carpet sellers often acted as reconnaissance parties, spying out the land for their burglar associates. And there is always the possibility that the carpets will be fakes or stolen.

Source: A Year in Provence by Peter Mayle

Stereotyping occurs for all of the following reasons:

➡ **Through the averaging of statistics**. The most commonly used statistics tend to show averages for countries and it is then assumed that the data applies to everyone. In reality, very few people match Mr or Mrs Average.

➡ **Through history**. People's view of other people is built up over time, and reinforced by repetition and re-telling. In this sense history is responsible for many stereotypes, reflecting what has become tradition and custom.

A game of two horns

Bull-fighting both in Spain and in south-west France is now more popular than ever before. Last season, one man – Jesulin de Ubrique – established a new record by killing 341 bulls in the course of 161 afternoons in the ring. Señor Ubrique is the idol of many teenage girls; bull-fighting is big business, with national television coverage and annual earnings for a top-rank matador of about £3.5 million . . .

Because of television the fights, or rather the individual matadors, are regularly discussed in offices and supermarkets. Such is the popularity of Jesulin de Ubrique that, when he fought six bulls before an all-female audience, some of them threw their underwear into the ring, others themselves.

Last month, Cristina Sanchez became the first woman to achieve full matador status. Her first encounter with grown-up four-year-old bulls took place at Nîmes, one of the many places in south-west France where bull-fights are conducted along the same rules as in Spain.

In France, it is technically illegal to kill a bull in the ring, but this is not a rule the French take very seriously. The payment of a nominal fine on each occasion to the municipal authority seems to satisfy everyone.

Bull-rings are to be found up the Mediterranean coast as far as Arles, and on the Atlantic coast to within 40 miles of Bordeaux. The best matadors traditionally come from the south of Spain.

Source: The Daily Telegraph (June 1996) from *Spanish Hours* by Simon Courtauld

What it does not do is take into account the huge impact of new influences such as telecommunication, higher incomes and travel to other countries, which are all constantly changing the way people live and think.

➡ **Through nationalism**. Sometimes stereotypes come from people trying to show that their nation is better than others. This can be done in humour, as with jokes about Germans getting up early to get the best places by the pool, but sometimes it is done with spite and reveals prejudice.

The general rule that should be followed, whenever stereotyping occurs, is to be suspicious of it, check the details and data very carefully and only make generalisations where they can be justified.

The role of the family

With very few exceptions, people are born into and brought up by families. The influence of the family on the way we think and behave is considerable, and usually pervades our lives from birth to the grave. The following list gives just some idea of how wide this influence may be:

➡ The family provides the first part of our education, giving us our language, the moral rules by which we live and many of our beliefs.

➡ The family provides the main support for children up to when they leave school.

➡ The family often provides support for, and looks after, the old.

➡ Customs and culture originate from the family.

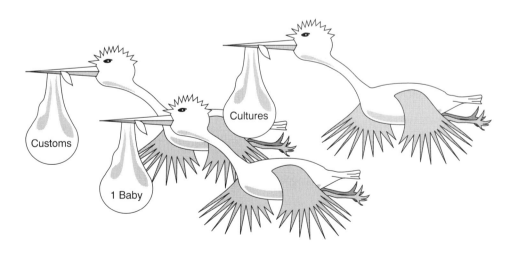

- The family often influences what jobs people choose to do.

- The family may provide wealth to relatives through gifts and inheritance.

- Frequently the family is the major factor in deciding how we will vote, where we go on holiday, what our favourite food and drink is, and what recreation we take.

Families can be very disruptive, and can also give children values that are anti-social, but in the vast majority of cases families are supportive and provide the first real experience of how to behave in society and get on with other people. It is therefore worrying that families seem to be so much under threat, not just in the UK but throughout the EU. In the last twenty years, more people have been getting divorced, there are more single parents, the middle-aged frequently put their parents into old people's homes rather than look after them at home, and more mothers (or fathers) go out to work and leave their children to look after themselves.

The real differences between the EU countries are in terms of how far down this road their societies have travelled. In the UK there has been a distinct move away from the **extended family** to the **nuclear family** and even to the **one-parent family**. This has happened as couples have moved away from their family roots in search of work. It has also happened because people have become more independent and do not expect to live at home when they grow up and have their own jobs. Older people now provide for themselves with pensions and want their independence for as long as possible.

> *Definition*
> An **extended family** is one where more than two generations live together, e.g. grandparents, parents and children.
>
> A **nuclear** family is one where only the parents and children live together.

In many EU countries, and especially in rural areas, the extended family is still very much in evidence, with three and sometimes more generations living in the same house. This is still common in Italy, Portugal and Greece. In Austria the normal family unit is nuclear, with both parents working. There is also a tendency for children to live with their parents until the children get married, which perhaps explains why Austrians tend to marry at such a young age. In Denmark, by contrast, the nuclear family is not the norm and indeed over 40 per cent of children are brought up in single-parent families.

For most people the 'family' and 'marriage' go together, although there is a growing number of unmarried couples having families. Figure 10.1 shows how the rate of marriage (measured by marriage/1000 people) has changed in the twelve years between 1981 and 1993. Denmark and Luxembourg are the only countries that have rising figures over this period, and both have had falling figures in the last five years.

Figures published in August 1995 show that the divorce rate in the UK is at an all-time high and marriages at an all-time low. Couples are getting married later than ten years ago. Men now marry at 28.2 years of age compared to 25.7 years, and women marry at 26.2 years of age compared to 23.4 years. Nearly 40 per cent of marriages end in divorce.

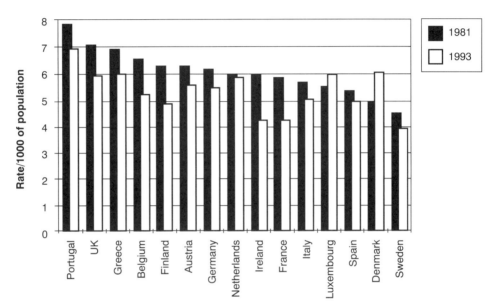

Fig 10.1 Changing popularity of marriage in EU countries,1981 to 1993
Source: Adapted from Eurostat

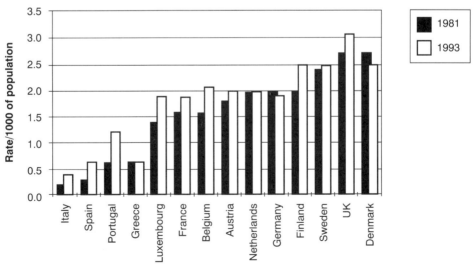

Fig 10.2 Changing frequency of divorce in EU countries, 1981 to 1993
Source: Adapted from Eurostat

The countries with the lowest rates of divorce remain those in which the Roman Catholic religion is still important, but even in Italy, Spain and Portugal the general trend is upward (*see* Figure 10.2). The importance of religion in dictating family life is also indicated by the number of children who are born outside marriage. Figure 10.3 shows that this is still considered unacceptable in Greece and Italy. In Denmark and Sweden it is marriage that is in danger of becoming the unusual family unit.

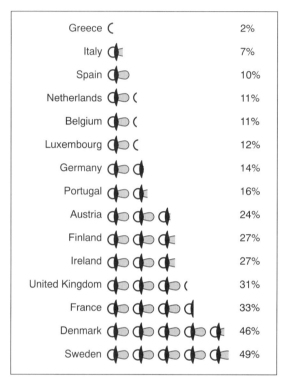

Fig 10.3 Percentage of births occurring outside of marriage in EU countries, 1992
Source: Adapted from Eurostat

The changing patterns in the family also affect the make-up of households. As there are more nuclear families, and as people live longer, there is a growing number of people who finish up living on their own, especially in countries like the UK (*see* Figure 10.4). More people are also choosing to have children and bring them up on their own. Sometimes this is because the father or mother walks out, but more and more frequently it is because the mother does not want the father involved, or that the state makes it easier to gain benefits if one is a single parent.

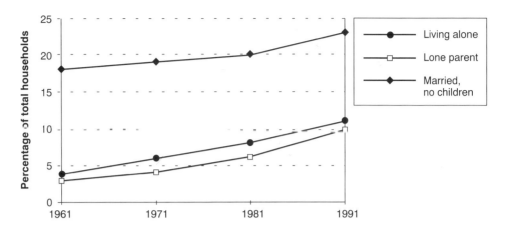

Fig 10.4 Percentage of UK households with people living alone, lone parents, or married with no children, 1961 to 1991
Source: Adapted from the UK population censuses

Another growing trend, also shown in Figure 10.4, is for people to marry but have no children. This allows both partners to work. This group is often referred to as **DINKs** – **D**ual-**I**ncome-**N**o-**K**ids. Delaying having children also contributes to childless relationships. In the UK the percentage of women who were childless at the age of 30 had risen from 18.5 per cent in 1977 to 30 per cent in 1987, and to 36 per cent in 1992.

Definition
A **matriarchy** is where the mother is the head of the family. A **patriarchy** is where the father is the head of the family.

Figure 10.5 shows that the stereotype of gender roles in the home is still very much in place in the UK. In other countries the divisions are even more extreme. In Italy, within the household, the family is still a **matriarchy**, with the mother deciding how the household will be run and laying down the rules of behaviour for the children. Outside the home the family in Italy is still considered a **patriarchy** with the man making the major family decisions. In France the traditional gender division in household chores is being broken down, but it is not as advanced as in the UK. In Denmark and Sweden roles are far more evenly spread and in Sweden it is fairly common for the man to stay at home and look after the children.

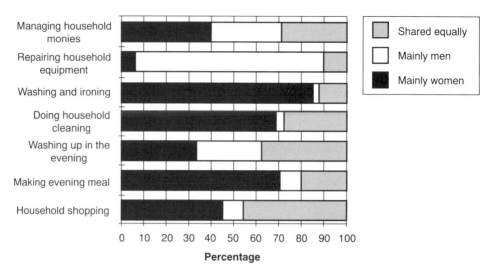

Fig 10.5 Division by gender of household chores, 1995 (UK)
Source: Adapted from Social and Community Planning Research

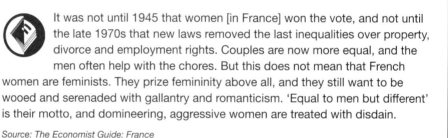

It was not until 1945 that women [in France] won the vote, and not until the late 1970s that new laws removed the last inequalities over property, divorce and employment rights. Couples are now more equal, and the men often help with the chores. But this does not mean that French women are feminists. They prize femininity above all, and they still want to be wooed and serenaded with gallantry and romanticism. 'Equal to men but different' is their motto, and domineering, aggressive women are treated with disdain.

Source: The Economist Guide: France

The impact of the family and the changing nature of the family on lifestyle has been shown with all of the examples above. Chapter 11, on lifestyle, will give other examples. The impact of the family, and the individuals' role within it, will also affect who is available for work, when they are available, the kind of work that can be done, etc. Working conditions will be affected in all of the following ways:

➡ The expected role of the woman within the family as mother, wife, housekeeper and provider of a source of income. Expectations differ considerably from one EU country to another. This is a major reason why countries like Denmark and Sweden have such a high proportion of women working, and why countries like Ireland and Italy have such a low proportion of women working (*see* Figure 3.6, page 49).

➡ The structure of the family will have a major effect on the mobility of labour (*see* page 51).

- For many families where mothers are expected to be responsible for the children, women may not be available for work until their children are of school age. In all EU countries this limitation is being eased as the state, and private sources, provide more nursery schools (*see* Figure 9.1, page 136).

- Even where mothers do work, their hours of work are often limited to school hours, and the work is frequently part-time.

- The decision to delay having children until later has meant that many women have established careers before they start their families, and when this happens they are far more likely to return to the workforce when their children are still young.

- The family is primarily responsible for establishing the **work ethic** in children. If girls see their mothers out at work they are likely to wish to work when they grow up. Where children see parents who are unemployed, they often finish up being unemployed as well.

- The family dominates the work environment when it is a family business that is being run. In Greece, Portugal and France, family businesses are still important. In countries like the UK they are beginning to come back into fashion because people are being made redundant and there is a growth of home working and contracting out.

Many smaller firms in France are still family firms and are run on clear patriarchal lines. The head of the firm, the *président-directeur général*, is chairman and managing director. He makes all important major decisions and they are to be obeyed without question. The firm is organised on strict hierarchical lines through the *cadres supérieurs* and then the *cadres moyens*, and down to the clerks. All job roles and responsibilities are clearly defined and delegation downward is rare.

The impact of religion

Belief in one god, or many gods, has a deep-rooted place in the minds of most people. For some people, religion and the creeds laid down by their faith become the main guidelines by which they live their lives. For others, religion is little more than a custom which, for example, encourages them to go to carol services at Christmas. Sometimes the impact of religion can destroy countries, as it is doing in the former Yugoslavia, and has come close to doing between the Catholics and Protestants of Northern Ireland. Generally, however, the impact of religion is less dramatic, but nevertheless still widespread in many EU countries.

For centuries religion has played a key part in the division of Dutch society. Even today being a Protestant or a Catholic can influence the choice of newspaper, political party, school and even hospital.

Source: Focus on the Countries of Benelux by Ed Needham

The customs and cultures of religion are expressed through all the following:

➡ **What clothes people wear**. Many Catholic widows in Italy still wear black for years after their husbands have died.

➡ **What people eat**. Muslims should not eat pork, Hindus should not eat beef, and Jews should only eat meat killed in a certain way (kosher). During Lent, Christians were expected in the past to eat only basic foods, but now they tend to give things up almost as a token. During Ramadan, the ninth month of the Muslim year, a rigid fast is observed where Muslims do not eat between sunrise and sunset.

➡ **The role of men and women in society and in the home**. There are no Catholic women priests, and no women Buddhist monks. In the Jewish religion women have both a restricted and a highly respected position in the family.

➡ **What days of the week and year believers are allowed to work on**. For Christians Sunday is the traditional day of rest, whereas for Jews it is Saturday. Throughout the year each faith has sacred days of celebration when followers are expected to worship or celebrate, and not work.

➡ Three events in people's lives dominate most others, especially where families are concerned. These are **birth, death** and **marriage**. For most religions these are marked with particular ceremonies, and in some religions the coming of age or acceptance into the faith is similarly marked.

➡ Religion has also tended to bring people together, and this has led to **ghettos, separate schooling**, and even **religious and racist persecution**.

For all of the reasons mentioned above, it is important to know what the religious breakdown is in each country, and how this will influence custom, culture, the way of life and how the impact of religion is changing over time.

Quick Quiz No. 5

Which EU country used to be part of the Roman Catholic church until the ninth century but now acknowledges the Patriarch of Constantinople as the head of the church, and not the pope?

The answer is given on page 224.

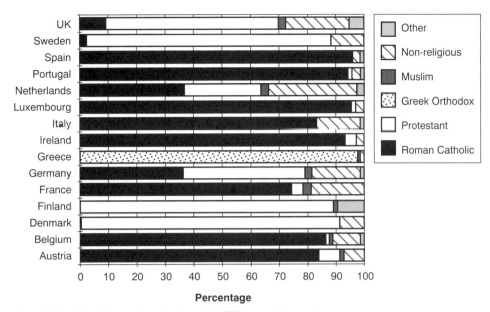

Fig 10.6 Division of religions in EU member states
Source: Adapted from OECD

Figure 10.6 shows how the EU countries are divided in terms of their major religions. It must be remembered that this simply records who calls themselves Protestants etc., and does not indicate how strong their belief is.

Religion provides codes of behaviour based upon what the believers feel is good and right, but these beliefs do not just have to come from religion. Many people who truly do not believe in any religious doctrine are often just as moral and good as those who do believe. Morality and beliefs which are not based on religion are therefore also important elements of a nation's culture and way of life.

Mixed messages on Italian morals?

After 16 years of fruitless campaigning and debate, women MPs in the Italian parliament have finally forced through a bill to change the definition of rape from a '*crime against public morality*' to a '*crime against the person*'. The latter carries much harsher sentences, with the minimum sentence raised from 3 to 5 years' imprisonment.

The same bill, however, lowers the age for legalised sex between consenting minors from 16 years of age to 13. The Catholic church is, understandably, worried by this part of the bill, seeing it as a '*teenage free-love charter*'.

Source: The Times (February 1996)

In some countries, such as Ireland and Italy, religion still has a significant impact on daily life and on customs and cultures. In many other countries the impact of religion has become a great deal less in recent years. In the UK, 55 per cent of people say they are members of the Church of England but 93 per cent of these people also say that they are not 'practising' Christians. In The Netherlands only 20 per cent of believers regularly attend church. It is also generally the case that teenagers and young adults are less interested in religion than people of a similar age ten or twenty years ago.

Church Tax

As in some other European countries, the municipalities impose a church tax on members of the Danish Christian Church which amounts to between 0.5% and 1.7% of an individual's income depending on the area. It is somewhat surprising that although most Danes hardly set foot inside a church during their lives, 88% of them elect to pay the church tax. You have to formally opt out of the church in order not to pay it.

Source: Live and Work in Scandinavia

Within most EU countries some of the most influential religions for the people who practise them are the minority religions. Examples include Judaism, Islam and Sikhism.

Quick Quiz No. 6

Christianity was founded by Jesus Christ about 2000 years ago. Which religions were founded

a) by Abraham about 4000 years ago?

b) by Prince Siddhartha Gautama about 2500 years ago?

c) by the prophet Muhammad about 1400 years ago?

d) by Guru Nanak about 500 years ago?

The answers are given on page 224.

The effect of religion on working conditions will be seen in all of the following:

➡ The days on which people can work. This applies to both the days of the week and religious holidays during the year.

- Times of breaks, and facilities for worship. Islam requires that believers worship five times a day facing Mecca.
- What clothes must and can be worn. The wearing of turbans by Sikhs instead of helmets is permitted in the UK police force.
- Whether women are allowed to work outside the home. Some Islamic sects have very strict rules.
- What foods can be eaten and, therefore, what foods should be provided in staff canteens.
- Whether membership of trade unions is allowed.

The impact of language

You only have to visit a foreign country where people are speaking a language that means absolutely nothing to you to realise just how important this basic form of communication is. Without language the major means of communication has been taken away from you and you are cast into the role of an outsider. For the individual this is inconvenient and uncomfortable, but where business is concerned lack of language can exclude firms from the marketplace. And it is not just language but all forms of communication that are open to misinterpretation.

 Few companies today can expect to avoid some form of international partnership: whether it be from acquisitions, mergers, joint ventures, alliances or international projects. This involves very special talents. Communicating with people from the same culture can sometimes be difficult even when they speak the same language but when there is a different language and culture, the possibilities of miscommunication are compounded dramatically.

Culture and language are, however, intertwined. We depend on trade for our survival and although our trade figures are extremely good, we cannot afford to be complacent. Our future depends on our ability to sell our goods and services in a way that is culturally acceptable. Choice of colour on the packaging of a product, the shape of the box – even the choice of typeface – can all be crucial to how the product is perceived.

Think of the power of imagery, too. If you were to stick a picture of a black cat on your wrapper to mean good fortune, you will soon discover it has the opposite meaning to most other European consumers.

Source: Ian Lang, President of the Board of Trade (1996)

Figure 10.7 shows the percentage of people speaking the main language in each EU country. With the exception of Belgium and Luxembourg, the first language is the main language of the vast majority of the people. In Belgium, 58 per cent of the population speak mainly Flemish, and 42 per cent speak French. In Spain, the four main languages are similar and all Spaniards are able to speak Castilian. In Austria, German is spoken, and in Ireland, English is the first language. All other countries have their own first language.

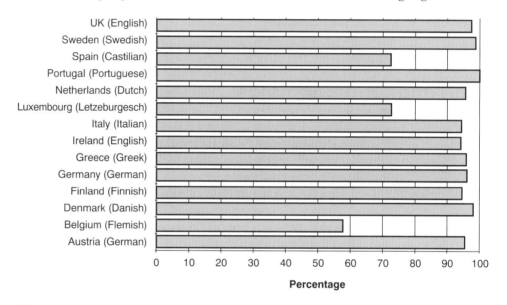

Fig 10.7 Percentage of nationals speaking the first language in EU countries
Source: Adapted from OECD

Figure 10.7 does hide the fact that a great many people in all EU countries have a major second language which they use almost as well as their first language. They are bi-lingual, and in many cases multi-lingual. The figures also hide the impact that apparently relatively minor differences in language may have on communication and culture. Often regional dialects may be so strong that they are almost different languages, and even different accents can cause confusion and misunderstanding.

Quick Quiz No. 7

German is the official language of Germany and Austria. English has also come in part from German. Which five EU countries have languages that come directly from German?

The answers are given on page 225.

Where languages are closely related to ethnic origins, as with immigrants, they will form an important part of their culture. It is therefore important to recognise the minor languages in countries as well. These are shown in Table 10.1.

Table 10.1 Minor languages spoken in EU countries

	Minor languages spoken
Austria	Slovene, Croat, Hungarian, Czech
Belgium	German
Denmark	Faeroese, German
Finland	Swedish, Lapp
France	Arabic, German, Portuguese, Breton, Basque, Corsican
Germany	Turkish, Frisian, Sorb
Greece	Macedonian, Turkish, Albanian, Vlach
Ireland	Gaelic
Italy	Sardinian, Rhætic languages
Luxembourg	German, Portuguese, French
Netherlands	Frisian, Turkish, Ambonese
Portugal	(There are no significant other languages spoken)
Spain	Basque
Sweden	Lapp
United Kingdom	Bengali, Gujarati, Hindi, Urdu, Welsh, Gaelic

These minor languages fluctuate in importance over time, as new immigrants increase their importance, and then are slowly integrated into the general society. In the past language also changed over time because of invasions, as with the Roman, Viking and Norman conquests of Britain. Alsace in France has belonged to France, Prussia and Germany in the last 200 years, and it is still the place where German is spoken in France. At the other end of France, the Basque country has been split between France and Spain and the people taught to speak French and Spanish (although some Basque remains). In South Jutland (Denmark) some people still speak German.

In some regions within EU states the original indigenous (see definition on page 185) language remains despite the imposition of a different national language. This has happened in the Basque area. In Ireland, Gaelic is the first language of people in the 'Gaeltacht' of Kerry, Galway, Mayo and Donegal. In parts of Wales, mainly in the north and west, Welsh is still the first language. In the far north of Finland, Lapp is the first language. The continued existence of these local languages has occurred because they formed such an important part of the culture. Not only does the language still exist, but also distinctly different local customs and cultures.

Today the main causes of changing language are the influences of other nations through trading, tourism and closer contact. When people find a foreign word for which they have no good equivalent, they adopt that word. In the UK we use French words, e.g. *café*, *matinée* and *cul-de-sac* and they use our words, e.g. *week-end*, *télévision* and *football*.

Examples of mistranslation from English

Come alive with Pepsi	– Rise from the grave with Pepsi (German)
Body by Fisher	– Corpse by Fisher (Flemish)
Cleans the really dirty part of your wash	– Cleans your private parts (French)
Avoid embarrassment, use Parker pens	– Avoid pregnancy, use Parker pens (Spanish)

Language does have a significant impact on culture and customs, and at the same time reflects the customs and cultures of countries. All of the EU countries use the words football and golf because they come from English, and until recently were not part of their culture. Other activities and words are adopted from foreign countries but are changed to fit the existing culture. Bowls and boules both come from the same French stem but the words and the game have developed in quite different ways. All EU countries have a phrase for Father Christmas and most have adopted the practice of present-giving from Saint Nicholas (Santa Claus). The Dutch still celebrate the original day of 6 December. In France *le Père Nöel* is associated with presents but not as widely as in the UK.

Language will also affect working conditions in all of the following ways:

➡ Certain jobs will require specific languages, as when working in another country, teaching a foreign language, working as a bi-lingual secretary.

➡ Language is the main form of communication and even when working in one's own country the standard of one's use of language often dictates what jobs one can do. Particular skills are required by journalists, writers, sales people, teachers and trainers.

> **MULTILINGUAL PA/SEC**
>
> £21K + benefits. Excellent opportunity for an English PA/SEC to use both fluent SPANISH and FRENCH in a dynamic environment.
>
> Duties will include translating/lots of liaison with Spain and France. You will be an excellent communicator, flexible and possess superb secretarial skills.
>
> Fantastic career prospects.

- For many 'migrant', or 'guest workers', the jobs that they are doing may not require language skills, so they may still be employed. When this happens warnings, health and safety notices, fire regulations, etc., will need to be understood. Employers will have to take account of this, especially where the number of foreign speakers is large.

 Language will even affect the layout of a computer keyboard, where the letters are laid out to make it easier to touch the most commonly used letters. In the UK the first line of letters starts QWERTY, while in France it starts AZERTY. In Germany, there are additional keys for ö, etc.

- Many professions develop their own forms of language, generally referred to as *jargon*. Without knowledge of these, potential employees will find it very difficult to find a job. The ultimate example of this is computer programming, where programmers have to learn specific languages such as Delphi and C++. Most computer languages are international and can be used effectively in all EU countries. Most jargon is very specific and cannot be easily understood outside the country, and even the region where it is used.

Quick Quiz No. 8

In GNVQ, like many other specialisms, jargon and the use of acronyms (words formed from the first letters of other words) are common. What do the following GNVQ acronyms stand for?

a) GNVQ **b)** BTEC **c)** RSA **d)** QCA

The answers are given on page 225.

Multicultural and indigenous influences

Definition
Indigenous populations are ones that are native to the area, and this implies that the people have lived in the same place for generations.
Multicultural society refers to a society in which there are many different cultures and all have some impact on the other cultures.

Customs and cultures are made up of a mixture of indigenous influences and imported influences which, over time, gel together to form **multicultural societies**.

The term '**indigenous**' is difficult to define because originally there were no people in what is now Europe. All cultures were imported. It is literally a question of time. Generally, if people have lived in an area for many generations they will be thought of as being indigenous, but other commentators might argue that many centuries are needed before this is the case. For this unit 'indigenous' should be taken to mean those people who have been in the area for generations and who have developed a distinct culture of their own. They can then be distinguished from more recent arrivals whose cultures have not yet been fully integrated into the general culture.

 The fact that the Basque Country is referred to as a 'country' is significant and reflects the Basques' long tradition of self-sufficiency and democratic ways. Although the Romans came here, they found the coast harsh and inhospitable and moved on. Likewise, the Arabs came but never conquered, and the Basques once again managed to preserve their jealously guarded freedom. Independence, however, also has its drawbacks – it meant that the Basque Country was not subject to the powerful and dynamic cultural and artistic influences of Roman and Moorish Spain; in later centuries Basques lacked these traditions to build upon. And for this reason you will not generally find great monuments and works of art in the Basque Country; artistic endeavours have never been an important focus of life.

Source: Discovering Spain by Penelope Casas

It is the indigenous culture that forms the basis of the culture, which is then slowly changed to absorb the influence of foreign cultures. Occasionally the change is very rapid, especially where one country or region is conquered by another. Generally, however, it is a slow process and it is possible to trace back the influences of the different cultures. Where various cultures exist together in one place there will be a multicultural society. This describes both integrated and non-integrated cultures.

As we saw above, languages tend to cross national boundaries and become part of a universal language, or get absorbed into the national language and change it from within. The same is often true of other aspects of culture and custom. With the increased number of international firms and more trade across national borders, working practices are also taking on a more multicultural look. This is dealt with on page 194. With all of the following the mixing of cultures can be seen:

➡ Clothes	➡ The role of the family	➡ Attitudes to religion
➡ Diet	➡ Music	➡ Goods and services
➡ Hairstyles	➡ Entertainment	➡ Games and sports
➡ The arts	➡ Building designs	➡ Methods of cooking

To show how these reflect both multiculture and the influence of indigenous customs and cultures, we will look at diet and music in more depth.

Diet and food

Many of the places in the UK where one eats out or buys take-aways reflect the influence of other countries and cultures:

➡ Chinese and Indian restaurants come from Asian and Indian immigrants to the UK
➡ Burger bars come from America
➡ Kebab houses come from Turkey, and through German
➡ Pizza restaurants come from Italy
➡ Cafés come primarily from France

The changing diet is also reflected by what we eat at home (*see* also Chapter 12), what is available in shops and supermarkets, and what are the main recipe books for sale in bookshops. All reflect a growing cosmopolitan (from many parts of the world) approach to our diet.

Variety is the spice of life

A survey of French eating habits, published in the *Journal of the American Dietetic Association*, found that the French eat so much fat in their normal diet that they should be leading the EU in coronary heart disease. In fact less than one in 1000 die from this disease in France. The UK record is over five times this figure.

The survey found that the French, on average, gain 30 per cent of their calories from fat, most of which is the saturated kind that causes heart disease. But they also found that the French normally eat a very wide range of food and drink. It is this, the experts believe, that is keeping the French healthy.

The normal diet includes meat, fish, cereals, vegetables, fruit and dairy products, which is much like the British diet, but we tend to eat the same products in each range, day in and day out. The French eat a wide range of different cheeses, fruits, patés, fish including shellfish, and they even eat a wide range of meats including horse and snails, and practically anything that flies.

Diet is also a reflection of national and ethnic characteristics. In the UK we have a reputation for eating fish and chips, Sunday roasts with gravy and two vegetables and endless cups of tea. But in the Soho Road in Birmingham, which is dominated by the Asian community, rice, spices, fresh vegetables and meats are the staple foods. In Lisle Street in London, every shop sells ethnic Chinese foods and provisions to cater for the dominant local Chinese community. In Paris, the influence of Arabic culture is found in Bobigny and Porte de la Chapelle, and the influence of Afro-Caribbean culture is found in Clignancourt and Porte Pontin.

Eating habits also spill over into the workplace and reflect the culture from which they have come.

➡ In large firms it has been the norm in the past to have separate canteens for the workers and the managers. This is less common now as large firms adopt Japanese and American work practices.

➡ The lunch break tends to reflect how important the midday meal is in different cultures (*see* inset).

➡ Eating is an important expression of social contact. It is like taking the first step to inviting someone into one's home. Business lunches, where colleagues or customers are invited to eat with you, are therefore an important part of how business is done.

The office lunch break

The approach to the midday lunch break in offices varies considerably across the EU. In the UK many people still eat a quick lunch and get straight back down to work. Others see it as a time to socialise with a roll and a pint at the local pub, but not for more than one hour. A growing number of businessmen and businesswomen are taking business lunches with clients. Here it is not considered wise to rush the meal and lunch may go on for an hour and a half or two hours.

In Sweden the traditional light meal is still very much in evidence. Luncheon vouchers are popular and are used to buy soup or a roll. Lunch is strictly a one-hour break, and alcohol is not to be consumed.

In Italy lunch is a time to socialise with colleagues or clients. Long full meals, sometimes up to five courses, are still common, and the lunch break is frequently two or more hours long. Several glasses of wine may be drunk to help the food go down and liven up the conversation.

■ Music

Popular music has now become international, generally dominated by UK and USA performers. Occasionally the French or the Swedes, and more often the Irish, manage to top the UK, USA and international charts, but generally that is only done when they sing in English. Indeed, English is the accepted international language of pop music, and as such it has become pan-European.

But there are other important musical influences going on. Paris is the centre for the development of Afro-Caribbean music in Europe, originating from immigrants living in Paris. In the UK, Bhangra has developed from the mixture of Asian music and western music, also from immigrants. Music, especially for the young, reflects a very dynamic force, one that is changing all the time. It is here that culture is at its most receptive to new influences. Frequently, music reflects the feelings and often frustrations of significant sections of society, and with this comes a kind of sub-culture in which the music symbolises and even drives behaviour and lifestyle. In the UK in the 1990s, this is reflected in 'rave' music, and the nightlife culture that goes with it.

Equally, the more traditional forms of music reflect cultures that people wish to emphasise and preserve. Some forms of regional music are fiercely preserved by the countries or regions that originally developed them. These include flamenco in Spain, fado in Portugal and rembétika in Greece.

Other music reflects nationalism, where music is taken to symbolise the nation, and people seem to feel that any erosion of the music also means that the nation is becoming less important. The most obvious examples are national anthems. Sometimes what is really just a regional musical form, such as flamenco in Spain, is also taken to express a form of national pride. Flamenco is really part of the gypsy culture of Andalucía, with a strong Arabic influence, but it is now associated generally with the culture of Spain, and most Spaniards are quite happy to accept this wider association. Where countries feel that their national musical symbols are under attack they can become very protective.

French music police are putting up barriers to foreign rock on the radio

The French government is on the warpath defending the nation's culture against the onslaught of Les Anglo-Saxons. Until recently French FM radio stations played 90% imported music, mainly in English. Since 1994, 40% of the music played must be in French, although this is only just being enforced now. Managers of French radio stations complain that their listeners are simply turning the radio off, or tuning into foreign radio stations. Supporters point out that half the pop music sold in France is in fact French and without this support new French talent will be unable to develop.

Source: *Time Magazine* (February 1996)

Quick Quiz No. 9

The national anthem of the United Kingdom is called 'God Save The Queen (or King)'. Which EU countries have the following national anthems?

a) The Marseillaise

b) This Is A Lovely Land

c) Thou Ancient, Thou Freeborn

d) The Soldier's Song

e) Land Of Mountains, Land Of Rivers

The answers are given on page 225.

■ Integration failures

The integration process of different cultures described above does not, unfortunately, always occur. Sometimes the existence of different groups in the same area leads to mistrust, segregation and even violence. Usually this occurs when one group feels threatened by another. In Germany, the Turkish immigrant workers are the violent target of the new right-wing political groups who see them as a source of cheap labour that is keeping German people out of work. In the UK, it is frequently Indians, Pakistanis and West Indians who are discriminated against in the workplace and find it hardest to get jobs. In the south of France, Algerian immigrants are discriminated against and have much higher levels of unemployment than the indigenous French population. In all three countries the minority groups find it difficult to live in the general community and tend to live in areas with other people from the same ethnic groups. Despite the EU legislation on free movement and the right to live where one wants, very real barriers of prejudice still prevent real integration.

Foreign minister Klaus Kinkel claimed some of his country's guests had "declared war" on their host. He was referring to extremists among the 500,000 Kurds who have come to call Germany home because they have been denied a homeland of their own within Turkey.

Kinkel's claim was hard to dispute after nearly three weeks of violent protests, front-page photos of bleeding German police, hundreds of Kurdish demonstrators arrested and widespread property damage.

Source: Time Magazine (April 1996)

11 Specific working conditions in EU member states

Chapter 10 has given many examples of how customs and culture affect working conditions, and many more are to be found in other parts of this book. For the effects of stereotyping, linguistic skills, equal opportunities, etc., readers should use the index to find where these are covered. This short chapter deals with certain specific working conditions, and changes to working conditions, that have not been covered elsewhere.

Customs and cultures affect so much of our lives that it is not surprising that they also affect the conditions in which we work. They also affect who works, where they work, how long they work for, what rates of pay they receive and so on. Some of these conditions have been covered in Chapters 3 and 4, and readers should refer to these chapters as well.

Effects on mobility of the workforce

The ability of workers to move from one job to another, or from unemployment to employment, is vital in an economy which is constantly changing and improving. Many of the jobs that dominated the economies of the EU in the 1970s and even 1980s have declined and new industries have grown to take their place. Much of the heavy secondary industry has almost disappeared and industries in computer technology, communications and leisure, recreation and entertainment have expanded. To meet these changes, labour needs to be much more flexible and mobile.

Definition
Geographical mobility is the ability to move from one country to another country, or one part of a country to another part.
Occupational mobility is the ability to move from one job to another.

Labour can be mobile in two ways – **geographically** and **occupationally**. Each of these has conditions that either help mobility or hinder it. Many conditions will depend on education and training, but others arise from the culture and customs that create the labour market.

■ Geographical mobility

People will move away from where they live only if they want to, and only if they are able to. Various factors will determine whether or not they can do this, and many of them will be influenced by customs and culture.

Table 11.1 Factors helping and hindering the geographical mobility of labour

Factors helping mobility	Factors hindering mobility
➡ Knowledge of other languages	➡ The language barrier
➡ Sufficient income to move	➡ The need to sell one's house
➡ Knowledge of available jobs	➡ Lack of details on job opportunities
➡ Independence from family ties	➡ Family ties, e.g. older dependants
➡ Internationally accepted qualifications	➡ Qualification not recognised abroad
➡ Friends and relations in other areas	➡ Inability to get residence permit
➡ Better living conditions	➡ Discrimination against foreigners
➡ Higher rates of pay elsewhere	➡ Lower rates of pay elsewhere

The structure of the family will have a considerable effect on geographical mobility. For example:

➡ Workers living in extended families will find it difficult to move because of the family ties. In countries like Greece and Italy there is less movement from area to area than in countries like the UK where the nuclear family is now the norm.

➡ Where both husband and wife are working, mobility may be restricted because movement for one person means that the other person will have to give up his or her job and may not be able to find a new one. As women generally earn less than men it is very rare for families to move so that the wife can find a new job.

➡ In countries like Austria, Greece and Italy children have tended to live with the family until they are married. This tied them into the family and made young workers far less mobile. In Italy, as in France, it is now far more common for couples to live together in their own homes before marriage. It is also more common for young people to move out of home into their own flats and houses, as happens in the UK. These developments tend to increase labour mobility.

■ Occupational mobility

People will move from one job to another when they feel that another job will be better for them, or when they are moving from unemployment to employment. Again there will be factors that help and hinder this process.

Table 11.2 Factors helping and hindering the occupational mobility of labour

Factors helping mobility	Factors hindering mobility
➡ Multi-skilled, many qualifications	➡ Lack of required skills or qualifications
➡ No special skills required in job	➡ The barrier of language
➡ Training provided with the job	➡ No information on vacancies
➡ Easy access to vacancy details	➡ Barriers created by trade unions
➡ Higher rates of pay in other jobs	➡ Jobs not available in local area

As with geographical mobility, many of the factors listed above relate directly to culture and customs, for example, the level of language skills or the custom of what is taught in schools. When movement is from unemployment to employment, stereotyping is often a major barrier. Many employers believe that people are unemployed because they are lazy. Other employers, despite anti-discrimination laws, will not employ people from other races and ethnic backgrounds. As countries have different levels of unemployment (*see* page 218) and different levels of ethnic minorities, the mobility of labour is also variable.

Figure 11.1 shows how the education systems in four EU countries offer different routes into work. The level of qualification that a person has is likely to have a major effect on his or her ability to move from one skilled job to another.

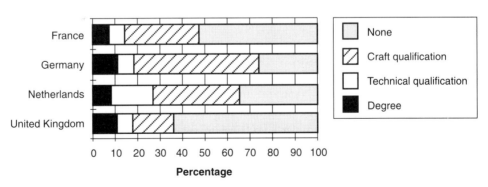

Fig 11.1 Qualifications of those in employment, 1990
Source: Adapted from OECD

Imported working conditions

As we saw in Chapter 6, many working conditions are imposed through Community law, and in that sense they are imported from the Council of Ministers or the Commission. Many other working practices are imported because the people running the businesses see some advantages in this. Others are imported because the firms that are set up are owned by foreigners, and they bring their working practices with them.

The most dramatic change in working practices has come from the influence of Japanese firms. The free trade within the EU has encouraged many Japanese firms to set up within the EU, and thereby escape the import tariffs. In the UK we have manufacturing firms like Toshiba, Toyota and Nissan. In other EU countries there is now a strong presence in the service industries of banking and insurance. Other EU firms have seen the success of Japanese work practices and have copied them.

The Japanese approach includes:

➡ The Japanese work ethic, where work is something that one should be proud to do, not just a way of earning income.

➡ Commitment of workers to the firm, which they are expected to see as a job for life.

➡ The rejection of trade union activity and even the signing of no-strike agreements.

➡ The use of team work and greater decision-making roles for workers, including quality circles.

➡ The use of total quality management and practices such as just-in-time systems, all designed to improve the quality of the final product.

➡ Close contact with suppliers of raw materials and components, and an expectation that these suppliers will be totally committed to the firm.

In other areas of work the conditions are changing because firms are adopting practices from other EU countries. The development of supermarkets and hypermarkets as a means of selling food, drink and an ever-increasing variety of other goods, came from France. With it has come the change, for the consumer, from being served to self-service and a change, for the staff, from having to deal with most aspects of retailing to specialising in one or two areas such as shelf stacking, working at the checkouts, collecting trolleys, warehouse duties, and even just cleaning.

The changing production process in the EU motor vehicle industry

1 Manufacturers and suppliers now work very much closer together, often developing improved systems of production jointly, and frequently using just-in-time supply systems.
2 Inside the workplace, management and the workforce now have shorter lines of communication, having removed some of the middle management. Total quality management, quality circles and continuous improvement programmes are now standard.
3 Flexible shift working is common and making better use of plant facilities.
4 Multi-discipline teams now work on design, using Computer-Aided Design (CAD) and Computer-Aided Engineering (CAE).
5 Automation is replacing the hardest and most repetitive areas of work, such as robotic paint-spraying and welding.

Many of the changes referred to above reflect the growing use of technology in the workplace. These changes have tended to take place first in large and often international firms. This is because they are the ones that can afford technology. Today, however, most firms will have some form of technology, even if it is only the use of a computer.

➡ In retailing, where products are bought on the premises, nearly all firms will have cash registers, and many firms have facilities for the use of credit and debit cards, and links to EPOS systems.

➡ In offices, technology will exist with computers, copying machines, fax machines, etc.

➡ In manufacturing, technology is present in CAD, CAM, CAE, and so on.

➡ In primary industry, many farms now use technology to monitor performances of livestock and to help with the cultivation of the land.

As technology has a significant cost it tends to be the richest countries that introduce it first. Portugal and Greece still have comparatively little technological development in their small businesses, and the same is true of rural areas of Spain, Italy and France. The success of hypermarkets in Portugal has only occurred because nearly all of them are French.

In **France** the spread of supermarkets is to be checked as planning permission is tightened for supermarkets over 300 sq. m. The 1000 hypermarkets currently have 34 per cent of the country's food sales.

In the **UK** Sunday opening has given supermarkets even more of the market share and has driven a large number of small firms out of business.

In **Denmark** there are few hypermarkets and most food and drink sales take place in local shopping centres.

In **The Netherlands** the local grocer is very much the norm and planning permission for large stores is almost impossible to obtain.

In **Italy** the expansion of hypermarkets has forced many small grocers out of business in the 1990s, but hypermarkets still only number a quarter of those in France.

In **Portugal** hypermarket sales form a very high percentage of total grocery sales, greater than in any other EU country.

In **Spain** hypermarkets are common and have caused a major decline in the number of small shops.

The working day

The norm for the working day in the UK is said to be 9 a.m. to 5 p.m., although this pattern is frequently changed with shift work, flexible hours, overtime, part-time working and working from home. The tradition in the southern countries of the EU was to work from early in the morning up to lunchtime, stop working for four or five hours in the hottest part of the day, and then work again into the evening. This is still the case in the more rural areas but major industries have needed to fit in with the working hours of their major customers. Many now work a similar pattern to that in the UK.

Quick Quiz No. 10

Because the earth is revolving, the sun rises at a different time in Ireland than it does in Greece. What is the normal time gap between these two countries?

The answer is given on page 225.

Table 11.3 shows the average opening times for main shops. In cities many shops will stay open over the lunch hours and large supermarkets will tend to have late-night shopping as well. There will also be significant local variations.

Table 11.3 Opening hours for main shops in EU countries

	Monday to Friday	Lunch break	Saturdays
Austria	0800/0900 to 1800	1 or 2 hours	0800 to 1300
Belgium	0900 to 1800	Some close 2 hrs	0900 to 1800
Denmark	0900 to 1750		0900 to 1300/1400
Finland	0900 to 1800		0900 to 1400/1600
France	0900/0930 to 1800/2200	1 to 4 hours	0900 to 1300
Germany	0830/0900 to 1830		0900 to 1300/1400
Greece	0900 to 2000	3 to 4 hours	0900 to 1400
Ireland	0900 to 1730/1800		0900 to 1730/1800
Italy	0900 to 1900/1930	2½ to 3 hours	0900 to 1900/1930
Luxembourg	0830 to 1800	2 hours	0830 to 1800
Netherlands	0830/0900 to 1730		0830/0900 to 1600
Portugal	0900 to 1900	2 hours	0900 to 1300
Spain	0700 to 2000	3 to 4 hours	0700 to 1100
Sweden	0900 to 1600		0900 to 1300/1600
United Kingdom	0900 to 1730		0900 to 1730

Source: RAC and Fodor's Europe

With the increasing number of mothers working, there has been a growth in flexible working hours and part-time work. These tend to be fitted around the school day. The increase in the number of women working has also meant that they cannot get to the shops in working hours, and supermarkets now tend to have late-night shopping every day (except Sundays). In countries like Portugal, where relatively few women work, the shopping patterns have not changed as much.

 In June 1996 the law changed in **Germany** to allow shops to stay open until 8.00 p.m. on weekdays and 6.30 p.m. on Saturdays. In November, **Austria** raised its permitted opening hours to 8.00 p.m. on weekdays and 4.00 p.m. on Saturdays.

In the UK we now have many shops that open on Sunday, although not usually in town centres. Local shops in other countries are sometimes open, but generally the large shops and supermarkets are closed. This is particularly the case in countries where religion still has a strong influence on the culture. In all EU countries, Sunday is a day of rest for most businesses, and most firms also close on Saturday.

For more and more people in the EU, the working day has become one of part-time work. In some cases this is because workers do not want full-time work, as with mothers who still have children at school, but in many other cases part-time work is all that is being offered. Figure 11.2 shows how part-time working has increased as a percentage of total work in all of the original twelve EU countries. Other work practices that are being brought in include the use of home workers, a great deal more use of telesales, and temporary work contracts which escape the need to pay redundancy payments.

A sharp break with tradition

It is about two hours by car from Deutsche Bank's imposing headquarters in Frankfurt to its direct banking subsidiary in a converted grain mill in Bonn. But the two are worlds apart.

The bank's twin-towered sky-scraper is the traditional face of banking, with the atmosphere one of restraint, discretion and respectability. The former mill building contains its new direct bank, Bank 24, where staff are friendly, energetic and informal – characteristics not always associated with German banks.

Many Bank 24 staff work part-time and come from outside banking. They have shorter holidays than Deutsche Bank staff and a different pay scale. 'Our people are young, with an average age of 27 and a strong service credo,' says Thomas Holtrop, Bank 24's head of marketing.

Source: The Financial Times (August 1996)

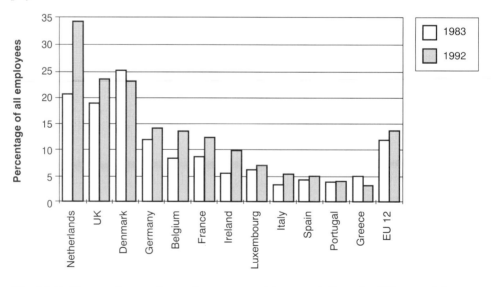

Fig 11.2 Percentage of employees working part-time in EU countries
Source: Adapted from EUROSTAT

The huge variation in **part-time working** shown in Figure 11.2 reveals a dramatic difference in working practices across the EU. In most cases the percentage of people working part-time is growing. This is, in part, explained by the increased number of women working (*see* Figure 3.6, page 49). Many women do not wish to work full-time.

There is also a very distinct divide between countries in the north and south of Europe. This division reflects a cultural division where many southern Europeans see their jobs as a way of life, and therefore something that they should be fully involved in. Many northern Europeans see their jobs as simply a method of earning money, and if a part-time job will earn enough, then that will do.

12 Differing lifestyles in EU countries

The lifestyles chosen by people, unless they are hermits, reflect the customs and culture of the area, region or country in which they live. The factors that affect this lifestyle are huge, but include all the customs and cultures examined above. In this chapter we will consider various measures of lifestyle. Some are good, which tend to improve our 'standard of living', some are bad, which are usually referred to as part of our 'cost of living'.

'Lifestyle' describes the way in which people live their lives. Each person will tend to have his/her own unique lifestyle but there will also be characteristics that apply to larger groups, such as the family, clubs, certain types of workers, men or women and even whole nations. This is shown by stereotyping (*see* page 169). There will also be an almost endless list of headings under which lifestyle might be considered. A few are given below:

➡ Age	➡ Religion	➡ Role in the family
➡ Diet	➡ Recreation	➡ Level of education
➡ Sport	➡ Type of work	➡ Experience of other cultures
➡ Health	➡ Marital status	➡ Membership of clubs, etc.
➡ Wealth	➡ Environment	➡ What is allowed by law

Lifestyle depends very heavily on three main factors:

➡ The customs and culture in the country

➡ The effects of the physical environment, particularly climate

➡ The levels of income enjoyed by the people who live there

Together these will dictate the **standard of living** that people can enjoy, but also the **cost of living**. They will also dictate what **types of lifestyle** are possible. These three aspects are considered separately below. For each section the reader should remember that it is customs, culture and laws that have created the lifestyles that are being shown.

Standard of living

The most commonly used measure for the **standard of living** is Gross Domestic Product (GDP) per head of the population. This measures the value of everything produced in a country in a year and then divides it by the number of people to provide an average. In the 1960s the UK had the second highest GDP/head of the EU countries but Figure 12.1 shows that we have not fared very well since then.

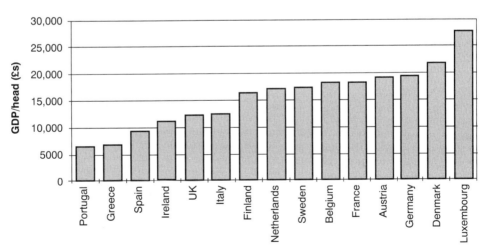

Fig 12.1 GDP/head for EU countries, 1995
Source: Adapted from Main Economic Indicators (OECD)

In 1994 Sweden had the second highest GDP/head in £s, but by 1995 it had fallen back to sixth highest. This did not happen because production in Sweden suddenly fell, it simply reflected a fall in the value of the Swedish krona against the pound sterling. This is a major problem when trying to compare GDP levels in different countries. What really matters is what people's incomes mean inside their own country and to measure this, **purchasing power parity (PPP)** is used. This compares incomes by working out what the average levels of income can buy in the country where they are being earned. Where prices of products are relatively cheap, as in Portugal and Greece, this will make the income figure rise. Where prices are relatively expensive, as in Luxembourg and Denmark, this will make the income figure fall.

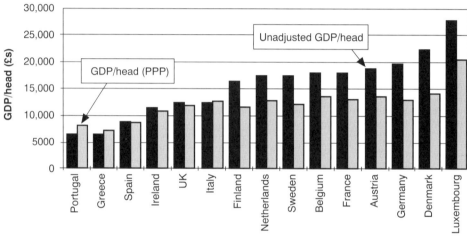

Fig 12.2 GDP/head and GDP/head (PPP) for EU countries, 1995
Source: Adapted from Main Economic Indicators (OECD)

Figure 12.2 shows how using purchasing power parity changes the figures for the EU countries, making the GDP/head figures very much closer together. All but four of the countries now come between £10,000 and £15,000 GDP/head. These are, however, all averages, and within each country there will be very wide regional variations. This is shown in the cutting from *EUR-OP News*. This uses the terms GNP and PPS, but they are very similar to GDP and PPP.

For people who work, their take-home pay is more important than the average level of GDP/head, so the levels of wages, income tax (*see* Table 8.1, page 122), state benefits, etc., are also important. Table 12.1 shows the starting point for EU workers in manufacturing.

Richest and poorest regions

Gaps in purchasing power in the EU continue to be high: whilst Hamburg reaches the highest per capita GNP in purchasing power standards (PPS) with 196%, Thuringen, also in Germany with 38% is the lowest. Seven regions are 1.5 times above the average, while 12 are below 50%. EUROSTAT figures show that only one region in Spain – Balores – reaches the EU 15 average, and in Greece and Portugal not one region reaches the average. High GDPs are recorded for Brussels (174%), Île de France (169%), Vienna (166%), Oberbayern (157%) and Bremen (155%). The regions below half the EU 15 average were Thuringen (38%), Alentejo (Portugal – 41%), Açores (Portugal – 41%), Mecklenburg-Vorpommern 41%, Sachsen 42%, Sachen-Anhalt 43%, Brandenburg 44%, Madeira (Portugal – 44%), Voreio Aigaio (Greece – 45%), Ipeiros (Greece – 47%), Centro (Portugal – 48%).

Source: EUR-OP News (Summer 1995)

Table 12.1 Comparative wage rates and hours of work in manufacturing, 1992

Country	Manufacturing as % of GDP	Wage/ hour (£)	Hours/ week	Weekly wage (£)
Sweden	22	9.60	38.5	370
Luxembourg	31	8.78	40.3	354
Norway	14	9.19	36.8	338
Austria	25	10.54	31.9	336
Germany (West)	23	8.19	40.7	333
Denmark	19	10.18	31.5	320
Netherlands	20	6.85	39.9	273
United Kingdom	30	5.98	43.2	258
Ireland	3	5.73	40.5	232
Spain	30	6.00	36.3	218
Belgium	22	6.42	32.7	210
Finland	22	6.63	29.6	196
France	21	4.48	38.7	173
Greece	14	2.32	41.1	95
Portugal	29	1.35	37.5	51

With all of the data given above it is the average figure that has been given. In reality, people receive a wide range of different incomes depending on what job they have, or if they are unemployed and having to rely on state benefits. Figure 12.3 gives a little more breakdown, in terms of wages, for seven of the EU countries. The wage rates shown here are the basic rates for the minimum guaranteed working week. Many employees will earn higher average rates because of overtime.

Quick Quiz No. 11

The two highest-paid European Union sports personalities in 1994 received £8.9 mil. and £7.5 mil. respectively. They both came from the same sport. What was it?

The answer is given on page 225.

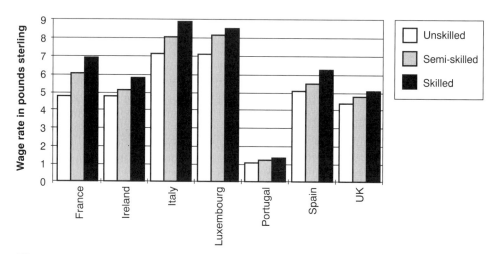

Figure 12.3 Wage rates per hour for different skills, 1994
Source: Adapted from the International Cost Survey

Income is only part of the standard of living – the part that is received each week, month or year. Our total **wealth** includes things that we own, such as cars and swimming pools, and things that will give us benefits and incomes in the future, such as houses – and pension rights.

Income and wealth distribution in the UK

The two tables below show how final income/person and marketable wealth/person were distributed in the UK in 1991. The population has been divided into sections and the figures show the average that each section receives or owns. The income distribution is divided into fifths. The wealth is divided into highly unequal sections because that reflects how wealth is actually distributed in the UK.

Income Distribution

Bottom fifth	Next fifth	Middle fifth	Next fifth	Top fifth
£6230	£8450	£12,500	£16,380	£26,910

Wealth Distribution

Bottom 50%	Next 25%	Next 15%	Next 5%	Next 4%	Top 1%
£4678	£24,533	£40,890	£75,938	£139,939	£508,200

In the EU, the patterns of wealth are very variable. Wealth is something that has to be accumulated and this is done slowly over time. In Italy, the level of savings is the highest in Europe and on average Italians had about £50,000 of saved wealth in 1995. In France this was about £43,000 and in the UK about £39,000. In Finland, the figure was only about £9000, but the figures did not include ownership of houses and for most people that is the major form of their wealth. Figure 12.4 shows the percentage of housing that is owned by the occupiers. Other housing is rented. Where the numbers are low this may indicate one of three things:

➡ That people are too poor to own their own houses, as in Greece.

➡ That people prefer to rent rather than tie their wealth up in houses, as in Germany.

➡ That there is a lack of housing available to buy rather than rent.

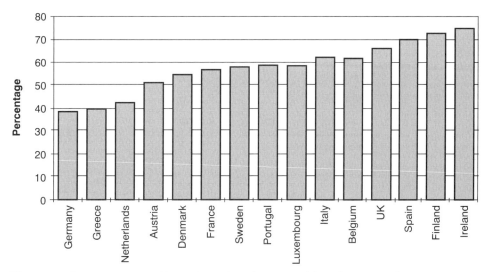

Fig 12.4 Percentage of housing that is owned by the occupier
Source: Eurostat

The standard of living can also be measured through the ownership of other goods and services that we receive. Table 12.2 shows figures for ownership of three common major household durable goods in the EU. Cars, televisions and telephones have been selected because these are considered to be good international measures.

The table shows that differences between countries are quite extreme, with nearly four times as many cars/person in Germany than in Portugal, three times as many televisions/person in Luxembourg than in Ireland, and nearly five times as many telephones/person in Sweden than in Portugal. In Sweden there is a telephone for each of the 8.8 million people who live there. Many of these figures may seem rather small but it must be remembered that they are per person, and not per household.

Table 12.2 Number of selected durable goods owned per person in the EU

Country	Cars	Country	TVs	Country	Phones
Germany	0.45	Luxembourg	0.71	Sweden	1.00
France	0.40	Denmark	0.42	Denmark	0.83
Italy	0.40	Germany	0.42	Finland	0.71
Sweden	0.40	France	0.37	Luxembourg	0.71
Austria	0.36	Netherlands	0.37	Italy	0.67
Belgium	0.36	Austria	0.36	France	0.63
UK	0.36	Spain	0.36	Germany	0.63
Finland	0.35	UK	0.36	Netherlands	0.63
Netherlands	0.34	Belgium	0.35	Austria	0.53
Denmark	0.31	Greece	0.33	U K	0.53
Spain	0.26	Finland	0.30	Belgium	0.45
Ireland	0.21	Italy	0.29	Greece	0.40
Greece	0.14	Sweden	0.29	Ireland	0.27
Portugal	0.12	Portugal	0.27	Spain	0.24
Luxembourg – no data		Ireland	0.23	Portugal	0.21

Source: Adapted from Eurostat

Ireland is in the bottom three countries for each of the measures, which might suggest a low standard of living, but there would be many people who would argue that having few cars, no television and no phone actually improves living conditions.

It is also very common to measure standards of living by specific types of service, such as health care, where the usual measure is how many doctors, nurses or dentists there are for every 1000 people in the country. This does give a rough guide to the levels of care we can expect in different countries. Figure 12.5 shows the number of doctors for every 1000 people in the fifteen countries of the Community. As with so many of the international comparisons, the UK comes out very poorly, but it should be remembered that the number of doctors does not automatically determine the quality of the service that they give. It is also important to know what medical back-up doctors have, how many nurses there are, what hospital facilities there are, and so on.

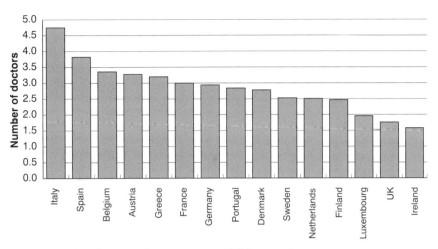

Fig 12.5 Number of doctors per 1000 people
Source: Adapted from WHO

Other common measurements of the standard of living, such as life expectancy, infant mortality or population density, have been covered in other parts of this book, and readers should check these to build up a fuller picture. The United Nations has attempted to combine some of these measures to provide a wider picture of the standard of living in different countries. This is called the **Human Development Index**, which measures GDP/head on a PPP basis, life expectancy and literacy. The leading country is then given an index value of 100 and all the other countries are measured against this. Table 12.3 shows how the EU countries fare on this measure. All are relatively high, but again this is only an average for each country.

Table 12.3 The Human Development Index for EU countries (1993)

	Index		*Index*
Sweden	98	Finland	95
France	97	Luxembourg	94
Netherlands	97	Ireland	93
Denmark	96	Italy	92
Germany	96	Spain	92
United Kingdom	96	Greece	90
Austria	95	Portugal	85
Belgium	95		

Source: Adapted from the United Nations

The many different ways of measuring the standard of living given above show how difficult it is to make accurate comparison between countries.

Way of life in EU countries

One way of identifying what people think is important, is to look at how they spend their money. Figures 12.6(a) and 12.6(b) show the average percentage of consumer spending on major types of product. They reveal some interesting contrasts, but also hide some important points:

➡ The high spending on food in Greece and Portugal reflects the relatively low incomes that they have and the need to buy necessities first.

➡ The low spending on health care in many countries reflects the fact that health in these countries is provided free by the state.

➡ All the figures include taxes and reflect different prices, so they do not show how much of each product consumers are receiving.

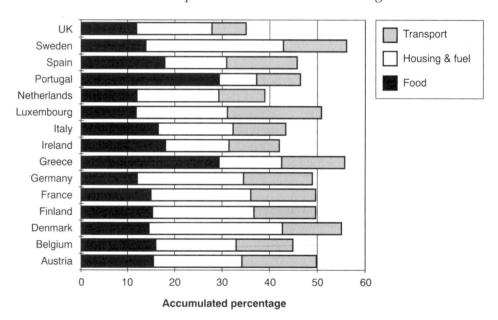

Fig 12.6(a) Percentage of consumer spending on selected products, 1993
Source: Adapted from Eurostat

Table 12.4 gives the actual amounts of five main products that are consumed by people in the EU. They tend to contradict some of the stereotypes that are associated with nations. The British may be thought of as the home of fish and chips, but the table shows that we consume less fish/head than any other EU country. The Germans are thought of as great meat eaters but they are only halfway up the table. On the other hand, they clearly do like their beer!

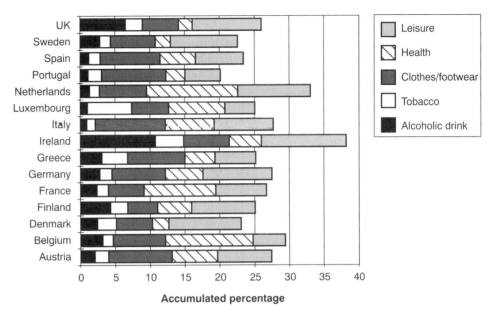

Fig 12.6(b) Percentage of consumer spending on selected products, 1993
Source: Adapted from Eurostat

Table 12.4 also reflects what products are available in each country and therefore reflects both national tastes and natural resources. The major wine producers are Italy, France, Portugal and Greece. Portugal and Denmark have large areas of shoreline and a long tradition of sea fishing. Luxembourg has many people from other countries living there, which helps to explain their high consumption of fish. Readers must note, however, that these figures are only for 1993, and the patterns can change dramatically from year to year. The figures should only be thought of as a rough guideline.

Eating through the day

For most Germans, breakfast may include a boiled egg, muesli and yoghurt, but more probably bread with cheese, jam and/or cold meats. Lunch, the main meal of the day, could include a juicy schnitzel (cutlet) – usually pork – roast potatoes and a salad. Dinner is often a cold and light meal of bread, a larger variety of meats and cheeses than at breakfast and, in colder weather, perhaps soup or a small stew. A popular stew is a combination of lentils and sausage. German desserts are almost always fruit or cream-based dishes. The amount of bread consumed by most Germans will astound visitors.

Source: AA Essential Explorer: Germany

Table 12.4 Quantities of major products consumed per head per year (kgs or litres), 1993

	Fish		Meat		Beer		Wine		Bread
Port.	35.5	Dk.	102.1	Ger.	151.9	Port.	77.2	Ger.	106.9
Dk.	26.2	Aust.	97.1	Ire.	137.1	It.	63.4	Port.	74.0
Lux.	18.8	Bel.	91.7	Dk.	116.0	Fr.	62.6	Ire.	69.2
Bel.	18.7	Lux.	90.6	Bel.	115.0	Gr.	56.8	It.	67.4
Sp.	16.1	Ire.	90.5	Lux.	111.5	Sp.	37.7	Gr.	64.8
It.	12.7	It.	71.9	UK	103.9	Aust.	31.4	Dk.	58.9
Sw.	10.4	Port.	61.2	Neth.	91.9	Bel.	28.1	Fr.	58.8
Fr.	9.8	Fin.	60.1	Fin.	89.3	Lux.	27.2	Sp.	56.1
Gr.	9.1	Gr.	59.3	Sp.	71.6	Ger.	26.8	Sw.	51.6
Fin.	8.7	Sw.	57.5	Sw.	67.2	Dk.	24.6	Bel.	46.4
Ger.	6.6	Ger.	43.2	Port.	56.5	Neth.	15.2	Lux.	44.9
Neth.	5.7	Sp.	38.9	Gr.	41.9	Sw.	12.9	Neth.	42.8
Ire.	4.3	Fr.	36.9	Fr.	39.5	UK	12.9	Fin.	31.7
Aust.	2.4	UK	34.1	It.	22.1	Fin.	9.9	UK	31.6
UK	1.2	Neth.	19.8	Aust.	19.2	Ire.	5.5	Aust.	19.2

Source: Adapted from Eurostat

For local differences in food and drink, menus and recipe books provide a very useful source of information. Generally, people will tend to use what is most easily available.

 There is an old saying in Piedmont that even in the condemned cell a man should not be refused a cup of broth, for broth is another of the region's specialities. Unlike the majority of Italians, the Piedmontese are inclined to prefer broth or soup to rice and pasta.

Source: Italian Regional Cooking by Ada Boni

The Frenchwoman, characteristically thrifty, displays her skill with pleasure. It begins with the choice of ingredients. Potatoes are chosen as carefully as peaches, value for money demanded, and good quality insisted upon in every cut of beef and bunch of radishes.

Source: French Cooking by Eileen Reece

Lifestyle is also shown by such public facilities as the number of libraries that a country has, or the number of newspapers. Figure 12.7 shows the number of libraries per one million people and the number of daily newspapers per 1000 people. The UK publishes more books than any other nation in the world – even the USA. Germany ranks fifth and France and Spain are eighth and ninth respectively in terms of book production. Combined with the figures for public libraries, this does suggest that the Britons and Germans are the greatest readers of books, whereas the Scandinavians are the greatest readers of newspapers.

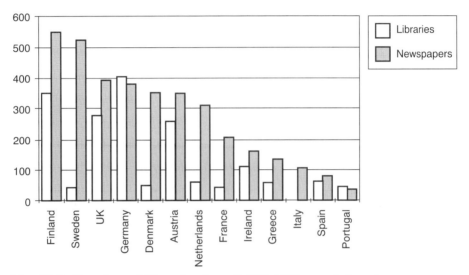

Fig 12.7 Number of libraries (per 1,000,000 people) and newspapers (per 1,000 people)
Sources: Various

Leisure activities also reflect the wide variety of lifestyles across the EU. Some of these are common to most countries. For example, most of the sports that are featured in the Olympic Games are to be found somewhere in each EU country. Sports that rely on specific conditions, such as skiing or surfing, will only be found in countries where those conditions exist. Other sporting activities are to be found in individual countries, as with hurling in Ireland, or in particular regions, as with *pétanque*, which is the Provençale variant of boules. Others are highly local (*see* inset on Örnsköldsvik).

Quick Quiz No. 12

Which of the four Grand Slam tennis tournaments are held in EU countries?

The answers are given on page 225.

Until 1970 an international sporting competition was held in Örnsköldsvik in Sweden. This competition was staged to see who could eat the most rotten herrings. Unfortunately, the herrings were so bloated and rotten that they caused most of the foreign competitors to have to be hospitalised. They also created such a strong smell of rotting cheese that competitors practising late into the night were in danger of breaching the health regulations in their own countries. It seems that only the Swedes can truly stomach such a competition and, understandably, the record of 53 whole fish in one hour is still held by a Swede.

Cost of living

The other side to the standard of living is the cost of achieving it. The obvious cost of living is how much is paid for goods and services, but there are a great many other factors that also affect how we live:

➡ The price of products and inflation

➡ The level of unemployment accepted by the country

➡ The environment that we live in and how polluted it is

➡ How safe our society is and how much crime there is

➡ What we have to give up to gain our standard of living, e.g. leisure time

➡ The levels of illness and disease in the country

Below we will take a brief look at some of these.

■ Inflation

The **retail price index** is probably the best known cost of living index. It is the one that the news media use, especially when they are talking about **inflation**. In other countries it is often called 'the consumer price index' because it measures how much it costs consumers to buy a certain '**basket of goods**'. The basket reflects all the major things that a household will spend money on, from food and drink to petrol and eating out.

Figures 12.8(a) and 12.8(b) show how the cost of living, as measured by the retail price index, has changed over the five years from 1990 to 1995. Note that two different scales have been used on the two graphs. The inflation has been given here as annual changes. When these changes are accumulated over the five years it shows just how wide the gap in inflation is between countries like Greece and Portugal and France and Denmark. This is shown in Figure 12.9.

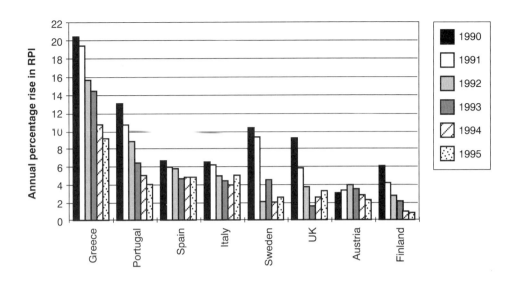

Fig 12.8(a) EU countries with the highest inflation, 1990 to 1995
Source: Adapted from Eurostat

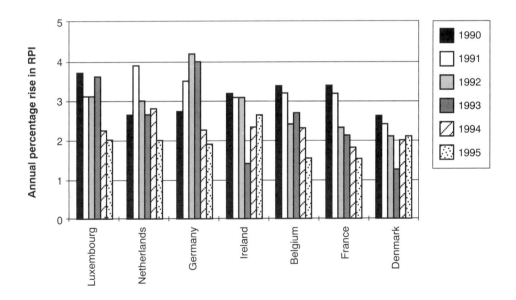

Fig 12.8(b) EU countries with the lowest inflation, 1990 to 1995
Source: Adapted from Eurostat

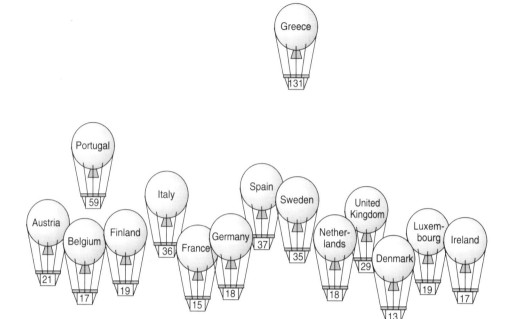

Fig 12.9 Percentage increase in inflation in EU countries, 1990 to 1995
Source: Adapted from Eurostat

In the UK, and most EU countries, there has been inflation every year since the war. This is something that is now considered as normal. Even in Germany there has been inflation nearly every year, but generally it has been low. The Germans will not allow inflation to get out of hand, because they still remember the madness of 1923 when they had a rate of over 75,000,000 per cent inflation in the space of five months. In Italy in the 1970s, there was a pay agreement with the unions called *scala mobile*, which meant that workers always got a pay rise of at least the inflation rate. All this did was to fuel the following year's inflation. Today the Italians have abandoned this foolishness, and have become the leading savers in the EU.

■ Taxation on goods and services

In 1993 it was agreed that by 1997 all EU countries would have a minimum charge of 5 per cent VAT on all items and that the EU should be working towards common taxation on good and services. The current situation is, however, that all the countries have different rates and systems, and they also charge VAT on different ranges of products. The UK is one of the few countries to charge no VAT on children's clothes, but it is also one of the few to charge 5 per cent VAT on domestic fuel. Germany, Luxembourg, Portugal, The Netherlands and France have no zero-rated items. Figure 12.10 shows how the VAT rates in the EU were broken down into different rates in 1994. The top of each section of the column indicates the rate for the band, e.g. the standard rate of VAT in Austria is 20 per cent.

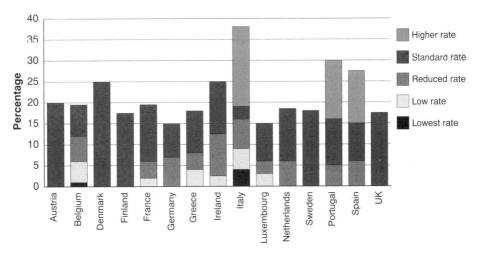

Fig 12.10 The range of VAT rates in the EU, 1994
Sources: Various

It is still the intention of the European Commission to move towards a standard indirect tax system for the whole of the EU. At the moment, however, not just VAT but the tax on cigarettes, petrol and alcohol varies considerably from one country to another. This explains why so many people go across the Channel to buy cheap wine and beer in France, and why it is still possible to buy exactly the same model of car in Germany as in the UK, but at £2000 or £3000 less.

Table 8.1, on page 122 showed the range of income tax in EU countries. This reveals a great deal about how different countries think about the role of taxation. In the UK the top rate of income tax is only 40 per cent, reflecting the belief of the Conservative government, and the electorate that voted them into office, that high rates of tax on people earning large incomes are not acceptable. In Belgium, Sweden, Denmark and The Netherlands, the top rate of income tax is over 70 per cent, and reflects the belief that people earning high levels of income should be made to contribute more to the general benefits given by the state. The attitude to businesses is, in part, reflected by the levels of corporation tax charged in each country (*see* Table 12.5).

Table 12.5 Rates of corporation tax in selected EU countries

	% tax		% tax
Belgium	43	Denmark	50
Finland	19	France	37–42
Germany	50	Greece	46
Italy	36	Netherlands	35–40
Portugal	36.5	Spain	35
Sweden	30	United Kingdom	23–35

■ The environment

The environment is a major factor in raising our standard of living, such as when it:

➡ creates pleasant and productive climates
➡ provides recreational facilities that people want, e.g. snow for skiing
➡ encourages lively nightlife
➡ leads to spectacles such as the *aurora borealis*

Quick Quiz No. 13

The *aurora borealis* or *northern lights* is the name given to the coloured lights that can be seen in the far north of Europe at night. What is the other name given to the *southern lights*, which can be seen in the southern hemisphere?

The answer is given on page 225.

and in lowering our standard of living, such as when it:

➡ creates asthma through air pollution
➡ leads to oil spills that destroy wildlife
➡ pressures workers so much that they have heart attacks
➡ encourages lifestyles that lead to the development of cancer

As a cost of living index, the environment is not very reliable. Austria and France have the healthiest trees and the UK the most polluted, yet France and the UK have the worst emissions of sulphur dioxide (about 3.5 million tonnes/year). Germany has the highest emissions of hydrocarbons into the air, which is not surprising as it has over 35 million cars, yet Germany tops the EU league for the use of unleaded petrol. When data for environmental conditions is used it needs to be considered with a wide degree of scepticism.

All the same, some standard measures, especially where they are shown per capita, do give some guide as to where pollution is worst. The emissions for carbon dioxide, CO_2, are shown in Figure 12.11.

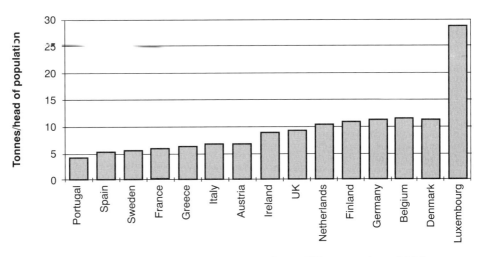

Fig 12.11 CO_2 emissions (tonnes/capita) for EU countries, 1993
Source: Adapted from Main Economic Indicators (OECD)

Does capitalism make you ill?

New medical research shows that former East Germans have become sicker since the collapse of communist rule and are picking up physical and mental diseases common to the West.

The popular assumption that East Germans would become healthier after the heavily polluted former communist state was cleaned up has been dashed by research in Erfurt and Hamburg. There has been a rapid increase in asthma, hayfever, respiratory diseases and serious allergies. Some cancers – especially those of the breast and colon – have increased in the east, as have a range of stress-related psychological disorders such as anorexia and clinical depression.

Source: The Times (August 1996)

■ Unemployment

Definition
Unemployment occurs when people who want jobs and are able to work cannot get jobs.

For most people unemployment is not a problem, but for the unemployed, and the families that depend on them, unemployment can be devastating. Unfortunately, most EU governments now think that even relatively high levels of unemployment are inevitable, and simply a necessary cost of achieving growth without inflation in a modern economy. This is perhaps a rather short-sighted view, for all of the following reasons:

➡ Unemployment lowers the standard of living of the unemployed and their dependants.

- All EU countries pay benefits for those who are unemployed and qualify for benefits, and these have to be paid for out of other people's taxes.
- Unemployment, and payments to people for being unemployed, produces nothing, so a valuable natural resource, labour, is being wasted.
- Unemployment tends to affect the weakest in society – the young, people of minority races, the poorly educated, etc.
- The fear of unemployment makes people reluctant to spend money and therefore less is bought and this causes more unemployment.
- High levels of unemployment are related to high levels of crime.

Unemployment levels are very closely related to how the economy is performing and whether we are in boom or recession. When less is being produced, fewer employees are required. All EU countries have gone through recession in the first half of the 1990s. Table 12.6 shows how this has affected men and women in different countries. It also shows, particularly with Finland, just how dramatically the unemployment situation can change.

Table 12.6 Unemployment rates (%) for females and males in EU countries (1990 and 1994)

	Female		Male	
	1990	*1994*	*1990*	*1994*
Spain	24.0	30.9	12.0	18.5
Ireland	15.5	19.7	14.0	16.7
Italy	15.8	17.8	6.6	8.3
Finland	2.8	16.8	4.0	20.1
Belgium	11.9	14.5	4.8	7.0
France	11.8	13.6	6.8	9.4
Netherlands	10.5	13.3	5.6	7.9
Denmark	9.1	11.2	7.2	9.1
United Kingdom	6.5	7.4	7.4	11.2
Portugal	6.4	7.3	3.2	5.3
Sweden	1.5	6.9	1.6	9.3
Germany (W)	5.9	6.7	4.0	5.9
Austria	3.6	4.5	3.0	4.1

(Unemployment in Table 12.6 is measured as a percentage of the workforce, i.e. those who are working and registered as looking for work.)
Source: Adapted from Economic Survey of Europe (UN)

In recession, employment falls faster initially in the industry sector, so the relative position of women appears to improve. Generally, female unemployment rates remain higher than those of men in the majority of EU countries. This partly reflects the sharp increase in female participation rates in recent years.

Source: Economic Survey of Europe

Table 12.6 reflects a significant difference in the ways that countries react to unemployment. In Austria unemployment is not considered acceptable, and so the government manages the economy in order to keep people employed. In the UK many women are not entitled to register as unemployed, so the figures for men are higher. This also reflects the growth of service industries where women, rather than men, are employed.

What, however, reflects a country's attitude most in terms of unemployment is the percentage of people who are allowed to remain unemployed for more than one year. This is called long-term unemployment. In Figure 12.12, this is shown as a percentage of everyone who is unemployed in the country, and it must be remembered that countries start with widely differing rates of unemployment, e.g. the 43.9 per cent in Germany is made up of very much less people than the 45.6 per cent people in France.

Quick Quiz No. 14

In the UK unemployed people can seek jobs through the state-run job centres. Which EU countries have state job centres called

a) Gewestelijk Arbeidsbureau?

b) Ufficio di Collocamento Manodopera?

c) Arbetsmarknadsstyrelsen?

d) Agence Nationale pour l'Emploi?

The answers are given on page 225.

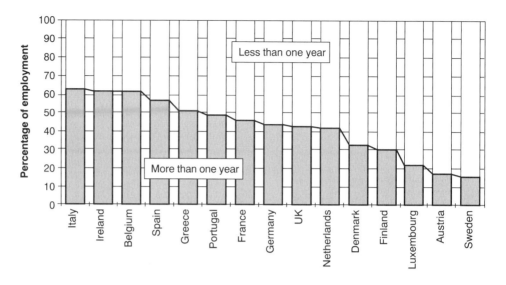

Fig 12.12 Long-term unemployed as a percentage of all unemployed within each country, 1995
Source: Adapted from Main Economic Indicators (OECD)

Some of Britain's most deprived inner-city areas will benefit from a £40m EU package to create more than 2,500 jobs and 8,500 training places, it was announced yesterday. Liverpool will be the biggest beneficiary, with £11.8m; Glasgow gets £10.9m, Manchester £6.4m, and Sheffield and Nottingham £5.4m apiece. The money was welcomed by council leaders for the boost it gives to areas plagued by high unemployment, crime and ill-health . . .

A spokeswoman for the European commissioner in charge of regional policy, Monika Wolf-Mathies, said: 'Britain is getting quite a good share.'

Parts of Naples and Venice in Italy, Lille and Paris in France, Magdeburg in Germany and Dublin and Cork in the Irish Republic are also to benefit under the programme.

Source: The Independent (August 1996)

■ Crime rates in the EU

Crime rates do vary considerably from year to year so the data given in Table 12.7 below is just a snapshot. It must also be remembered that different countries define crimes in different ways, and that crime varies from one region and area of a country to another. Ireland has the lowest rate of rural crime in the EU, but the relatively high rates of urban crime colour the final figures.

Table 12.7 Selected crime rates and ranking in EU (crimes/100,000 people)

	Murder	Rank	Rape	Rank	Theft	Rank
Austria	2	=11	7	=8	2900	9
Belgium	2.5	10	6	10	2600	11
Denmark	5	5	9	=3	8400	2
Finland	0.5	15	8	=5	3000	–7
France	4.5	6	8	=5	4000	6
Germany	4	7	8	=5	4400	5
Greece	2	=11	2	=13	500	14
Ireland	1	14	2	=13	2000*	=12
Italy	6	4	10	2	2800	10
Luxembourg	11	2	5	=11	3000*	=7
Netherlands	15	1	9	=3	5600	4
Portugal	3	=8	1	15	400	15
Spain	2	=11	5	=11	2000	=12
Sweden	7	3	16	1	8700	1
United Kingdom	3	=8	7	=8	6700	3

Two main groups of countries tend to have lower than average crime rates:

➡ Poorer countries like Greece and Portugal. Some crimes, especially theft tend to be a characteristic of rich societies where people have more to steal and the poor feel more alienated.

➡ Countries where religion and the family are still important, like Greece, Portugal and Spain. Italy is something of an exception to the rule.

The UK has the dubious distinction of being the country with the highest prison population in the EU.

In an attempt to establish who are the most honest Europeans, the *Reader's Digest* arranged for 200 wallets to be left in twenty European cities. Each wallet had the name, address and some personal details, but also about £30 in cash. On average 58 per cent were returned to the owner's address or to the police, etc., but the figures were widely different from one city to another.

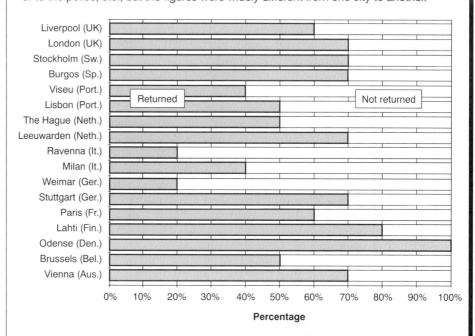

Fig 12.13 Number of wallets returned (1996)
Source: Reader's Digest

ASSIGNMENT 3
Examine customs and cultures in the European Union

TASK 1

Prepare notes on customs and cultures found in the EU. The notes should be presented in the appropriate form and must cover the following:

➡ Every item listed in the range for **customs** and in the range for **cultures**

➡ **One** example of a custom and **one** example of a culture for each of the EU member states

This will mean that 30 individual pieces of research will need to be done. These may be statistical, articles from newspapers or magazines, extracts from travel guides or recipe books, etc. You must identify which item in the range you are covering with your research and notes.

TASK 2

You must research, prepare and present a report on each of the following:

➡ A comparison of the effects of customs and cultures on the working conditions in the UK and one other EU country.

➡ A comparison of the effects of customs and cultures on the lifestyles in the UK and one other EU country.

The report should consider the similarities and differences between the UK and the other chosen country, for working conditions and lifestyle.

Sources of information

This textbook, newspaper and magazine articles, travel guides, country guides, recipe books, Eurostat publications, personal experience from holidays, visits and work (but remember to validate sources), contact with foreign nationals, etc.

Key skills available for testing

■ **Application of Number:** Statistical data can be collected, checked and presented in an appropriate form to achieve PCs in Elements 3.1 and 3.2.

■ **Communication:** Elements 3.2, 3.3 and 3.4 can all be covered in this assignment.

■ **Information Technology:** Information technology can be used to support all of the tasks in the assignment, and will cover Elements 3.1, 3.2 and 3.3. The presentation of your research should use graphs, tables, etc., where appropriate.

Answers to Quick Quizzes

No. 1

a) The words employ, employer and employee all come from the same basic **French** stem *emploi* meaning 'employment' and *employer* meaning 'to employ'.

b) Kindergarten comes from the **German** *Kindergarten* meaning, litererally, 'children's garden' but is now generally used for pre-school institutions and playschools.

c) Hurricane comes from the **Spanish** *huracan* meaning the same as in English – violent windstorms or cyclones.

d) Panorama, now used as the title of a BBC television programme, comes from two **Greek** words – *pan* meaning 'all' and *orama* meaning 'view'.

No. 2

The exact origins of both football and golf are unknown, but the modern games can both be traced back to the United Kingdom. Football started in England and golf started in Scotland.

No. 3

a) The Romans were centred on Rome, which is now the capital of Italy.

b) The Saxons came from around the River Elbe, now part of Germany.

c) The Vikings who raided Britain came mainly from what is now Norway.

d) King Canute was a Dane and King of England from 1016, King of Denmark from 1018 and King of Norway from 1028.

e) The Normans came from Normandy, now a region of France.

No. 4

It is the Swedish men who believe that they are 'God's gift to women'.

No. 5

The Greek Orthodox church broke away from the Roman Catholic church and is now practised in Greece, Turkey and parts of Russia. In Greece it is the official religion and it is against the law for anyone to attempt to convert members of the church away from this religion.

No. 6

a) Judaism

b) Buddhism

c) Islam. Muslims, or Muhammadans, are believers in Islam

d) Sikhism

No. 7

Danish, Dutch, Finnish, Letzeburgish (Luxembourg) and Swedish all come from German, developing into distinct separate languages over time. In Belgium, Flemish is basically a dialect of Dutch and so also comes from German.

No. 8

a) GNVQ stands for **G**eneral **N**ational **V**ocational **Q**ualifications
b) BTEC stands for the **B**usiness and **T**echnology **E**ducation **C**ouncil
c) RSA stands for the **R**oyal **S**ociety of **A**rts
d) QCA stands for the **Q**ualifications and **C**urriculum **A**uthority, and is the body that decides what the syllabus is for each GNVQ course, how it will be examined, etc.

No. 9

a) France
b) Denmark
c) Sweden
d) Ireland
e) Austria

No. 10

The normal time gap between Ireland and Greece is two hours, but it does depend on when the two countries change their own clocks. It is sometimes only one hour.

No. 11

Gerhard Berger (Austrian) earned £8.9 mil., and Nigel Mansell (British) earned £7.5 mil., both through Formula One motor racing.

No. 12

The French Open Tournament is played in Paris.
The British Open Tournament is played at Wimbledon, London.
The other two tournaments are played in the USA and Australia.

No. 13

The *southern lights* are known as the *aurora australis*.

No. 14

a) *Gewestelijk Arbeidsbureau* is found in The Netherlands.
b) *Ufficio di Collocamento Manodopera* is found in Italy.
c) *Arbetsmarknadsstyrelsen* is found in Sweden.
d) *Agence Nationale pour l'Emploi* is found in France.

PART FOUR

Element 16.4
Investigate different work opportunities among European member states

PERFORMANCE CRITERIA

A student must:

1 identify and give examples of the **tasks and responsibilities** for a work role in a specific occupational area

2 describe the **types of skills** required to carry out the **tasks and responsibilities** in selected work roles

3 **compare** the **employment and career progression opportunities** in the selected occupational area in two member states

13 Introduction – Collecting information

Investigating how work opportunities and specific work roles differ across the EU is likely to be the hardest part of this unit. This introductory chapter, therefore, lays out, in some detail, how to choose a specific work role to study and how you should set about collecting the data. Students are advised to read the introduction carefully and decide, early on, **what information they will personally need and where they will collect it from**.

It is equally important to know what is required in order to carry out specific work roles (jobs). This will be covered in Chapter 14. All of the following factors will be considered, both in general terms and with reference to specific EU examples:

➡ The qualifications required in order to be allowed to do a specific job.

➡ The skills required in order to be able to do a specific job.

➡ The tasks that are involved with carrying out a specific job, both routine and specialist.

➡ The responsibilities that employees/employers have in terms of their work roles.

➡ The expectations that employers will have about their employees in relation to loyalty, secrecy, health and safety, quality assurance, etc.

➡ What the employee is entitled to in terms of adequate training, health and safety, security, etc., and his/her expectations.

Many of these points have been covered, in general, in other parts of this textbook, and students should check for references in the index.

Chapter 14 will then examine, briefly, some specific examples of employment and career opportunities.

What career should be studied for this element?

The information technology industry has expanded at an unprecedented rate over the past decade, and the number of competent professionals in this field has not kept pace with demand; so if you are a qualified and experienced computer programmer, systems analyst, systems designer or computer engineer, you certainly have an extremely marketable skill and can be quite choosy as to where you want to work.

Source: How To Get a Job Abroad by Roger Jones

Most advanced-level students do not know what they will be doing after they have finished their GNVQ or 'A' level courses. If they are thinking about going on to university, they are even less likely to know exactly which career they will be following in the future. Unfortunately Element 16.4 of the BTEC course supposes that students have a very clear idea of what career path they wish to follow and that is what they will be researching for this element. The reality is quite different. Most students, at this point in their education, will be undecided about what they will be doing in the future and career choices will still be at best vague, and possibly not seriously considered at all.

All of this makes it very difficult for the students trying to complete Element 16.4. This element then adds to that problem by insisting that students restrict their research to a very narrow area of the total job market – **a work role in a specific occupational area**. This inevitably means that the choice of which work role to study, in which specific occupational area, will have a major impact on how well students are able to do in their assignments.

Choosing which work role and which occupation you wish to study may be based on all of the following factors:

➡ The actual career that you have already decided to follow in the future.

➡ Any career that might be of interest to you and which you want to find out more about.

➡ A career that you have experience of through either visits or work experience in another EU country.

➡ Contacts that you have with people in other countries, or contacts that you have with people in the UK who themselves have foreign contacts.

➡ Any career that you have a wide range of data on.

Ideally, the job that you choose to research will be one that you are interested in and will help to develop your own career prospects. Unfortunately that job may not be the one that you can access most information about, especially in up to three other EU countries. When choosing which job to target your research on, one factor will outweigh all the others, and that is, '*Do I have access to all the data that I need?*'

Quick Quiz No. 1

Which UK industry employs more people than any other UK industry?

The answer is given on page 259.

When you choose which occupational area to study you should keep in mind the following points:

➡ Choosing an occupation that you are interested in will make your study much more enjoyable and therefore you are likely to produce better work.

➡ Finding information about job roles, tasks, career progressions, etc., in other countries is generally very difficult indeed and the primary consideration must be a question of how much data you have access to.

➡ You must make your decisions about which occupational area to study early on in the course. Gathering information often takes months rather than days.

➡ Many of the institutional sources of information that you need, e.g. professional bodies, chambers of commerce, consulates, etc., will require you to contact them directly. This is done most efficiently by telephone, fax or letter. You are not likely to find all the information that you require in textbooks.

➡ Ask for guidance and support. As long as you quote your sources you cannot be penalised in terms of your overall grade (unless your sources are doing all the work for you). Suitable sources will include:

● Your teacher/lecturer

● Careers advisors

● Parents

● People who work in the chosen industry

● Professional bodies

Perhaps the most helpful hint that can be given, in terms of choosing which work role to study, is that **nothing is ruled out**. The recommendation may be that you choose a work role from within the technical, administrative or supervisory spheres, but work roles from any other sphere are equally acceptable. What really matters is that the work role is clearly identified and that details are found for the same work role in other EU countries. If you wish to research and compare EU farm labourers or hairdressers or fashion designers or casual workers in the tourist industry, or even teachers, you may do so within the specification of this element.

The jobs and the pay

In French ski resorts Ski Total have provided the following details for 1996/97 for seasonal workers looking for jobs in the tourist industry.

Resort managers (£80–£120 per week, plus commission). The job is to organise all aspects of clients' holidays, supervise other staff and ski guiding up to about three days a week. Age: 22 min. 'This is the most demanding job in the resort,' says the company. 'Applicants must be hard-working, resourceful, patient, outgoing, efficient and be able to get along with and handle people well at all levels.'

Cooks (£60-£100 per week). Cooking to a high standard for 21-30 people, manning kitchen, supervising junior staff. Driving licence and French or German useful. Age: 21 min.

Chalet girls/boys (£50-£65 per week). Catering to a high standard, cleaning, washing up, bed making, etc., for 8-12 people in self-contained chalet. Age: 21 min.

Chalet helper/assistant cook (£40 per week). Cooking, cleaning, washing up, making beds, etc. Age: 19 min.

Source: Overseas Job Express (June 1996)

Sources of information on work opportunities in the EU

■ Books

There is a wide range of general and specialist books available in public libraries and good bookshops and these are worth an early inspection. For example, *The Directory of Job and Careers Abroad*, edited by André De Vries, gives details of the following areas of work:

- Banking and accounting
- Journalism
- Medicine and nursing
- Secretarial
- Teaching

- Computer services
- The law
- Oil, mining and engineering
- Translating and interpreting
- Transport, tourism and hospitality

It also gives details of contacts and addresses for more detailed study.

Working Holidays 1996, published by the Central Bureau for Education, provides brief job profiles on all of the following temporary work roles:

- Archaeology
- Au-pair work and childcare
- Community work and children's projects
- Work in the field of conservation
- Farmwork
- Teaching
- Travel and tourism

Grape picking in the South of France, tasting the product, living at the vineyard, taking *déjeuner sur l'herbe* with the grower and his family – all this may conjure up a colourful and idyllic scene. With proper planning a job in the grape harvest may live up to this standard. However, the hours are long, and you need to be very fit as the work is hard, involving lots of bending, stretching and carrying. The accommodation may be very basic and during bad weather only those hours actually worked will be paid.

Source: Working Holidays 1996

There are also books that specialise in a particular profession, e.g. *Teach Abroad* also published by the Central Bureau for Education, or *European Engineering Yearbook* published by Cambridge Marketing Intelligence Ltd. These provide details of the qualifications and skills needed for UK residents to work in their own chosen field abroad.

Other books will specialise in one country and should provide information on a range of work roles and occupational areas. Examples include:

➡ *How to Live and Work in Spain* by Robert A.C. Richards (*How to* Books)

➡ *Living in Spain* by John Reay-Smith (Robert Hale)

➡ *Long Stays in Spain* by Peter Davey (David & Charles)

➡ *Setting up in Spain* by David Hewson (Merehurst)

Books of this kind are produced for each EU country. Check the sources listed at the back of this textbook, and your local library.

In UK libraries and bookshops there are many career books that deal specifically with jobs and career progressions in the UK. All EU countries produce these, although they are difficult to track down and they will, of course, be published in the foreign language. They will give details of job roles, qualifications and career progressions. Examples include:

➡ *Guide des Opportunités de Carrière*, which gives details of opportunities for graduates in France.

➡ *Intermediair Jaarboek*, which gives details of opportunities for graduates in The Netherlands.

■ Newspapers and magazines

Many national papers provide details on careers abroad as part of their regular items on general career news. They will also run advertisements for overseas jobs on certain days of the week. Usually these are written in English, but where another language is required for the job, they may advertise in that language.

The Financial Times runs international appointments on Thursdays. *The Times* has a special section for secretarial jobs on Wednesdays, often including jobs abroad. *The European* publishes a few EU jobs but also publishes details of jobs that people are looking for. Where jobs are advertised, even in foreign languages, they usually provide very useful details of qualifications required, likely levels of pay and benefits, and details of what the job roles entail.

There are also specialist publications that deal only with jobs, such as *Jobsearch*. This paper has a page or two on overseas jobs and agencies at the end. *Overseas Jobs Express*, which is a fortnightly publication, concentrates solely on overseas jobs, many of which are in the EU.

Most UK papers and magazines advertise UK jobs, and the same is true of foreign newspapers. They are a valuable source of information, but they will of course be in the country's own language. Table 13.1 shows a list of major newspapers that carry job adverts in the EU press.

The papers listed in Table 13.1 tend to be the national papers. As in the UK, local papers are also a valuable source of data on available jobs. There are also specialist English-language newspapers in other EU countries, such as *Athens News* in Greece and *Portugal Post* in Portugal. These do make it much easier for UK citizens who don't know the foreign language well. The papers will give details of what jobs are available and what the requirements and conditions are.

There are also specialist foreign newspapers/magazines that only deal with jobs, such as *Markt und Chance*, which is a weekly publication by the German Labour Institute giving details of jobs on offer. There is also a growing number of newspapers, with job details, that are published abroad, but are written in English. Examples are given in Table 13.2.

 The post of **technical engineer** in Portugal was advertised in *The European* of July 1996. The post, which offered progression to technical director, asked for a degree in technical engineering, good knowledge of English and German and BASIC CAD knowledge. The job specifications listed skills in problem solving, self-sufficiency and innovation. A major restriction was that the candidate had to be between 25 and 30 years old.

Table 13.1 Major newspapers carrying job advertisements

Austria	*Die Press, Der Standard* and local papers such as *Wiener Zeitung*
Belgium	*Le Soir, La Meuse* and *Antwerpse Morgen*
Denmark	*Politiken, Ekstra Bldet* and *Belingske Tidende*
Finland	*Helsingin Sanomat* and *Turun Sanoma*
France	*Le Monde, Le Figaro* and *France-Solr*
Germany	*Frankfuter Allgemeine Zeitung* and *Die Welt*
Greece	*Kathermerini* (*Athens News, Athens Daily Post* – both in English)
Ireland	*The Irish Times, The Irish Independent* and *The Irish Press*
Italy	*Corriere della Sera, La Repubblica* and *Il Messaggero*
Luxembourg	*Luxemburger Wort* and *Tageblatt*
Netherlands	*De Telegraaf, De Volkskran* and *Het Parool*
Portugal	*Correio da Manha, O Diario* and *Jornal de O Dia*
Spain	*La Vanguardia, Diario 16* and *Diari de Barcelona*
Sweden	*Svenska Dagbladet, Dagen, Expressen* and *Dagen Nyheter*

Quick Quiz No. 2

In which EU countries are the following regional newspapers to be found?

a) *Il Giornale di Napoli*

b) *Göteborg Postern*

c) *Le Provençal*

d) *Neues Salzburger Tagblatt*

The answers are given on page 259.

Table 13.2 Examples of foreign newspapers published in English

Country	Titles	Address
Belgium	*The Bulletin*	329 av Molière, 1060 Brussels
France	*The News* and the *Dordogne Telegraph*	Universal Media Ltd, 67 Chiltern Street, London W1M 1HS
Greece	*Athens News*	23-25 Lekka St, Athens 10557
Spain	*Iberian Daily Sun*	Universal Media Ltd (see above)

■ Work experience

Ultimately the tasks, skills, qualifications, job roles, etc., that really matter are the ones that actually have to be carried out in the workplace. The best way to study these is to research the job of work being done in the office, factory or other work environment. Where work experience abroad is possible it should be readily taken up. This may provide highly valuable data for one country, but few students are likely to be able to experience work in four different EU countries. All the same, be prepared, and work out what data you need to collect before you start work.

The same is true if you are able to arrange visits to foreign workplaces, but here you need to be even more prepared. You are unlikely to be there long and it may be difficult to talk to the people who really know about the job role you are studying.

■ Professional bodies

Generally, even the best books only give a broad picture of tasks, responsibilities and required skills. At some point you will almost certainly need to contact some outside source – either an individual or an institution.

In many professions there are specific institutions or governing bodies. Normally one thinks of professions such as law, architecture, dentistry or accountancy, where entry is usually only possible if one has passed the required examinations. But there are also institutions that help to control, advise and support professions which members have joined because they are already working in that industry. Examples would include the Institute of Exporters, the banking profession and the teaching unions. With the growth of NVQs, and the testing and recording of a wide range of practical skills, there are now many institutions that monitor and control standards in vocational jobs, such as hairdressing, catering and retailing.

Quick Quiz No. 3

What is the basic difference between GNVQs and NVQs?

The answer is given on page 259.

All of these institutions will have offices and personnel whose primary function is to provide members and would-be members with information on their profession. The same is true of similar institutions in the other EU countries. Your first jobs, however, are to:

➡ choose the occupational area that you are interested in

➡ find out which UK institution is responsible for the area you are interested in

- find out, either through the UK institution, or from other sources, which foreign institutions are responsible for your chosen occupational area
- decide what information you require and contact them

Most people who know what is going on in a specific occupational area are busy people, and therefore it is important that you know exactly what information you would like before you contact them. You should think carefully about what you need to know in advance. All of the following points need to be considered:

- Which job(s) you are interested in.
- Which countries you want details for. The *evidence indicators* ask for research on four EU countries.
- What information you need about the job(s) that you have chosen to study and in particular what information you need about tasks, responsibilities, skills, qualifications, career and progression opportunities, etc.
- What date you need to have the information by. But do not be pushy, otherwise sources will simply ignore you.
- Where you want the data sent. You should be explaining, as you ask for information, that you are a student and that the data will help you with your studies. Some sources may be more willing to provide information if it is to be sent back through the school/college. Alternatively, you may choose to take the line of asking for information for yourself, because that is the career you are thinking about following.

Some of the major professional bodies are listed in the resources guide at the end of this book. Many of the UK professional bodies have specific departments that deal with working overseas, such as The Royal College of Nursing, International Section, Cavendish Square, London, W1M 0AB. Other professions have created international links which also provide details of working conditions in other countries, such as The International Confederation of Midwives, 10 Barley Mow Passage, Chiswick, London, W4 4PH.

■ Personal contacts

The best sources of information are often personal contacts. The people who you know personally are often more willing to give you the information than strangers are. They are also more likely to be able to give you the data you require when you need it.

The most reliable personal contacts are people who are actually doing the job that you are researching. Parents and friends may also have contacts, and may be able to place additional (friendly) pressure on colleagues, etc. Two examples of the kind of details that can be gained in this way are given in Figures 13.1(a) and (b), one for a full-time job, one for a part-time job. Do think carefully about what questions you ask. Questions about age and salaries may offend some people.

Name	Country worked in	Job title
Emmanuel Renauld-Dehlinger	France	Responsible Bureautique
Age	Industry	Years of work
31	Town Hall	1992 to 1995

What day-to-day tasks were involved in the job?

Buying equipment and software. Suppliers relationships.
Looking after the computers to fix what was going wrong.
Network administration.
Software writing.

What specialist skills were required in the job?

Computing skills.
Organisational skills.

Who were you responsible to?	Where did your job fit into the structure of jobs in the firm?
The Computer Department Manager	Major Cabinet ↓ General Secretary ↓ Computer Department ↓ Office Automation
Who were you responsible for? Three computer technicians	

What health and safety factors were involved in your job?

Health: Screen radiation protection. Position of people sitting at a desk in front of a computer.
Safety: Protection of the equipment from theft, fire, flood, electrical surge, vandalism. Protection of the data and the software.

What qualifications/skills were required for your job?

Computer Engineer

Fig 13.1(a) Sample questionnaire completed by Emmanuel Renauld-Dehlinger

What training was provided 'on the job'?		
At the workplace	Through courses? *Various software packages* *Communication*	New skills learned? *Software and network skills*

What is the normal route of progression in the type of job you were doing?

Engineer

↓

Project Manager

↓

Computer Department Manager

Which professional organisations control the training, quality, entry qualifications, etc., for the type of job that you were doing?

The Engineer Diploma is controlled by the State.

Fig 13.1(a) *cont.*

Name	Country worked in	Job title
Benoît Imhauser	*Belgium*	*Teacher*
Age	Industry	Years of work
36	*School – Ceran*	*1996*

What day-to-day tasks were involved in the job?

Teaching French 3 hours a day using a technique based on the students answering questions whose answers would make them produce a certain type of structure or vocabulary.
Giving 45-minute grammar workshops and listening comprehensions.

What specialist skills were required in the job?

The Ceran technique for teaching.
Knowledge of French grammar and vocabulary.

Who were you responsible to?

The Head Teacher

Who were you responsible for?

Directly responsible only for the students

Where did your job fit into the structure of jobs in the firm?

Directors
↓
Head Teacher
↓
Teacher
↓
Assistants
↓
Activity Leaders

What health and safety factors were involved in your job?

General care of the students but nothing else.

What qualifications/skills were required for your job?

A degree or certificate of the Superior School (Taken after 'A' levels).
Teaching experience.

Fig 13.1(b) Sample questionnaire completed by Benoît Imhauser (Belgian)

What training was provided 'on-the-job'?		
At the workplace	Through courses?	New skills learned?
A 2-week course to introduce new teachers to the Ceran technique.		*Use of videos and tapes. Use of specific grammar exercises.*

What is the normal route of progression in the type of job you were doing?
The staff is mainly composed of qualified teachers. After a certain number of years teachers usually become responsible for a department, or for the organisation of the Junior Summer School. Some teachers are asked to train newcomers in the Ceran techniques.

Which professional organisations control the training, quality, entry qualifications, etc., for the type of job that you were doing?

Fig 13.1(b) *cont.*

■ Libraries and careers centres

Libraries have limited funds available and even the restricted range of books referred to in this textbook are unlikely to be found in all UK public libraries. The best approach to choosing the work role to be studied may, therefore, be to find what countries and professions are covered in the local library and then to look for other sources that will add further details about the specific qualifications, skills, career progressions, etc., that are required.

European Information Centres (EICs)

have been set up across the European Union, with over 200 centres linked with the latest technology. They have been set up, primarily, to aid businesses seeking expansion into the EU markets, providing details on Community law, available markets, inter-company links, etc. But they also store data on professional links, standardisation of qualifications, foreign professional institutions, etc. Details of the nearest EIC will be provided by the local public library.

Another possible approach is to contact the careers service, or check the careers data in the school/college/public library. These will provide good sources of information on jobs, qualifications, required skills, etc., in the UK, and may also provide EU comparisons. UK job centres are now linked to EU employment offices and have computer facilities that allow people to access details about jobs that are available in other EU countries.

European Document Centres (EDCs) have also been set up across the UK with the express objective of 'stimulating European awareness and the study of Europe in academic institutions'. Most of these are attached to universities, and usually allow students from outside to access data. Details are given in the resources section at the end of this book.

The publication of details of the qualifications needed for specific professions and jobs has now been unified in the **Official Journals of the European Communities** available from HMSO, 51 Nine Elms Lane, London SW8 5DR (Tel. 0171 873 8373). Publications cost between £4.75 and £19.50 and are available for all of the career areas listed in Table 13.3. The publications may also be available at the EDCs and the EICs.

Table 13.3 Career areas through the Official Journals

	Code number
Agricultural	C83 volume 33
Chemical industry	C262 volume 35
Clerical/administration, banking, insurance	C108 volume 35
Commerce	C42 volume 35
Construction	C292 volume 32
Electrical/Electronic	C321 volume 32
Food industry	C292 volume 35
Hotels and catering	C166 volume 32
Iron and steel	C182 volume 36
Leather	C223 volume 36
Metalworking	C196 volume 34
Motor vehicle repair	C168 volume 32
Printing/media	C295 volume 36
Public works	C20 volume 36
Textile clothing	C253 volume 33
Textile industry	C318 volume 34
Tourism	C320 volume 35
Transportation	C338 volume 35
Wood	C330 volume 36

Source: Department for Education and Employment

The list shown in Table 13.3 is being constantly updated and many more career areas are now covered.

14 Tasks, responsibilities, skills and career progression opportunities

This chapter will consider how **different** or **similar** the work roles of specific jobs are across the EU. With many work roles there will be very close similarities, and the jobs will essentially be carried out in exactly the same way in all EU countries. With other work roles the duties, commitment, responsibilities, skills, etc., will vary considerably from country to country. With all jobs it will be the **benefits** (such as income, power and future career prospects) and **constraints** (such as the law, basic skills and personal capital) that determine what roles individuals have.

This chapter will consider the general similarities and differences in work roles across the EU. It will then examine how the work roles compare in terms of **tasks and responsibilities**, and **types of skills**.

Uniform and varied work roles

Some jobs are carried out in almost the same way in all of the EU countries. The job of a hotel receptionist, for example, is essentially the same in every country. It will require telephone skills, the handling of payments, customer service, etc. In larger hotels additional knowledge may be required, such as how to cash travellers cheques, or the ability to speak one or more foreign language. The essential requirements and structure of the job will change primarily with the size of the hotel, and not with the country where the work is being done.

Other jobs reflect the culture, customs or climate of particular countries and are only found in certain parts of the EU. Bull-fighting is now practised almost exclusively in Spain and Southern France. The growing of saffron (the dried stamen of the cultivated crocus) is also concentrated in Spain and France. Only in Scandinavia are reindeer farmed. Whisky is still the specialised brew of Scotland and Ireland.

Quick Quiz No. 4

In which EU country did bull-fighting originate?

The answer is given on page 259.

Where certain types of production are highly localised, the way in which jobs are carried out and the skills, qualifications, responsibilities, etc., that are expected are likely to be unique to that local area. However, the local, and indeed national, distinctions are rapidly being broken down as products become standardised across the EU. A firm like McDonalds, that now has its own or franchised outlets in every EU country, insists that all McDonalds' products are the same, with no regional or national differences. Globalisation is all too rapidly destroying the distinctions between national products, and with that the distinctions in national work roles. In all of the following industries the work roles are becoming standardised across the EU:

➡ Supermarkets and fast food retailers

➡ Banking, insurance and finance

➡ Telecommunications and major transport systems

➡ Much of the car industry, which now uses Japanese work practices (*see* page 195)

➡ Heavy industry, such as iron and steel, which uses standard manufacturing techniques

Other industries and professions retain a healthy individuality where there are distinct regional/national differences in the work roles and the ways in which jobs are carried out. These include:

➡ The legal profession

➡ Professors and lecturers in universities

➡ Farming, where scale, owner/tenant status, full-time/part-time commitment, etc., vary considerably from country to country

➡ Many crafts remain individual to particular regions or countries – lace making is quite different in different parts of the EU, and is either hand made or machine made

Quick Quiz No. 5

In which EU country did lace making originate?

The answer is given on page 259.

Many other work roles have a mixture of common factors, and factors that are specific to the country or region. In English pubs the roles are still, generally, distinctly divided between the following people:

➡ The **owner**. Sometimes this is the person who runs the pub, but usually the pub is owned by a brewery (e.g. Bass Charrington), or a limited company (e.g. Fortes). The owner has no work role in the actual running of the pub.

➡ The **manager**. The manager's job is to see that a team of workers is doing its job and providing the proper services for customers. Many pub managers will also carry out pub service duties.

➡ **Bar staff**. Usually part-time, their main function is to serve customers, stock the bar, and clear up when the pub closes.

➡ **Cleaners**. Most UK pubs will employ people whose sole work role is to ensure that the pub is clean. This does not include washing glasses, etc., which is usually the job of the bar staff.

➡ Where there are catering facilities, specialist **cooks/chefs** and even **commis-chefs** may be employed.

In many EU countries, cafés, restaurants and bars are generally owned by the person who manages them. Frequently they will be family businesses, and because of this the work roles will be quite different. They are more likely to be split on gender roles, with the women cooking and the men serving. Owners will take on most of the roles. Many landlords will have no other job.

Differing tasks and responsibilities across the EU

The details given below should be used to identify, from your own research, how tasks and responsibilities across the EU compare.

■ Tasks and responsibilities

Routine tasks are ones that form parts of a set procedure of work and ones that are likely to be repeated over and over again. Routine tasks would include:

➡ For **teachers** – teaching, setting work, marking work, and registering classes

➡ For **bricklayers** – keeping their equipment in good order, laying and cementing bricks, and ensuring that walls are straight and safe

➡ For **bakers** – preparing the dough, heating the oven, and cooking the bread

Because these roles are often different in different countries there will be some variation in the routine tasks.

As a farm labourer on a pig farm, the author had the **routine** tasks of mucking out the sows' pens before breakfast, feeding the porkers and baconers, and renewing the straw.

➡ Some countries have assistants working with teachers and these assistants will do some of the routine tasks.

➡ In the UK and Germany, many building firms are large and there will be a clear division of labour so that the bricklayers will not be expected to mix their own cement or carry and stack their own bricks. In Austria and Greece many building firms are small and builders will carry out many tasks, including bricklaying, cement mixing, carpentry, plumbing and so on.

➡ In many French towns and villages, and even cities, small bakeries still exist and the bakers will not only routinely make the bread, pastries, etc., but will also serve customers, clean the shop, etc.

Non-routine tasks or **specialised tasks** are ones that do not occur regularly or that require some specialist skills. These would include:

➡ For **teachers** – predicting students' final grades, dealing with a fight, and teaching a specialist subject

➡ For **bricklayers** – adding a decorative finish on the orders of the owner of the house, helping a mate nail plasterboard to the ceiling, and driving the van to pick up more cement

➡ For **bakers** – preparing special breads for the harvest festival, checking the books to see that they balance, and catering for a Christmas party

As a farm labourer on a pig farm, the author had the **non-routine** tasks of driving the tractor and loading straw bales, and of laying the drainage system for the farmhouse.

What will determine whether tasks are routine or non-routine will be how the jobs are done, what is expected of the workers, what is specified in the contract of employment, etc. As these conditions vary from country to country, the routine and non-routine tasks will also vary.

Hierarchical positions indicate where in the management structure of a firm the work role is placed. For most UK schools, the hierarchy is as shown in Figure 14.1, although this is rather simplistic.

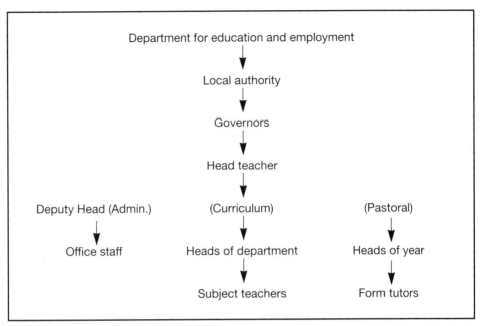

Fig 14.1 **Usual mechanistic hierarchy of UK state schools**

Many firms still have a very mechanistic structure (as shown above for education), but a growing number of firms are adopting Japanese practices where a more organic structure is practised. Here decisions are made through joint consultation, and workers of different status have access to each other and management. When this happens management tends to delegate responsibility downward so that workers become responsible for their own decisions.

Quick Quiz No. 6

In the UK political system, one person has the ultimate right to decide what the law in this country will be. Who is it?

The answer is given on page 259.

In the EU the move away from the linear hierarchy to an organic flat model depends mainly on the amount of contact that countries have had with the new management techniques. In Austria and Greece many firms are still owned by families and the mechanistic structure is still there. In the UK, Germany and France there are growing Japanese and multinational influences and more organistic work practices. In Finland, industry has been influenced by practices in the Soviet Union and work roles are far more level there.

The status of an employee is often dictated by his or her job title and description, as with engineers in the UK:

Engineering Technician (Eng. Tech.)

Usually works under guidance as part of an engineering team. Requirements:

1 Educational qualification, e.g. BTEC National Diploma or Certificate
2 Two years' training on a structured programme
3 Two years of engineering experience
4 Minimum age, 21

Incorporated Engineer (I.Eng.)

Works independently or under general directions. Requirements:

1 BTEC Higher National Diploma or Certificate
2 Two years' training on a structured programme
3 Two years of engineering experience
4 Minimum age, 25

Chartered Engineer (C.Eng.)

Works at the highest level and is responsible for his own tasks. Requirements:

1 Honours Degree in engineering, or the Engineering Council's Part 2 Examination
2 Two years' training on a structured programme
3 Two years of engineering experience
4 Minimum age, 25
5 Corporate membership of a nominated chartered engineering institution.

■ Specific tasks

Certain work roles expect a range of tasks and responsibilities to be carried out. The *range* suggests such areas as health and safety, quality assurance and financial management. In the actual workplace, the range of functions that employees are expected to carry out is likely to be very much wider. A lock keeper would be expected to:

➡ Ensure that boats pass through the lock safely and quickly, thereby giving tourists the quality they expect. (Quality assurance)

➡ Open and close the lock, maintain water levels, record daily changes in conditions. (Procedures)

➡ Check water levels, maintain safety equipment, operate the locks carefully, ensure that staff are properly trained and equipped. (Health and safety)

- ➡ Manage the accounts of any sales of refreshments and snacks that might be made. (Financial management)
- ➡ Train staff up to the required standards to operate the lock gates, weir controls, etc. (Staff training)

but also to:

- ➡ Provide information to users, and promote the services given by the water authority. (Publicity and promotion)
- ➡ Ensure that the lock and surroundings are protected from vandalism. (Security)
- ➡ Record the water traffic that passes through the lock each day. (Administration)
- ➡ Keep the lock area clean and ensure that spillages, oil leaks, etc., are cleaned up. (Environmental protection)

All jobs will have unique responsibilities, and some of this will reflect the culture and physical environment in which they occur. Across the EU the conditions will vary and so will the specific tasks and responsibilities.

Types of skills

As has been said repeatedly above, many jobs across the EU are essentially the same, as are the skills required, irrespective of the country in which the jobs are being done. There will, of course, be many examples of variations because people do different jobs in different countries. The skills required by a bull-fighter, a downhill skier and a fly-half for the Welsh rugby football team are obviously not the same.

Skills can be classified under general headings and then applied to specific work roles. Three examples are given below, but generally most work roles require a range of skills.

Social skills are particularly important when the work role requires contact with either other workers, or with suppliers, advisors, officials or customers. Very few jobs require no social skills. Certain jobs, however, require particularly good social skills, as with people working in direct marketing, personnel departments and entertainment.

Numerical skills will be associated with banking and finance but also with turf accountants at race courses and market makers in the stock exchanges.

Analytical skills are required by people working in problem-solving industries such as research, criminal investigation and economic forecasting. But most people who assess data will need these skills, such as market researchers, psychoanalysts and bank managers.

When comparisons are made across the EU, the skills required will help to confirm how different or similar work roles are in different EU states. Differences will also occur because of the benefits and constraints that arise in different EU countries due to laws, customs and cultures. Readers should check back to Parts 2 and 3 to see how these affect different countries.

> ### Dutch-speaking operations/logistics manager
>
> Wanted for work in Holland. Two to three year contract. £50K + package.
> *Personal status:* Single or married.
> *Experience:* Logistics or materials management.
> *Skills:* Linguist, technical experience, leadership.

Examples of differing work roles in the EU

A list of institutions that provide details for a wide range of professions is given in the resources section on page 260. Below are a few examples of how work roles, qualifications, etc., differ across the EU. Students may find that the examples given below deal with their chosen area of study, but it is more likely that these will simply offer examples of the kind of information that is available.

■ Secretarial jobs

Some jobs, such as secretarial work, are essentially the same in all EU countries. Mainstream secretaries will require all of the following skills:

➡ Basic keyboarding skills, generally measured by typing speeds and accuracy

➡ Initiative in terms of correcting, processing and filing work

➡ Communication skills in term of recording and interpreting information

➡ Language skills, especially in the national language of the firm, but ever more frequently, bi- or tri-lingual skills

Higher grade secretaries will be expected to have shorthand skills, and personal assistant skills such as organising meetings. For most secretarial roles it will not be the country that changes the skills required, but the rank that the person has risen to. All EU countries have secretaries with specialist areas of knowledge, such as bi-lingual secretaries, medical secretaries and legal secretaries.

Quick Quiz No. 7

Which two institutions are mainly responsible for testing the skills and qualifications for secretaries in the UK?

The answers are given on page 259.

Most careers in Germany require training and recognised qualifications. Secretarial work is an exception, but generally secretaries do attend secretarial college to gain qualifications. Examinations are available twice a year, put on by local chambers of commerce. As in the UK, secretarial work is graded by qualification and experience. Bi-lingual secretaries will be one of the following:

FremdsprachlicheSekretarin: with reasonable typing skills and a basic knowledge of another language.

FremdsprachenSekretarin: with excellent secretarial skills, typing, shorthand, office practice. Language skills good enough to compose letters, answer the phone, etc.

FremdsprachenKorrespondentin: Good secretarial skills, with typing. Excellent language skills and translating skills.

■ Retailing jobs

Retailing jobs require basic skills that satisfy the customers (e.g. providing the service that customers expect, providing a complaints procedure, and ensuring that goods are available when customers want them). But retailing also requires basic organisational skills which ensure that the business is being run efficiently (e.g. ensuring that products are delivered on time, raising finance to buy the stocks, and effectively advertising the products). Most of these skills will apply to all EU firms, and the career progression available will follow the pattern shown on page 252.

Other jobs are very specific to the country where they are found. Because each country has its own laws, the legal system in each country is slightly different. The UK is very different from the majority of the EU because our system of law is not based upon Napoleonic law. In the UK the roles of the barrister, solicitor, judge, magistrate, clerk of the court and representatives in industrial tribunals are very different. We also distinguish between criminal and civil law, and between private and company law. Each division creates different work roles for the people involved. In the EU widely different divisions occur.

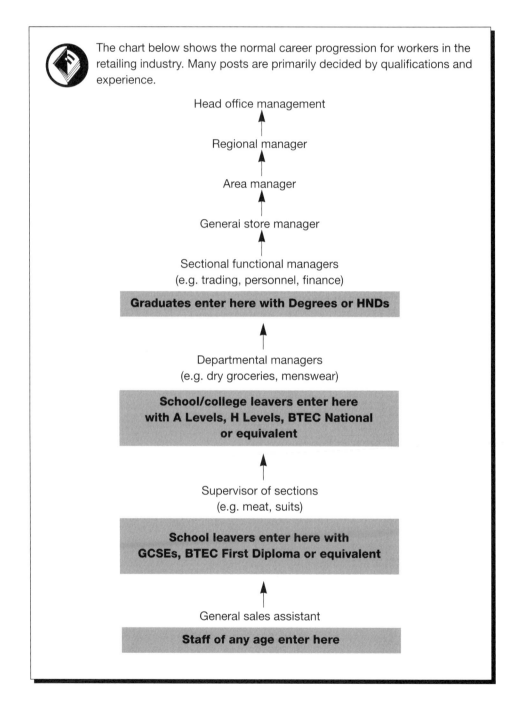

The chart below shows the normal career progression for workers in the retailing industry. Many posts are primarily decided by qualifications and experience.

Head office management

↑

Regional manager

↑

Area manager

↑

General store manager

↑

Sectional functional managers
(e.g. trading, personnel, finance)

Graduates enter here with Degrees or HNDs

↑

Departmental managers
(e.g. dry groceries, menswear)

**School/college leavers enter here
with A Levels, H Levels, BTEC National
or equivalent**

↑

Supervisor of sections
(e.g. meat, suits)

**School leavers enter here with
GCSEs, BTEC First Diploma or equivalent**

↑

General sales assistant

Staff of any age enter here

Two types of lawyer, *avocats* and *conseils juridiques*, exist in France, as well as the legal public officials, called *notaires*, who draw up certificates, etc., related to some parts of the law such as house sales. Court officials also exist, similar to our *registrars* and *clerks of the court*.

Avocats can appear before the lower courts, but only those *avocats* with the highest status can appear before the higher courts. The *conseils juridiques* are far more restricted. They cannot generally plead for clients in the court, except in certain commercial proceedings and arbitrations, and before administrative bodies.

Lawyers in France, generally, practise alone or in partnerships. As in the UK, the highest rewards are for those in commercial or financial law. Hourly charges for clients will go from 500 francs per hour for a junior lawyer, and 900 francs per hour for a senior lawyer, to 1,500 francs per hour for a partner. Firms usually have between five and twenty lawyers.

Teaching qualifications in the EU

Teaching is one of the specified professions in which the qualifications gained in one EU country are supposed to be recognised in all EU countries. The reality is often quite different as individual countries question the value of the qualifications awarded in other countries.

All EU countries require some recognised qualification or experience before teachers may take up posts in the mainstream primary, secondary or higher education establishments. The length and quality of the training and experience do, however, differ considerably from country to country. Generally the training and qualification required are different for primary and secondary school teachers. The main details for each EU country are listed below.

Austria

➡ Primary school teachers follow a three-year course at teacher training college and must pass an examination (*Lehramtsprüfung*).

➡ Secondary school teachers follow a four-year course, studying two subject areas and taking the *Lehramtsprüfung* in both. They are then awarded the *Magister* degree.

Belgium

Because there are two languages in Belgium there are separate education departments for each of the two language areas. Below the French qualifications are given, but they are very similar for the Flemish language.

➡ Primary school teachers study for three years at teacher training college leading to a diploma (*Diplôme d'Institutrice(eur) Primaire*).

➡ Lower secondary school teachers study for three years at teacher training college and take an examination (*Diplôme d'Agrégé de L'Enseignement Secondaire Inférieur*).

➡ Upper secondary school teachers must be graduates. They must pass an educational examination, the *Agrégation de L'Enseignement Secondaire Supérieur*. This may be taken at the same time as their final degree examination or some time afterwards. No separate training or course is required.

Denmark

➡ Primary and lower secondary school teachers study at teacher training institutions for four years.

➡ Upper secondary school teachers require a degree and then study for five months to receive the *Paedagogicum*.

 Seminars, given in English, are offered by Det Danske Selskab in Copenhagen to foreign students. These seminars explain how the Danish education system works.

Finland

The standard training to teach in primary or secondary schools is a four-year degree course in education, specialising in the appropriate level.

France

Teaching posts are competitive and one can only take exams for becoming a teacher if there are posts available.

➡ Primary school teachers follow a two-year training course.

➡ For secondary school teaching in the *collèges*, prospective teachers take an internal examination and are awarded the *Certificat d'Aptitude au Professorat d'Enseignement Général du Collège (CAPEGC)*. With a degree it is possible to take an external examination set by universities, which allows specialist teaching in specific subjects and requires one year of teacher training. This leads to the *Certificat d'Aptitude au Professorat d'Enseignement du Second Degré (CAPES)*.

➡ For secondary school teaching in the *lycée* it is necessary to have a degree and the CAPES. Some take the competitive *Agrégation* examination which is similar to our master's degree and also allows people to teach in universities.

Germany

➡ For teaching in primary, lower secondary or comprehensive schools, teachers follow a three-year teacher training course with an examination, then a two-year probationary period teaching in schools followed by a second examination, the *Zweite Staatsprüfung*.

➡ For teaching in lower and upper secondary schools, the route is a four-year teacher training course, although many students take up to ten years to complete this, with an end examination, two years' probation and then a second examination, the *Zweite Staatsexamen*.

 Following the implementation in Germany of the 1992 EC directives on the mutual acceptance of qualifications within the EC (including teaching qualifications), British teachers will be able to compete freely for positions in German schools and should reasonably expect that their applications will be favourably scrutinised.

However, one crucial difference will remain between the status of German nationals and foreigners employed as teachers in state schools. Teachers who are German nationals are *Beamte* (civil servants) and as such are entitled to job security for life and perks such as reduced national income contributions.

Source: Live & Work in Germany by Victoria Pybus

Greece

➡ Primary school teachers follow either a two-year course in higher education or a four-year course as part of a degree at university. Alternatively teachers can be trained on the job over a period of one year.

➡ Secondary school teachers must be graduates and are then trained to be teachers in schools through in-service training.

Ireland

Primary school teachers can be qualified through a two-year diploma, a three-year *Bachelor of Education* or a four-year honours degree.

➡ Secondary school teachers must be graduates and take a one-year postgraduate course to gain a *Higher Diploma in Education.*

Italy

➡ Primary school teachers can qualify with four years at upper school (i.e. from the age of fifteen to nineteen), gaining the *Diploma di Abilitazione Magistrale.*

➡ Secondary school teachers require no pre-service training but must be graduates. They must, however, pass a competitive examination, the *Concorso Abilitante.*

Luxembourg

➡ Primary school teachers must follow a three-year teacher training course leading to the *Certificat d'Aptitude Pédagogique.*

➡ Secondary school teachers must have a degree and then have studied for three years to become a teacher, passing the final examination, the *Examen de Fin d'Études Secondaires.*

Netherlands

➡ Primary school teachers must study for four years to gain the *Pedagogische Academie voor het Basisonderwijs (PABO).*

➡ Secondary school teachers must be graduates. They must then successfully complete a one-year teacher training course, leading to the *Eestegraads Bevoegdheid* (which allows teaching at all levels in secondary schools) or to the *Tweedegraads Bevoegdheid* (which only allows teaching up to certain levels).

Portugal

➡ Primary school teaching requires a three- or four-year teacher training course.

➡ Secondary school teaching requires a relevant degree and the teachers are trained on the job.

Spain

➡ For primary and lower secondary teaching, students follow a three-year degree course leading to the *Diploma de Profesor de Educacion General Basica.*

➡ Upper secondary teachers must have a degree in their subject and the *Certificado de Aptitud Pedagogica (CAP).*

Sweden

In Sweden the teacher training is geared to the type of school that one wishes to teach in. Throughout the teacher training course, which may last for three years (for the *högskola*) or four years (for the *gymnasieskolan*), the students build up points and the number of points dictates the highest level that one is allowed to teach at.

United Kingdom

➡ Primary school teachers normally have a *Bachelor of Education (B.Ed)* degree, gained after three years of study, or an honours degree gained after four years of study.

➡ Secondary school teachers are now expected to have a degree in the relevant subject and then follow a one-year teacher training course to gain the *Postgraduate Certificate of Education (PGCE).*

 The Teaching As a Career Unit (TASC) has the job of promoting teaching as a career and providing advice and guidance to those who wish to become teachers. This advice includes details of training courses and of career progression. TASC Publicity Unit, Sixth Floor, Sanctuary Buildings, Great Smith Street, London, SW1P 3BT (Tel: 0171 925 5880/5882).

The details above should make it clear just how difficult it is to ensure that qualifications gained in one country are of the same value as those gained in another country. These details, however, only deal with mainstream primary and secondary school teaching. The EU countries will also have different regulations for pre-school (nursery) education, ranging from no qualifications at all to the same stringent qualifications as for primary schools. Most countries also have vocational courses, for example, specialising in technology, or art, or music, and these may require different qualifications and experience from mainstream teaching.

When the whole field of the education profession is considered across the EU, the range of qualifications, examinations, degree requirements, experience, training, etc., is remarkably varied. The time taken to qualify to be a teacher and the age range one is then allowed to teach also change from country to country. So when it comes to teachers from one EU country applying for jobs in another EU country it is not surprising that so few actually succeed.

ASSIGNMENT 4
Investigate different work opportunities among European member states

Write a report on the differing work opportunities in different EU states. The report must cover all of the tasks given below.

TASK 1

➡ Select **one** specific work role and four EU member states in which this role will be studied.

➡ Identify, with examples, how the tasks and responsibilities for this work role are carried out in the four member states.

TASK 2

➡ For the same work role, describe the specific skills required to carry out the tasks and responsibilities identified in Task 1.

TASK 3

➡ Select one occupational area, e.g. teaching, nursing, retailing, etc.

➡ Take the UK and one other EU member state.

➡ Examine and compare how employment and career progression opportunities differ between the two countries.

Sources of information:

☞ This textbook, libraries, specialist books, newspapers and magazines, professional institutions, personal contacts, consuls, EICs, EDCs.

Key skills available for testing

■ **Application of Number:** There is little opportunity for gaining these skills here.

■ **Communication:** Elements 3.2 and 3.4 will form major parts of your work here.

■ **Information Technology:** Information technology can be used to support all of the tasks in the assignment, and will cover Elements 3.1, 3.2 and 3.3.

Answers to Quick Quizzes

No. 1

The National Health Service has the highest number of employees of any industry in the UK.

No. 2

a) *Il Giornale di Napoli* (The Naples Journal) is Italian
b) *Göteborg Postern* (The Gothenburg Post) is Swedish
c) *Le Provençal* (The Provencal) is French
d) *Neues Salzburger Tagblatt* (The Salzburg Daily News) is Austrian

No. 3

GNVQ is vocational, but because it is studied and assessed in schools and colleges, it is based more on theory than on practice. NVQ is also vocational but is carried out in the workplace and it therefore tests work skills that are actually being practised.

No. 4

Bull-fighting was originally practised in ancient Greece and later by the Romans.

No. 5

Lace making originated in Italy around 1500 AD. It is now widely practised in the EU, with major centres in Belgium (Brussels), France (Alençon, Valenciennes), Germany (Saxony), Italy (Venice) and the UK (Honiton – hand made, Nottingham – machine made).

No. 6

Theoretically, the monarch can decide whether or not laws are passed in the UK. In reality, if the Queen decided to use her powers to stop a law being passed, and it was one which the government really wanted passed, her powers would be taken away from her. The top of the political hierarchy in the UK is the cabinet.

No. 7

The two main bodies that set tests for secretaries in the UK are **Pitman** and the **Royal Society of Arts** (RSA).

Sources of information

The sources of information given below have been divided into broad types. Some sources will provide data that is particularly useful for specific elements and assignments. These sources will be indicated by the '⌖' sign, followed by the element number, e.g., [⌖ 16.2]. Other sources will provide data that can be used for most assignments, as with newspapers, country profiles, etc. These will have no sign and will come at the beginning of each list.

General EU sources and general sources for specific countries

■ Commission of the European Communities

(providing general information and materials).

- London Office, 8 Storey's Gate, London, SW1P 3AT (Tel: 0171 973 1992)
- Belfast Office, 9/15 Bedford Street, Belfast, BT2 7EG (Tel: 01232 240 708)
- Cardiff Office, 4 Cathedral Road, Cardiff, CF1 1SG (Tel: 01222 371 631)
- Edinburgh Office, 9 Alva Street, Edinburgh, EH2 4P (Tel: 0131 225 2058)

■ General institutional sources

- DTI European Division, Ashdown House, 6th Floor, 123 Victoria Street, London, SW1E 6RB (Tel: 0171 215 5000)
- European Commission Information Office, Jean Monnet House, 8 Storey's Gate, London, SW1P 3AT (Fax: 0171 937 1900)
- European Commission, Publications Unit, rue de la Loi 200, B-1049 Brussels (Tel: 32 2 235 1111)
- European Movement, United Kingdom, Europe House, 158 Buckingham Palace Road, London, SW1W 9TR (Tel: 0171 824 8388)
- **European Document Centres (EDCs)** – The EDCs, which are mainly located in universities, hold a wide range of data on many aspects of the EU which apply to all elements. Contact your local university library for details [⌖ 16.1 to 16.4]

➡ The Central Bureau for Educational Visits and Exchanges, Seymour Mews House, Seymour Mews, London, W1H 9PE (Tel: 0171 486 5101) [✠ **16.2**]

➡ **European Information Centres (EIC)** – The EICs hold details on Community legislation, and also economic and statistical data on EU countries. Local libraries will provide details of the nearest EIC [✠ **16.2**]

➡ Employment Branch: Overseas Placings Unit, 4th Floor, Steel City House, Moorfoot, Sheffield, S1 4PQ (Tel: 0114 2739 190) [✠ **16.2**]

➡ Employment Conditions Abroad Ltd., Anchor House, 15 Britten Street, London SW3 3TY (Tel: 0171 351 7151) [✠ **16.2**]

➡ International Training and Recruitment Link, The Old Coach House, 56 High Street, Harston, Cambridge, CB2 5PZ (Tel: 01223 872747) [✠ **16.2, 16.4**]

➡ European Centre for International and Regional Culture, Parade Street, Llangollen, Clwyd [✠ **16.3**]

➡ The Employment Service, Overseas Placing Unit, Level 4, Skills House, 3–7 Holy Green, Off The Moor, Sheffield, S1 4AQ (Tel: 0114 259 6051) (Provides pamphlets on "working abroad" for each EU country.) [✠ **16.3, 16.4**]

➡ The Overseas Branch, Department of Social Security, Newcastle Upon Tyne, NE98 1YX [✠ **16.3, 16.4**]

■ EU Embassies/Consulates in London

(These provide contact points for specific countries, and will have details on most aspects of living and working in those countries.)

➡ Austrian Embassy, 18 Belgrave Mews West, London, SW1X 8HU (Tel: 0171 235 3731)

➡ Belgian Embassy, 103–5 Eaton Square, London, SW1W 9AB (Tel: 0171 235 5422)

➡ Royal Danish Embassy, 55 Sloane Square, London, SW1W 9SR (Tel: 0171 235 1255)

➡ Finnish Embassy, 38 Chesham Place, London, SW1X 8HW (Tel: 0171 235 9531)

➡ French Embassy, 58 Knightsbridge, London, SW1X 7JT (Tel: 0171 201 1030)

➡ German Embassy, 23 Belgrave Square, London, SW1X 0PZ (Tel: 0171 235 5033)

➡ Greek Embassy, 1A Holland Park, London, SW1 3TP (Tel: 0171 221 6467)

➡ Embassy of the Republic of Ireland, 17 Grosvenor Place, London, SW1X 7HR (Tel: 0171 235 2171)

➡ Italian Embassy, 14 Three Kings Road, W1 (Tel: 0171 312 2200)

➡ Luxembourg Embassy, 21 Wilton Crescent, London SW1X 8SD (Tel: 0171 235 6961)

- Royal Netherlands Embassy, 38 Hyde Park Gate, London, SW7 5DP (Tel: 0171 584 5040)

- Portuguese Embassy, 11 Belgrave Square, London, SW1X 8PP (Tel: 0171 235 5331)

- Spanish Embassy, 24 Belgrave Square, London, SW1X 8QA (Tel: 0171 235 5555)

- Swedish Embassy, 11 Montagu Place, London, W1H 2AL (Tel: 0171 724 2101)

■ General statistical sources

- *Euromonitor*
- *European Business Information Sourcebook* (Headland) – provides a detailed list of all major sources of information across the EU.
- *EUROSTAT: Basic Statistics of the European Union* (Office for Official Publications of the European Communities, Luxembourg) – provides a wide range of general data on the EU.
- *Labour Force Statistics* (OECD)
- *Labour Market Trends* (Office of National Statistics)
- *Main Economic Indicators* (OECD) – good basic data on all EU countries, and the other major countries of the world, e.g., USA and Japan.
- *Monthly Digest of Statistics* (CSO)
- *Regional Trends* (CSO) – Section 2 gives regional breakdowns for EU countries for many major indicators.
- *Social Trends* (CSO)
- *Statistical Yearbook* (United Nations) – wide range of data, but not just the EU.
- *Demographic Yearbook* (United Nations) – For all countries providing figurs for population, age, gender, births, deaths, marriages, divorce and location. Census data is also given for specific countries. [✠ **16.1.1**]

Details of major OECD statistical publications are provided by the OECD Data Extraction Services, 2 rue André-Pascal 75775 Paris CEDEX 16, France.

■ Major records of national statistics

These provide basic statistical data for each country. (N.B. these are nearly all only published in the national language) [✠ **16.1**]

- **Austria** – *Statistisches Handbuch für die Republik Österreich* – Österreichisches Statistisches Zentralamt, Hintere Zollamsstrasse 2b, 1033 Vienna, Austria

- **Belgium** – *Annuaire Statistique de la Belgique* – Institute National de Statistique, 44 rue de Louvain, 1000 Brussels, Belgium
- **Denmark** – *Statistisk årbog* – Danmark Statistik, Sejrøgade 11, DK-2100, Copenhagen Ø, Denmark
- **Finland** – Statistical Yearbook of Finland – Central Statistical Office of Finland, PO Box 504, 00101 Helsinki, Finland
- **France** – *Annuaire Statistique de la France* – INSEE, 18 boulevard Adolphe Pinard, 75675 Paris Cedex 14, France
- **Germany** – *Statistische Jahrbuch für die Bundesrepublik* – Statistisches Bundesamt, Gustav-Stresemann-Ring 11, D-65189 Wiesbaden, Germany
- **Greece** – *Concise Statistical Yearbook of Greece* – National Statistical Service of Greece, 14–16 Lycourou St, 10166, Athens, Greece
- **Ireland** – *Statistical Abstract* – Government Publications Sales Office, Sun Alliance House, Molesworth Street, Dublin 2, Ireland
- **Italy** – *Annuario Statistico Italiano* – ISTAT Sistan Segreteria, Via Cesare Balbo 16, 00184 Rome, Italy
- **Luxembourg** – *Annuaire Statistique du Luxembourg* – STATEC, 19–21 Boulevard Royal, BP304, L-2031, Luxembourg
- **Netherlands** – *Statistisch Jaarboek (Netherlands)* – Netherlands Central Bureau of Statistics, Prinses Beatrixlaan 428, PO Box 959, 2270 AZ, Voorburg, Netherlands
- **Portugal** – *Anuario Estatistico* – Instituto Nacional de Estatistica, Av. Antonio Jose de Almeida 2, 1078 Lisbon, Portugal
- **Spain** – *Annario Estadistico de Espana* – Instituto Nacional de Estadística, Paseo de la Castellana 183, Madrid 28046, Spain
- **Sweden** – *Statistisk Arsbok* – SCB Forlag, 70189 Orebro, Sweden
- **United Kingdom** – *Annual Abstract of Statistics* – HMSO, 49 High Holborn, London, WC1V 6HB

Textbooks, guides, etc.

■ Books specifically related to living and working in Europe

These provide considerable detail on many aspects of living and working in EU countries, and many are written for individual countries. The list below shows which countries are available under each book heading.)
[✠ 16.2, 16.3, 16.4]

- *How to get a job in . . . Europe*; *France*; *Germany* (*How To* books)

➡ *How to live and work in . . . Belgium; France; Italy; Spain; Portugal* (*How To* books)

➡ *Live & work in . . . France; Italy; Germany; Scandinavia; Spain and Portugal; Belgium; the Netherlands and Luxembourg* (Vacation Works Publications)

➡ *Living and working in . . . Britain; France; Spain* (Survival Books)

■ Travel guides

Travel guides are usually provided for all EU countries separately, except Luxembourg which is usually covered with Belgium. Some publishers also provide guides for the whole of Europe. [✠ **16.1.4, 16.3**]

➡ *AA Essential Explorer* (AA Publication Division)

➡ *Baedeker* (Baedeker. Distributed in the UK by AA Publication Division)

➡ *Blue Guides* (A & C Black (Publishers) Ltd.)

➡ *Fodor's* (Fodor's Travel Publications Inc.)

➡ *Insight Guides* (APA Publications)

➡ *Let's Go* (Let's Go Inc. Published in the UK by Macmillan)

➡ *The Rough Guide* (Rough Guides Ltd. Distributed by Penguin Group)

➡ *The Versatile Guide* (Duncan Petersen Publishing Ltd.)

➡ *Thomas Cook Travellers Guides* (AA Publishing)

■ Other books

➡ *Country Profiles* (DTI Export Publications) – available for each EU country.

➡ *European Community Economies: A Comparative Study*, Frans Somers (Pitman Publishing)

➡ *Guide to the European Community*, Dick Leonard (The Economist Books Ltd)

➡ *OECD Economic Surveys* (OECD) – available for each EU country

➡ *Portrait of the Regions* (EUROSTAT)

➡ *The Economist Pocket Europe* (The Economist Books Ltd)

➡ *The Guinness European Data Book* (Guinness Publishing)

➡ *The Times Guide to the Single European Market*, Richard Owen & Michael Dynes (Times Books)

➡ *Vital World Statistics* (The Economist Books Ltd)

➡ *The Geography of the European Community* by John Cole and Francis Cole (Routledge, 1993) [✠ **16.1**]

➡ *Geographical Digest* (Phillip's) [✠ **16.1**]

➡ *European Business: Text and Cases* by Ian Barnes & Leigh Davison (Butterworth–Heinemann, ISBN 0 7506 1836 1) – case studies on different European Industries. [✠ **16.1.3**]

➡ *A Social Portrait of Europe* (EUROSTAT) [✠ **16.1, 16.3**]

➡ *Europe in Figures* (Eurostat) – a good general data base for the 12. Eurostat should now have data for all 15 EU countries [✠ **16.1, 16.3**]

➡ *Living and Retiring Abroad*, Niki Chesworth (Kegan Paul) [✠ **16.2**]

➡ *Law of the European Union*, Penelope Kent (Pitman), ISBN 0 7121 0851 3 [✠ **16.2**]

➡ *A Guide to Higher Education Systems and Qualifications in the European Community*, edited by Anita Wijnaendts van Resandt (Kogan Page) [✠ **16.2.1**]

➡ *The Daily Telegraph Guide to Working Abroad*, Godfrey Golzen (Kogan Page) [✠ **16.2, 16.3**]

➡ *Handbook of European Business Contacts*, Gerard P Dawson (Colt Books Ltd, with the British Chambers of Commerce) – now out of print but still available in public libraries. This provides details of all the vital contacts in the 12 EC countries in all major professions [✠ **16.2, 16.4**]

➡ *How to get . . . a Job in Hotel & Catering; a Job in Travel and Tourism; into Films & TV* (*How To* books). [✠ **16.4**]

➡ *The Directory of Jobs and Careers Abroad* (Vacation Work Publications). [✠ **16.4**]

➡ *The A–Z of Careers and Jobs*, edited by Diane Burston (Kogan Page) [✠ **16.4**]

■ Journals and newspapers with regular publications on EU matters

All quality newspapers have regular articles on Europe and should be checked regularly.

➡ *Export Today* (The Institute of Export)

➡ *Overseas Trade* (DTI)

➡ *The Economist*

➡ *The European*

➡ *European Focus* (KPMG) [✠ **16.2**]

➡ *EUR-OP News*, EUR-OP, Office 172, 2 rue Mercier, L-2985 Luxembourg (Fax (352) 29 29 – 427.63). *EUR-OP News* is currently provided free [✠ **16.4**]

➡ *Financial Times* – international appointments on Thursdays. [✠ **16.4**]

➡ *Jobs in Europe* (Workforce Publications) [✠ **16.4**]

Sources for specific careers

[✠ Providing data specifically for **16.4**]

■ Professional institutions

➡ **Advertising** – Advertising Association, Abford House, 15 Wilton Road, London, SW1V 1NJ (Tel: 0171 828 2771)

➡ **Architecture** – Royal Institute of British Architects, Education Dept., 66 Portland Place, London, W1N 4AD (Tel: 0171 580 5533)

➡ **Banking** – Banking Information Service, Careers Section, 10 Lombard Street, London, EC3V 9AT (Tel: 0171 626 9386)

➡ **Civil Aviation** – Civil Aviation Authority, 45–59 Kingsway, London, WC2B 6TE (Tel: 0171 379 7311)

➡ **Computing** – Institute of Analysts and Programmers, Charles House, 36 Culmington Road, London, W13 9NH (Tel: 0181 567 2118)

➡ **Dental Nursing** – British Association of Dental Nurses, 110 London Street, Fleetwood, Lancashire, FY7 6EU (Tel: 01253 778631)

➡ **Dentistry** – The British Dental Association, 64 Wimpole Street, London, W1M 8AL (Tel: 0171 935 0875)

➡ **Engineering** – Civil Engineering Careers Service, 1–7 Great George Street, London, SW1P 3AA (Tel: 0171 222 7722)

➡ **Estate Agency** – The National Association of Estate Agents, Arbon House, 21 Jury Street, Warwick, CV34 4EH (Tel: 01926 496800)

➡ **Farming** – Careers Education and Training Advice Centre, C/O Warwickshire Careers Service, 10 Northgate Street, Warwick, CV34 4SK (Tel: 01926 410410)

➡ **Information Technology** – Institute for the Management of Information Systems, IDPM House, Edgington Way, Ruxley Corner, Sidcup, Kent, DA14 5HR (Tel: 0181 308 0747)

➡ **Insurance** – The Chartered Insurance Institute, Careers Information Service, 20 Aldermanbury, London, EC2V 7HY (Tel: 0171 606 3835)

➡ **Journalism** – National Council for the Training of Journalists, Latton Bush Centre, Southern Way, Harlow, Essex, CM18 7BL (Tel: 01279 430009)

➡ **Marketing** – Chartered Institute of Marketing, Moor Hall, Cockham, Maidenhead, Berkshire, SL6 9QH (Tel: 01628 524922)

➡ **Medicine** – British Medical Association, BMA House, Tavistock Square, London, WC1H 9JP (Tel: 0171 387 4499)

➡ **Musicians** – Musicians' Union, 60–2 Clapham Road, London, SW9 0JJ (Tel: 0171 582 5566)

- **Nursing** – English National Board for Nursing, Midwifery and Health Visiting, Careers Service, Victoria House, 170 Tottenham Court Road, London, W1P 0HA (Tel: 0171 388 3131)
- **Personnel** – The Institute of Personnel Development, IPD House, 35 Camp Road, London, SW19 4UX (Tel: 0181 946 9100)
- **Pharmacy** – The Association of the British Pharmaceutical Industry, 12 Whitehall, London, SW1A 2DY (Tel: 0171 930 3477)
- **Public Relations** – The Institution of Public Relations, The Old Trading House, 15 Northburgh Street, London, EC1V 0PR (Tel: 0171 253 5151)
- **Statisticians** – Royal Statistical Society, 12 Error Street, London, EC1Y 8LX (Tel: 0171 638 8998)
- **Translation, Interpreting, Bi-lingual Secretaries** – The Institute of Linguists, 24a Highbury Grove, London, N5 2EA (Tel: 0171 359 7445)

Countries index

Generally the data provided for each topic in this book covers all EU countries. There are, however, some situations where individual countries are given as examples of particular points. These references are given below. The use of [ ] around the number indicates that the reference will be found in the articles or extracts rather than the main text.

General index

Benelux   4–5
Birth rate   *Definition* 18, 2, 18–20

Car industry   7, 48, 58, 65, 67, 195
Commission   98–9
Common market   *Definition* 4, 4–6
Communications   *Definition* 4, Chpt 5
   Postal   82–4
   Telecommunications   *Definition* 84, 84–88
Contract of employment   *Definition* 126, 126–9
Cost of living   200, 212–16
   Crime   220–2
   Environment   216–7
   Inflation   *Definition* 212, 212–4
   Taxation   103, 107, 122–3, 180, 214–6
   Unemployment   *Definition* 217, 217–20
Council of Ministers   97–8, 139
Customs and cultures   *Definition* 157, Part 3, 95
   Diet   163, 178, 187–8, 208–10
   Family   *Definition* 171, 170–7
   History   164–7, 170
   Imported   160–1, 194–6
   Indigenous and multicultural   *Definition* 185, 160–1, 183, 185–6
   Language   157–8, 161, 165, 181–5
   Local   163–4
   Music   188–9
   Physical environment   167–8
   Regional   162–3, 164–5
   Religion   177–81
   Stereotyping   *Definition* 169, 161, 169–70, 193
Customs union   *Definition* 4, 4–5

Death rate   *Definition* 18, 2, 18–21
Demographic profile   *Definition* 13
Demography   *Definition* 12, *see also* Population
Divorce   173–4

Financial Times Pitman Publishing produce a wide range of material for Foundation, Intermediate and Advanced GNVQ Business, covering mandatory units, optional units and core skills.

ADVANCED GNVQ BUSINESS
Mike Leake *et al.*
0 273 61067 8

This book has been written to follow the latest GNVQ specifications and is divided into eight comprehensive units, each covering one mandatory unit. Each unit is written by a subject expert and contains assignments and activities which have been thoroughly class-tested. In addition to activities and review questions, the text contains up-to-date test questions to assist and direct students towards success in end of unit tests.

BUSINESS: A STUDENT'S GUIDE
3rd edition
Desmond Evans
0 273 61770 2

A wealth of case studies and tasks are provided to give students the opportunity to collect evidence for their portfolio, in the third edition of this best-selling text for Advanced GNVQ Business. Each chapter includes both learning objectives and test questions similar to the kind that the student can expect for an 'end-of-unit' test. Written in an easy flowing style, key facts are available at the end of each unit to help students with revision and there are useful cross references to the performance criteria throughout.

Other GNVQ texts available include:

Advanced GNVQ Business and the Law
Ewan MacIntyre
0 273 61239 5

Behaviour at Work for Advanced GNVQ
2nd edition
Susan and Barry Curtis
0 273 62057 6

Financial Services for Advanced GNVQ
2nd edition
Keith Vincent
0 273 62056 8

Foundation GNVQ Business
Carole Jones
0 273 61327 8

Business for Intermediate GNVQ
2nd edition
Jon Sutherland and Diane Canwell
0 273 61772 9

Living in Europe for Intermediate GNVQ
John Evans-Pritchard
0 273 62541 1

FINANCIAL TIMES
PITMAN PUBLISHING